"This is as much an autobiography as a travel book. It records the reactions of an amiable 23 year old Peace Corps volunteer to his years in a primitive Himalayan village. Phil Deutschle well conveys the early sense of emotional and cultural isolation... the excitement of a recklessly brave solo conquest of Pharchamo (20,580 ft.)... Phil Deutschle gained a lot from his experience and he describes it agreeably."

The Good Book Guide

About the Author

Phil Deutschle—after surviving solo high-altitude climbing in the Himalayas and in the Andes, crossing Africa and the U.S. by bicycle, and paddling a dug-out canoe down the Congo River—has been described in the international press as everything from a "laid-back American guide" to a "hyperactive, exploring-mad psychopath." But his chosen career—teaching at impoverished schools around the world—makes him more an altruist than a mad adventurer. After working for years in Nepal, Denmark, Botswana, the Navajo Nation, and Bolivia, Deutschle now teaches high-school science in central California. He has never owned a car nor a cell phone.

Also by Phil Deutschle

Across African Sand: Journeys of a Witch-Doctor's Son-in-Law

THE TWO-YEAR MOUNTAIN

A Nepal Journey

by Phil Deutschle

Bradt

To Mette, to April, to Robyn,
and to my Mom

First published in 1986

This revised edition published 2012 by
Bradt Travel Guides Ltd
IDC House, The Vale, Chalfont St Peter, Bucks SL9 9RZ, England
www.bradtguides.com

Published in the USA by The Globe Pequot Press Inc,
PO Box 480, Guilford, Connecticut 06437-0480

Copyright © 1986, 2012 Phil Deutschle
Photographs and drawings copyright © 1986, 2012 Phil Deutschle
Maps redrawn by David McCutcheon
Edited by Caroline Taggart
Text design and typesetting by Adrian McLaughlin
Cover design: illustration and concept by Neil Gower
                    typesetting by Creative Design and Print.

ISBN: 978 1 84162 385 6

British Library Cataloguing in Publication Data
A catalogue record for this book is available from the British Library

Production managed by Jellyfish Print Solutions; printed in India

Acknowledgements

A wide range of people have helped me to live *The Two-Year Mountain* and then to write it. I am grateful to you all. The Peace Corps staff and my fellow volunteers gave me much more support than I have given them credit for. The U.S. Congress allowed the program to survive despite their cutbacks. The people of Nepal, the villagers of Aiselukharka, the teachers and students, and especially the family of Krishna Bhakta Himalaya took me into their homes and into their hearts. *Dhanyabaad.*

M. P. saw me through the first writing and all that's happened since. Lary Gibson of CSUN acted as mentor. Mr and Mrs B. proofread the manuscript. Innumerable persons gave support and advice, while Bob Stoneham alleviated fears and José Luis Vargas offered encouragement at the most unexpected and most needed of times. Roger D. helped me with myriad practical matters, and Hilary Bradt brought the project to fruition.

Many persons have allowed themselves to be described in these pages. I apologize for casting you in a light strongly tinted by my own prejudices and shortcomings. But then, if I had been unwilling to reveal a large part of myself, I would have had very little to say.

In the creation of this re-issue of *The Two-Year Mountain*, I am grateful to Hilary Bradt for once again believing in the value of this work, to Adrian Phillips for setting the project in motion, and to Caroline Taggart for putting all the pieces together. Thank you.

Krishna Bhakta and Philipsir

Foreword

The first edition of *The Two-Year Mountain* chronicled my experiences as a U.S. Peace Corps Volunteer in Nepal from 1977 to 1980. Since then, the most accessible regions of Nepal have changed dramatically—and generally for the good. But in the remote hills, far from roads and the influences of Kathmandu, life continues identical to my experiences of thirty years ago. In that regard, these pages contain a true depiction of current life in rural Nepal.

High-altitude mountaineering equipment and techniques have developed wonderfully over the past three decades. The climbing described here is, therefore, a retrospective to the days of thawing out frozen leather boots, tightening straps on crampons, and the endless chopping of steps up steep ice walls. While high climbing has become more comfortable, the Himalayan air is just as thin, the slopes are just as steep, and the climbs are just as dangerous. A warning to alpinists: My accounts of solo climbing should not—*must not*—be viewed as safe route possibilities for solitary mountaineers. Unroped climbing across crevassed glaciers and up steep ice is really, *really* stupid.

The glossary at the back contains translations of Nepali words and explanations of mountaineering terminology. The maps show major villages and general routes followed. Four supplemental chapters describe a startling homecoming journey to Nepal undertaken after a lapse of thirty-four years from when I first set foot in the Himalayas. All events related here are rigorously factual.

Phil Deutschle
September 2011

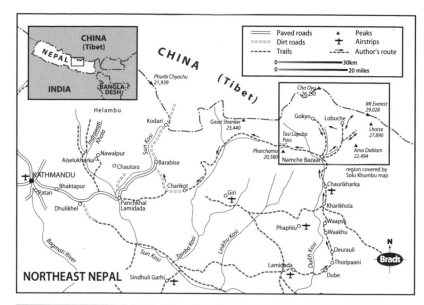

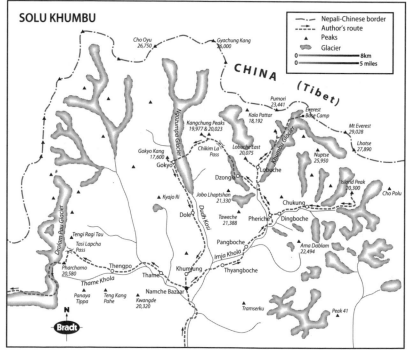

TRAINEE ASSIGNMENT CRITERIA

Country/Project Name:
NEPAL/Secondary Education Math/Science, 1977

Requirements:
BA or BS degree in mathematics or science, preferably with
a secondary education teaching certificate and teaching
experience.

Candidates must have a proven aptitude for learning a
foreign language, since all teaching will be in the
Nepali language. Must be willing and well able to walk
considerable distances, since schools will be in remote
areas.

Volunteer Assignment Description:
The goal of this project is to provide each year an agreed
upon number of math/science teachers to work in secondary
schools in Nepal, until such time as the local Ministry
of Education can meet its own manpower requirements for
qualified math/science teachers.

There are many potential frustrations to teaching in
Nepal. As in American schools, discipline is a problem,
and cheating on exams is all too common. Classroom
furnishings are minimal, consisting only of benches and
long, narrow tables. Blackboards are almost always in a
poor state of repair. The supply of science equipment is
meager. Teaching will be difficult for you, especially at
first, since you will be required to instruct in Nepali and
long hours will be spent on preparing lessons.

The rural community in which you will live will most
likely be Hindu with a variety of castes and ethnic
groups. Your village will be without many amenities like
electricity, running water, or indoor bathrooms. Houses
are usually of mud or stone with thatched roofs. Houses
contain little furniture although you may have some made.
You may eat with a local family or establish your own
simple kitchen. Your diet will consist of rice, lentils,
vegetables, and sometimes meat.

By serving as an education volunteer in Nepal, you will be
accepting a challenge matched by few which you might face
in the U.S. If you are willing to accept this challenge,
the Peace Corps and the Government of Nepal encourage you
to apply for this program.

Action Form A-731 (excerpt)

Swayambhunath Buddhist shrine with symbols of Wisdom and Compassion

March 15

Tribhuvan International Airport

L astly, two chickens and a string of fish are loaded into the plane's luggage compartment. The chickens, with their feet bound, are complacent as a large hand fits them into a space between a basket of sooty pots and a rolled-up mattress. Somewhere in that jumble of bags and boxes, crates and cartons, are my overweight backpack and, in a loose-weave basket with room for air, my special cargo. I hope they will be OK. The fish, being well dead, are unceremoniously tossed in.

Eighteen of us vie for the Twin Otter's eighteen seats—it's been booked for two weeks. With an inherent fear of being left behind, we push one another for position. My greater height and lighter skin give me an edge and I get the window seat just behind the pilot.

A man claims the spot next to me. He wears the brass buckle shoes and black *topi* cap of Nepali officialdom. Together we fumble with his seatbelt. When it clicks into place, he tilts his head to one side and thanks me with an untranslatable "*Laa.*"

I sit back and close my eyes. I'm relieved to be on the plane, but I'm also apprehensive over what the coming weeks will bring.

As we accelerate down the runway, I feel that sudden lack of vibration and heavy-in-the-stomach feeling that tells me we're in the air. The roofs of the city drop away as we climb into the midmorning sky over Kathmandu. Thatched farm houses, tiled-roofed homes of merchants, gilded pagodas and the gleaming royal palace all shrink, giving the very false impression of a storybook town.

I look about the cabin and I am surprised to see another foreigner; most flights of the Royal Nepal Airlines Corporation (RNAC) are of no interest to Western tourists. I wonder why he's going to Lamidada. It's a small village lost in the hills of eastern Nepal, whose single notable feature is a hilltop long enough and flat enough for a landing strip. My own destination is first a day's walk north to leave off my cargo and then much further and higher, to the high Himalaya, toward the top of the world, Mount Everest.

I look through the window toward the Himalayas, but only the hills are visible. It's funny to call them hills when they range in height up to 15,000 feet. Ridges rising up and streams running down, they stretch the length of Nepal. Slope after slope is carved into terraces. Tilled by hand or with oxen, they feed Nepal's twelve million.

I continue staring through the window. The hills are brown from the dry winter, and as I watch they become darker and darker, filling the window, turning it black... a different window in a different plane, a world away, two and a half years ago...

I looked through the blackened window at the terminal, trying to make out the dark shapes across the night. I wanted to know that Kay was looking back at me, pressing her hands against the glass, wearing a three-year-old silver and turquoise ring. I wanted to cry, but my eyes remained dry.

Our goodbye had been difficult. We had said that we loved one another and that we always would. Neither of us could really comprehend that I would be gone for two years. We had eaten a farewell dinner at a Chinese restaurant and from a fortune cookie had come a message:

YOU'LL BE CALLED TO A POST REQUIRING HIGH
ABILITY IN HANDLING GROUPS OF PEOPLE

The DC-9 began to move and I looked at the floor. *I'm gone. I'm gone.*

It was just a forty-minute hop from Sacramento to San Francisco, where I had an hour's wait for my flight to Chicago. Early morning saw the plane circling O'Hare Field, waiting for the fog to lift. A refueling detour to Milwaukee got me back to Chicago long after my connecting flight to Philadelphia had already left.

As I ran around the airport in search of another plane, I was accosted by two followers of the Hare Krishna faith. They wore saffron robes, and their bald heads gleamed.

"Do you have," they smiled benevolently, "some time?"

"No," I said, not lying for once, and rushed off.

Once in the air, I was accosted again. "Why are you going to Philly?" asked the man in the adjacent seat.

"I have a meeting," I said slowly. I didn't want to talk.

His eyebrows arched. Looking younger than my twenty-three years, I wasn't someone who would commonly be flying across the country to meetings.

Reluctantly I explained. "I'm on my way to be a teacher in Nepal with the Peace Corps. We're meeting…"

"What!" came a voice from the row behind us. "So am I!"

I turned around and we introduced ourselves. He was Ed from Chicago, with curly hair and a big smile. I was Phil from near Los Angeles, wearing a purple headband.

In Philadelphia we teamed up, both of us assuming that the other knew something more of what was going on. After reclaiming our luggage, we followed the directions on our mimeographed letters and took a taxi-van to the Ben Franklin Hotel.

The hotel, which appeared too big for itself and almost gloomy in its out-of-date posh, had a floor and a half reserved by the Peace Corps. Ed and I soon found ourselves in a conference room full of potential volunteers. Here the program for the next two days was explained in detail. This *staging*, as it was called, was in preparation to flying to Nepal for our three months of training.

There in the heart of beautiful Philadelphia, we were subjected to getting-to-know-you sessions, participated in group discussions on why we were there and what we expected, saw color slides of the Nepali countryside, registered our cameras and radios with customs, filled out various official forms, received our passports, and were vaccinated against smallpox, cholera, typhoid and polio. On a free afternoon I went to see the Liberty Bell, which made me feel very patriotic and full of momentousness for what we, as United States Peace Corps Volunteers, were endeavoring to do for the world. I also fed the pigeons.

During those few days, Ed and I shared a room but we didn't become close. We were from different spheres. After taking a degree in mathematics, he had worked the last half-dozen years as a computer technologist. He was nicely respectable, while I was more of a long-haired flower child come a decade too late. But strangely enough, I came equipped with a B. Sc. in Mathematical Physics, *magna cum laude.*

The volunteer that I got to know the best was Jim. We were both from Southern California, were equally thin, and had the same type of scraggly billy-goat beard that most men shave off out of embarrassment. We both played wooden flutes known as recorders and the last night of staging we played duets together until 1 a.m.

Of the other trainees I gained only hazy impressions; I hadn't done very well during the getting-to-know-you sessions. What I did notice was that few of them had concrete reasons for joining the Peace Corps. Many didn't have anything better to do, or didn't want a 9 to 5 job, or were just looking for some excitement and foreign mystique. But not me. I was an altruist, wanting to help educate Third World children for whom school would be an opportunity and not an imprisonment. Education was the foundation of development, and so on. That's what I told myself.

Regardless of our different motives, we were on our way to Asia. After a short flight to New York, we flew over the Atlantic in a Pan Am 747. We were three groups of volunteers: fisheries workers, math/science teachers, and

English teachers. The math/science teachers were the largest group, though our numbers were already dwindling. There were supposed to have been twenty-two of us, but one had never come to Philadelphia and another had withdrawn during staging. I knew that Peace Corps training programs had a world-wide dropout rate of 25 percent, and I now wondered who the survivors would be.

Across the Atlantic, we had forty-five minutes to explore London Airport. I sent a hasty postcard to Kay, and we continued toward Frankfurt. I sat between Jim, my newfound friend, and Dwight, one of the English teachers.

Dwight had been to Nepal before when traveling across Asia with money from an inheritance. He had stayed in India for six months and he now spoke basic Hindi, meditated regularly, and was a confirmed vegetarian. I never called myself a vegetarian, but other than Thanksgiving and Christmas dinners, I ate very little meat. So when meals came on the plane, I felt sheepish being confronted with a chicken leg while Dwight was busy with his specially ordered vegetarian meals. I would have felt less self-conscious if I had known that after six months in Nepal, Dwight would stop meditating, abandon his vegetarianism, and even learn to drink. In two years he would be engaged to marry a local Nepali woman.

We saw as much of Frankfurt as we had seen of London—the inside of the airport. We proceeded east. I dozed a bit and watched a movie without sound; I didn't want to invest two dollars in a set of headphones. The plane droned on as countries passed beneath us in a blur. We all sat in our individual seats while our thoughts became scrambled from crossing so many time zones.

The next stop was Tehran. In 1977, this was before world events would put Tehran in the headlines, and I had to look at a map to see where we were. A shuttle bus took us from the plane to the terminal. Cameras were not allowed inside since the airport doubled as a military installation. This was just as well, for the transit lounge was barren and unphotogenic. I walked around in circles, stretching my legs until I spotted a place to look outside.

A triple-wide entrance admitted the evening air and Tehran's 3,700-foot altitude made the breeze cool. As I approached, the guard turned his back to me. While he blocked a man from entering, I recognized my chance to escape the constraints of the terminal. Without really thinking, I stepped around the guard and slipped through the door—outside into Iran with no passport check and without a visa.

The guard didn't notice me, so I was free to meander down the street looking at the trinkets being hawked on the pavement. I gave an unwilling vendor two American quarters for four postcards, and I tried to explain with my hands that the price was fair. I was sure that he could change the money into rials somewhere.

Worried about the time, I returned to the entrance but a gate sealed the doorway. It held back a crowd, making it impossible to get through. Now I was more than worried; I was scared.

I ran, and I searched, and I eventually found a corridor that led into the building. A policeman in an office guarded the door. He worked at a desk, periodically looking down at his papers before surveying the corridor again. With heart pounding, I waited until his head was down, and I tried to walk by without being seen. Unbelievably he didn't spot me, and I immediately turned down a hallway to the right. Another turn, a dead end, and back again. Two more turns and I was lost. I was panicked about missing the plane and terrified of getting caught.

I came to an office with glass windows and acted as though I belonged there as I passed by. The people inside paid me no attention.

Then suddenly, miraculously, I was through the building to the other side. I could see the shuttle bus being boarded for the drive back to the plane. I hurried toward it, but was stopped by a shouted command from behind. I turned around and was confronted by two policemen. They both had guns, pointed vaguely in my direction. They yelled at me in Persian what must have meant, "Stop or we'll blow your head off!"

They bustled me off to a room where I was searched. Other guards checked my passport and boarding pass and then rechecked them. They seemed baffled as to how and why I had dodged the security patrol. No one guessed that I had been illegally outside. They struggled with their English to question me, but they soon tired. I carried no drugs and no bombs, so they begrudgingly let me board the plane.

Back in my seat I sat very still. I waited until we were in the air before telling Dwight what had happened. He heard me out and proclaimed that I had the makings of a true world traveler.

The plane droned on and I dreamily thought of Kay. We had been together for three years, and since my parents and brothers had been scattered by a divorce, Kay had been my entire family. All my papers listed her as the one to contact in case of an emergency. If we had lived at an earlier time, we would have been husband and wife.

As we flew over Afghanistan, I leaned back in my seat and saw Kay's long dark hair and bright green eyes. Why had I left? I loved Kay, but I disliked America—I was not interested in money, and I hated the automobile. It only pulled people apart instead of bringing them together. Joining the Peace Corps had been an easy decision. But I had never imagined how difficult it would be to leave Kay.

Another four hours brought us to New Delhi. We walked to the reception hall, and despite the late night hour, the air was stifling. Huge winged roaches flew everywhere. Someone stopped to examine them. That was Rob. He was over six feet tall and had massive hands. He was an amateur entomologist and he had brought a dissection microscope with him. He planned to make a complete insect collection, but he never would.

Our departure for Kathmandu wasn't till the morning, so I spent the remainder of the night trying to sleep on a bench. Each time the room was quiet I lurched up, fearful that everyone had gone and left me behind.

At 10 a.m. we boarded an RNAC 727 called the *Yeti*. Yetis, I knew, were the elusive abominable snowmen and snowwomen said to live in the Himalayas. What I didn't know was that the *Yeti* was the RNAC's only jet.

The take-off was flawless—I had learned a lot about flying in the previous six days. The weather was clear, giving a good view of the Ganges plain. The land was a smooth green and the sun reflected silver on the lace-like river systems. Further to the north the land bunched into mounds, and I knew that we were over Nepal when I saw the hills rising beneath us. Endless ridges and ravines made it clear why Nepal had so few roads. The hills mounted higher and higher, stretching as far as I could see in greenness.

They were much the same hills as I see now—a difference in color—they're now brown instead of green. The Nepali pilot takes the eighteen-seat plane through a tight turn and starts the descent. We must be at Lamidada, but I can't see the landing strip. He clears a ridge at tree-level and the ground rushes up. Suddenly we're down, bouncing to a stop on the dirt runway.

Stepping into the sunshine, I join the other foreigner to wait for the baggage to be unloaded. He's British and is going to visit his wife who's a doctor at a hospital two days' walk south. I have nothing to say to him. His presence is an intrusion on my uniqueness here.

When my things come out I'm relieved to see that the basket and its contents are all right. A man drops my pack upside down, but nothing is damaged. I change my mind about hiring a porter; I'll carry everything myself, as usual.

The families here live in a medieval world. They go everywhere by foot (the nearest road is five days away), they fetch water from a hole in the ground, cook on wood fires, and farm with hand tools. Each week a plane arrives, confronting them with the twentieth century. Those who live nearby stop their work every Saturday to come see what the *hawai jahaaj*, the air ship, will bring.

As I rearrange my load, a circle of onlookers gathers around. They watch me openly and expectantly, as though I'm about to perform magic. One man stands barefoot, with dirt between his toes and up his shins. He holds a local-made hand shovel and stares at me contentedly.

Another man, realizing that I'll be there a while to secure my pack, squats down and takes out a rolled leaf cigarette. He holds it vertically between two fingers and makes a fist, sucking the smoke through the opening formed by his thumb and forefinger. In this way the cigarette is never defiled by contact with his lips. After a few puffs, he passes it to a friend.

To one side stand two nearly-adult schoolboys. They watch me askance, pretending that they're too old and worldly to be interested. On their feet they wear matching white tennis shoes.

I tighten the straps that hold my sleeping bag to the pack frame and tie the basket firmly to the top of it all. Standing up, I look among the faces and ask the man with the shovel for directions to the villages of Dube and Thoripaani. He's both pleased and embarrassed to be singled out. But before he can answer, another man, who's better dressed, steps forward and explains the way.

I hoist the pack to my shoulders and start off. The trail is good—wide and smooth—so I'm able to hike without paying attention to the placement of my feet. Past the scattered fields and houses of Lamidada, I settle into an even pace. I look nowhere in particular. The load rests on my back, and my legs swing forward, one foot at a time. The rhythm of my stride relaxes me, step after step, almost hypnotic, trance-like...

The RNAC jet descended and I saw the roofs of Kathmandu for the first time. As we approached I could see people in the fields by the runway. A man without a shirt looked up from his work and watched the plane land.

As we coasted to a stop, the volunteers broke into spontaneous applause. It was a moment of ultimate arrival. We emerged from the plane, one by one, blinking and gawking like newborn babes.

We passed through customs and were met outside by members of the Peace Corps staff. A woman in a sari put a garland of flowers around my neck and another stuck a red glob of rice onto the center of my forehead. Pressing her hands together at chest height, she did a little bow of welcome and said, "*Namaste.*" I copied her, putting my hands together and returning her *Namaste*. We stood in the sunshine smiling and laughing at the wonder of being in Nepal.

Jim and I took pictures of each other and got into the back of a Peace Corps Land Rover for the drive into town. Turning onto the main road, a taxi raced around the corner, coming right at us from the wrong side of the road. I gripped the seat, expecting to crash, but it passed by harmlessly.

"They drive on the other side here," explained the driver.

"*Ahhh.*"

"And that on your forehead—" it was beginning to run down our faces in red streaks "—is called a *tikaa*. There are many types and they're given for different reasons. Those are a greeting and a sign of respect."

We would have much to learn.

He drove us to the Star Hotel where we would rest for three days before the start of training. We needed that long just to get into a normal sleeping pattern. I was time-lagged by thirteen hours, and my body didn't know day from night.

Jim and I shared a bleak little room, but we spent little time there. We were busy with orientation meetings, a reception dinner, explorations of the town, and best of all, more injections: gamma globulin against hepatitis and something from duck embryos against rabies.

Kathmandu amazed us. We saw something new every time we turned around: a woman carrying a stack of steel plates on her head, a cow dozing in the roadway, a friendly beggar with elephantiasis of the foot, and an ancient pagoda* said to have been made from a single tree. We listened to voices in many tongues and we jumped aside when we heard the rumbling of pushcarts coming down the back alleys. Each corner had a confusing combination of smells: incense and urine, mustard oil and motorcycle exhaust. We were too naive to see the depth of the city's problems. We just rejoiced in the excitement, like tourists on holiday.

The first half-month of language training was to be held in Dhulikhel, a town 30 kilometers away. The morning that we were leaving Kathmandu, Jim and I ate breakfast together at a nearby restaurant.

We had finished the meal and were sipping tea when a woman at a far table hailed us, "Are you N/71 trainees?" She was young, just slightly plump, and had long blonde hair. She wore a wraparound dress and she held a piece of toast in her hand.

"What, huh?" we said, looking puzzled at each other.

"N/71. Your group number. You're math/science teachers?"

"Yeah, that's right."

"So you're N/71."

This was the Peace Corps classification system. It meant that we were the seventy-first group of volunteers in Nepal.

"Are you a Peace Corps Volunteer?" asked Jim, having to speak very loud to be heard so far away.

"Yes," she said. "I'm almost finished."

"Do you want to sit here?" I asked, gesturing to the empty seats at our table. She didn't seem to hear me and she went on talking. "I have just three months left." The toast was still in her hand.

"Do you work in Kathmandu?" Jim called across the room.

"No. Up in Trisuli, you know."

---

* This pagoda, called Kastha Mandap and built in 1596, might be the origin of the city's name. *Kath* means wood, and *mandu* comes from the word for temple. Pagoda architecture originated in Nepal.

We didn't know, and we shook our heads with uncertainty.

She continued, "I work at a sheep farm up there, but it's going badly, you know. I was brought here to be a technical advisor, a specialist, but the job I'm doing could be done by anyone. They don't really need me at all."

As she spoke her eyes wandered about the room as though she was watching an invisible fly. She never looked directly at us, and this made us feel very ill-at-ease.

"But the worst thing," she resumed, "is the food, or lack of food. I just can't get any up there. I can have some carried in, but it's a lot of trouble and it's too expensive."

This made no sense; she looked well-fed to me.

"That's one of the reasons that I have to come to Kathmandu. To eat. Also I'm a little sick..." The toast remained in her hand, uneaten, and her eyes continued to wander.

Two hours past Lamidada, the path becomes rocky, which breaks my reverie by forcing me to concentrate on my steps. The trail descends to the river and ends at a makeshift bridge. It's built from bamboo poles lashed together with strips of cane. The bridge is only temporary and will be washed away in the summer monsoon, necessitating a long detour downriver to a steel suspension bridge built by the German volunteers. When the river subsides again in the fall, the bamboo one will be rebuilt in the same place.

The bridge is made of a large X-support on each bank and joined together by many lengths of stout bamboo which are tied end-to-end and bowed over the river. It looks dubious, so I let a porter who's coming from the other side cross first.

He carries a cone-shaped packbasket full of firewood that weighs at least 80 pounds. His load isn't carried by shoulder straps like my pack. Instead, it's supported by a single woven band that passes around the basket and up across his forehead. This characteristic tumpline is called a *naamlo*. The basket rests against his back with the weight pulling down on his head.

He takes off his rubber sandals and confidently scrambles across the bridge on all fours. When he gets to my side, I hear him reciting a low prayer.

My turn comes and I crawl on hands and feet across the rickety bridge. The bamboo struts creak under my weight and my oversized pack puts me off balance. I climb carefully down the other side and I'm relieved to be safely across.

From here, the trail follows the river then climbs the hillside towards Dube. The sun is already below the treetops and I must soon find a place to sleep.

A woman comes down the switchbacks carrying a large earthenware jug of water. She keeps one arm crooked around the jug's neck, while she rests its base on her hip. Her dark hair is entwined with red yarn and braided into a long pigtail. I think she's beautiful. She looks like Kay.

Almost an hour up the slope, I come to the source of her water. She must spend a quarter of her day just collecting water for her family. Sacred *pipal* trees encircle two cottages—the first houses of Dube. The rest of the village is spread across the hillside.

A rivulet of water trickles from beneath a cluster of bamboo, and I put down the pack to fill my water bottle. I drop in an iodine tablet, and begin the requisite 20-minute wait before I can consider it safe to drink.

While I'm waiting, a middle-aged woman emerges from the nearer house. She wears typical Nepali dress: a length of patterned cloth wrapped three times around her waist to form a long skirt and a tight short-sleeved shirt that covers her breasts but leaves her midriff bare.

I approach her and ask, "*Ma yahaa basna sakchhu?*—Can I stay here?" I gesture towards the house. It's already dusk.

She looks at me carefully. "*Tapaaiko ghar lyaanubhayo?*—Did you bring your home?" she asks smiling. She's not surprised that I speak Nepali. She wouldn't know what to do if I *didn't* speak Nepali.

"Ah, no, I didn't bring my home," I answer with confusion.

"Certainly not," she says, "so of course you can stay here."

"And can I get some food?"

"Yes, yes."

She shows me inside and gives me a place on the floor. I untie the basket from the pack as two children crowd in to see.

"*Musaa, musaa,*" they cry, "Rats, rats."

"*Musaa hoinaa*—Not rats," I correct, "*Kharaayo*—Rabbits."

"*Sailo!,*" hollers the woman. "Come see the rabbits."

Another child rushes in and joins the others repeating, "*Kharaayo, kharaayo*—Rabbits, rabbits." They're afraid to reach in and touch the rabbits for fear that they'll bite.

"How many are there?" asks the woman as she peers into the basket of white fur.

"Three."

"So you have three. Give me one."

"No. I can't. They're not mine. They're a friend's. I'm taking them to him."

"Oh, but you have three! Who are they for?"

"They're for Klaus-sir* in Thoripaani."

"*Aaiee... Klaus-sir .*" She knows of him. Teachers, and especially tall white ones, are greatly honored.

She goes now and begins to prepare the evening meal. The room soon fills with smoke and people. They are primarily members of the family, though others are porters who, like me, are just stopping for the night. This woman must be well-known for her hospitality. The smoke is due to the absence of a chimney. All Nepali homes are like this, which provides the single biggest advantage of sitting on the floor—being below the level of the smoke.

After an all-you-can-eat dinner, I spread my sleeping bag on the moonlit porch. I sleep well beneath a belly full of rice.

---

*All Nepali teachers have a respectful *sir* tagged onto their names.

March 16

Dube Village

I awake to the sound of chickens squabbling over breakfast. Two of them peck vigorously at my pack while the others attack the wooden door, intent on getting in. It opens a crack and a mottled hen squeezes through triumphantly. Suddenly a loud *thump* and *squawk* scatter the flock as their compatriot is kicked out the door. A handful of corn is thrown into the yard and the feathered troops rush out to eat as the door is slammed shut.

To try to sleep longer would be futile, so I get up and dress. Despite the early morning chill, I wear only my shorts and a long-sleeved shirt. I'll get warm as I hike. I retie the basket of bunnies to the pack and look around, as always, to see if I've left anything behind.

The woman is unsure of how much I should pay for the evening's meal, but she finally accepts four rupees, about thirty-two cents. "*Namaste*," she says with her palms held together under her chin.

"*Namaste*," I reply as I start up the trail.

Passing through the village, I'm greeted with calls of, "*Kharaayo, kharaayo*—Rabbit, rabbit." My fame has spread overnight.

Above Dube, the mountainside is bare—it's been stripped of firewood over the years—and I can see up the ridge that leads to Thoripaani. I'll be glad to talk with Klaus again, and I wonder if he'll look different. Sometimes he shaves off his thick dark beard. I wonder about his health too. He is never just so-so. He'll be either incredibly robust or incurably ill.

Klaus shuffled into the tiny room and slumped into a chair. I had been watching the clouds, hoping for a peek at the Himalayas north of Dhulikhel. I turned around when Klaus came in. We had never truly talked before.

"You don't look too good," I said. It was an understatement.

"I didn't sleep much," he muttered.

"Yeah, those dogs were really barking and fighting…"

"No, it wasn't that."

"You've got diarrhea?"

He leaned forward with his elbows on his knees and put his head in his hands. His face was ashen.

"Did you throw up, too?"

He shook his head. "Only once."

"That's too bad… I heard that Steve had to throw up in the middle of the night and only just got to an open window in time. But then it turned out to be a screen window. They said that it was a real mess."

Klaus's right eye looked up at me through his fingers. He didn't appreciate my humor.

Our talk was interrupted by the arrival of a short man whom we recognized as Karki, one of the language instructors. "*Namaste,*" he said to both Klaus and me. "*Namaste,*" we replied. We had already learned that much.

Karki took a deep breath and began. "*Mero naam Karki ho. Mero naam Karki ho.*" He pointed to himself and said it again and again, slowly and deliberately.

We had been in Nepal for four days and this was our first session of language training. Karki was nervous. He had never taught before, but with a class of only two students, he needn't have worried.

In nine other rooms of the lodge, similar classes were being held. The language instructors patiently repeated the words and the trainees tried to extract some meaning from the strange foreign sounds. No English would be spoken in class. We were expected to figure things out as we went along.

We would have class seven hours a day, six days a week. This was known as the *direct approach* to language training, but I preferred to call it the *sink-or-swim method*.

So much emphasis was put on learning the language because our work would be in rural Nepal where no English was spoken. At our assigned villages we would have to teach solely in Nepali, and we had just three months of training in which to become fluent.

Now Karki changed his intonation and said, "*Tapaaiko naam ke ho? Tapaaiko naam ke ho?*"

After six repetitions, I interjected, "*Mero naam Phil ho.*" Karki was delighted. I had answered his question, "What is your name?" with "My name is Phil," in correct Nepali. Karki was now convinced that he was a superb language teacher, and Klaus sank further into his chair, feeling stupid as well as sick.

Unfortunately for Klaus, I had a big advantage over him. Back in the States I had contacted a former Peace Corps Volunteer and had taken a score of Nepali lessons at three dollars an hour. Those lessons would put me ahead at first, but we were learning so quickly that in a few days I would be no better than anyone else.

I had taken those lessons in the U.S. because I had been so unsure of my ability at languages. In high school I had passed two years of Spanish but I hadn't exactly excelled; I had even insured that I would pass by stealing a copy of the final exam. I was a better thief than I was a linguist.

By the second day of class, Klaus and I could carry on such stimulating conversations as this:

"*Namaste.*"

"*Namaste.*"

"What is your name?"

"My name is Phil. What is your name?"

"My name is Klaus. Where do you live?"

"I live in California. Where do you live?"

"I live in Michigan. What is your father's work?

"My father is an engineer. Do you have brothers and sisters?"

And so on...

We plunged ahead, learning grammar, pronunciation, and spelling. Nepali was unlike any language we had encountered before. The verb was always at the end of the sentence and was conjugated according to person, number, affirmation, and status. Honorific verb suffixes were used when speaking to adults and informal suffixes were used for children. Each verb possessed fourteen forms in the present tense alone, then had another fourteen in the past tense, progressive, etc. The future tense was easy—just put "maybe" at the end of the sentence. We were fortunate that Nepali had no irregular verbs to memorize.

But we weren't so lucky with the pronunciation. Nepali words contained four different *D*'s, four *T*'s, three *S*'s, and so forth. We couldn't hear the differences between these sounds, much less produce them correctly. And some of the sounds, like the very difficult *Gh*, had to be aspirated with a blowing of air as we said them.

अमेरीकामा हुँदाखेरी फलिले पढाउने तालमि लनु भएको थियो । पढाउने तालमि लनु भएकोले वहाँलाई हसिाव र वज्ञिान राम्रोसंग पढाउने आउँछ । वहांले वधिार्थीहरुलाई सकेसम्म राम्रो बुभाउन कोशसि गर्नु हुन्छ । क्लाशमा जानु भन्दा पहिले वहाँ लेसन प्लान तयार गर्नु हुन्छ । लेसन प्लान तयार गर्नु भएपछि मात्र पढाउनु हुन्छ । नेपाली वधिार्थीहरुलाई वहांले पढाउनु भएको असाध्य मन पर्छ रे । वहाँलाई धेरै गफ गर्नु मन लाग्दैन ।

One hour each day was spent on reading and writing. The Devanagri alphabet—also used for Sanskrit and Hindi—has forty-five letters, plus half-letters. It has no similarity to the Roman alphabet, and though it looks outrageous, it is much more systematic than English. Mercifully, Nepali words are spelled almost exactly as they are pronounced.

By the end of the first two weeks of language training, we knew the basic verbs, numbers, family relations, foods, times of day, days of the week, colors, directions, emotions, and weather conditions. Even though we could struggle through a great number of situations, the thought of teaching in Nepali terrified us. We had just two and a half months left.

During this initial training, Klaus and I learned much about one another. He had a German mother and an American father, and he had solved the dilemma of choosing countries by coming to Nepal. He was as idealistic as I was, and he had once planned to become a doctor and to devote his life to work in the developing countries—the Albert Schweitzer of Asia. He wanted to save the world, or at least a part of it.

Can the world be saved with rabbits? Perhaps not, but Klaus is certainly the one to try.

As I hike, the rabbits scurry about in protest at the shaking of their basket. They are tired of being closed in and I am tired of carrying them.

The trail gains the top of the ridge shortly before Thoripaani. The houses are close set, straddling the trail in two long lines. Thoripaani is a large village and the houses are well kept. The window frames are painted red or yellow, and some have hanging flower boxes, though no flowers will be up until spring.

I'm directed to Klaus's house, and an excited boy rushes off to fetch him from school while I sit on a stone to wait.

Klaus strides down the trail, without a beard, but smiling broadly. He wears rubber sandals and has dirt between his toes.

"I got your letter," he says, "so we knew that you were coming to Lamidada on yesterday's plane. I guessed that you'd be here this morning, but I had some things to do at the school. I'm sorry that I wasn't here. I was…"

"What are you talking about? You're always apologizing about something. What's this?" I ask, grabbing a handful of flesh at his stomach. "You look fat!" I say this as an Asian compliment, meaning that he's healthy and strong.

"I eat well here."

"You must. Look, I brought you a present."

"Great, you got the rabbits. Where did you find them? I searched everywhere the last time I was in K'du."

"It was luck. The two females I got from friends, and then I scoured the bazaar till I found a male—that's the scruffy one."

"You must have had trouble getting them here. How much are you carrying?"

"About sixty-five pounds. I weighed it at the medical office before I left, but that was without the rabbits."

"You should have gotten a porter." He scrutinizes my rather substantial pack, noting the climbing equipment: crampons, ice axe, and over-boots. "So you really plan to do it."

"Do what?"

"The climb that you wrote about in your letter."

"Yeah. I guess so."

Klaus senses my reluctance to talk about it and he changes the subject. "Are you hungry?" he asks. "I got some special things last market day..."

Before eating, we collect some grass and leaves for the rabbits and set them free in his small side room. "This used to be my kitchen," says Klaus, "but now I always eat with the family. Didi is trying to get a teashop started, but first I want to build her a fireplace—one with a chimney—so she won't have to breathe all that smoke."

"And what about the rabbits? You'll breed them for the meat?"

"And use the fur! Did you see the hats that Pesout had made out of rabbit fur?" Klaus's eyes assume a dreamy look as he pictures those wonderful hats. "They were beautiful. I'm sure that the women here could start a good cottage industry by sewing things from the rabbit skins, once we get enough."

"I thought you were going into the leather business—tanning water buffalo skins left over from market days and selling them down in India."

"I still want to do that," he says with a trace of disappointment, "but we've had trouble getting acid to tan the skins."

The family's porch of dried mud feels smooth and cold as we sit outside eating pounded rice and drinking milk tea. Klaus's own room is in the government-leased house on the other side of the path, but he prefers to spend his time here. Village children pass by on their way home from school, and the afternoon shadows lengthen. We wear jackets and sweaters to protect us against the wind that blows across the ridge.

"What about the rabbit hutches? Have you started them?" I ask.

"No, there hasn't been time. But I have a design, and the two carpenters from the school will build them tomorrow. I've been busy with a proposal for a Peace Corps Partnership* project."

"But caring for rabbits doesn't cost that much. It…"

"The money won't be for that. It's to set up a lab-room. We'll outfit a room with tables, science equipment, and big windows for light."

"It sounds nice, but who'll use it after you're gone?" I ask.

"There's another science teacher who I hope will use it. He and the Headmiss are very excited about it."

"Headmiss? You have a *lady* Headmaster?"

"Yep."

We talk continuously, pausing only briefly for the evening rice. For both of us it's an orgy of English, and a lot has happened since we last talked three months ago. Klaus will be staying here for another year, but I've already finished my two years of teaching. He tells me of the village and the school,

---

* This was a program whereby an organization in the U.S. (a church, school group, club, etc.) could sponsor a special Peace Corps project. All the labor and a percentage of the cost came from the volunteer's village while the bulk of the material cost was donated by the sponsoring organization.

the students and the teachers. I tell him of my travels since I left my village in December: a journey to western Nepal to escort new volunteers to their schools, and a short trip to Darjeeling and Calcutta before flying to Lamidada.

As the night deepens so does the conversation. I ask a question for which I already know the answer; it's clear from the look in Klaus's eyes. "So tell me, how have you been?"

"All right," he shrugs. "You know."

I do know. One can enjoy life in the village and feel good about the work and have fun with Nepali friends, but it always comes back to one thing—loneliness. You can get used to new foods and a new language, but you always miss being with people from your own world, from your own century.

"What have you heard from Cindy?" I ask.

"She's married."

"What! Married? Just like that?"

"I got a newspaper clipping from her brother."

"How can she do that? Just because you're ten thousand miles away for a couple of years..."

"Yeah."

We have nothing more to say.

I join the rabbits in their little room and sleep, but not well. I'm troubled by broken dreams of Kay, something about a lost ring, and visions of a white mountain soaring into the sky—a mass of ice falling down with me underneath, doing nothing.

March 17

Thoripaani

Klaus is at school, teaching his classes and getting the carpenters started on the rabbit hutches. This leaves me to my own devices and I use the time to go through his collection of books. He's an intellectual with a supply of Camus, Dostoyevsky, and Marx (in German of course). I read Kafka's *Metamorphosis*, which still gives me a shudder.

Best of all, I find a detailed map of the area. I can pore for hours over a good map, especially a topographic map of high mountains. Tracing the contour lines with a finger, I look for solo climbing routes to the tops of the highest peaks. I close my eyes and picture the mountains, as vivid in my mind as my first view of Himalayan ice.

Chandra Man brought the motorcycle around a corner and there they were—the Himalayas stretched up to the sky. The air was crystal clear and the snow shone brightly in the sun. I craned my neck to look up. I was overwhelmed. How could any mountains be so high?

Chandra Man banked around a turn and they were gone. I held onto the seat. Another corner and they were back again. Majestic, magnificent, sublime. Clad in blue and white ice. Which one was Annapurna? I thought of the Frenchman, Maurice Herzog, who lost all his fingers and toes to frostbite when he first climbed Annapurna in 1950.

Chandra Man weaved the motorcycle down the twisting road. He was Administrative Assistant to the training program, and though I trusted his driving, I wished that he would slow down. Despite my fear, I enjoyed the wind blowing past my ears and being surrounded by the deep green hills. The road followed the bends in the river, and around each turn I gaped up at the mountains.

We had completed our two weeks of initial language training and we were now traveling to Sisuwa, a village 90 miles west of Kathmandu, near Pokhara in central Nepal. In Sisuwa our training would continue with a difference. Instead of staying together in a lodge, we would each be living with Nepali families— families that spoke no English and had never dealt with foreigners before. I knew only the name of the head of my family, Gopi Nath Baral, and that the household had two men, four women, and one child. I was grateful that my family didn't have more children. One of the trainees, Pesout, would be in a family with thirteen children and we all wished him luck. We could imagine him with an audience of small faces watching his every move. Children, we had learned, stared much more blatantly than did adults.

Most of us were apprehensive about being thrust into a non-English speaking family, but the language instructors tried to relieve our anxieties. They guaranteed that someone would accompany each of us to make introductions and to stay for a few hours to get everything settled. Fine.

Then the chartered bus had broken down halfway from Kathmandu to Sisuwa. Karki and the other language instructors stood idly around the crippled bus saying, "*Ke garne?*—What to do?" They gestured with a shrug that included a half-rotation of the wrist with the fingers pointed upward— almost like screwing in a light bulb—sometimes with one hand, sometimes with two. This didn't help the bus at all. *Ke garne* was both a belief in fated defeat and the total acceptance of a sad reality. In Nepal, it was an all-pervasive attitude of resignation.

To get to the village as soon as possible, some of us had piled into the attending jeep and others had climbed into the truck filled with baggage and teaching materials. Chandra Man's motorcycle had a place for a passenger, so I climbed aboard. I would learn two months later that I could have been summarily dismissed from the Peace Corps for riding on a motorcycle without a helmet.

We arrived in Sisuwa at a large house that was being rented for use as a training center. Most of our assorted homes were down two side roads a few kilometers away. The jeep returned to the crippled bus to fetch another load of trainees, and by the time we were all at the training center it was dark. Most of the staff was still with the bus, so we decided to go to our families without the aid of interpreters.

The jeep took some of the trainees up one road while I got into the truck for a short drive down the other. The moment we arrived, a chattering throng gathered around the truck. My name was called and I climbed out. In the darkness I could see only a mass of people. Someone pointed to a young man in the crowd, and that was all the introduction that I was ever given.

My things were on my back in a Kelty pack. It and a goose-down sleeping bag were mine to keep if I completed my two years of service. Under one arm I carried a metal box crammed with Nepali textbooks and their English translations. The young man took the kerosene lantern that I held, and after lighting it, he wordlessly led the way.

The walk seemed longer than it was. As my guide strode easily along, I stumbled behind him with my case of books. I was unaccustomed to walking in the dark and the lamp served more to blind me than to light the way. At the front of the house we had to jump a drainage ditch; I could hear—but not see—the water. The man took down the upper rung of a railed gate. After climbing over, he guided me into the yard and up a flight of concrete steps on the outside of the house. The stairs led to an open veranda covered by a low tin roof—so low that even though I was bent over, the pack snagged on it. I had to crawl in, pushing the case of books across the floor in front of me.

He pointed at two doors and asked me something that I didn't understand. I thought he was asking which room I would prefer. Not knowing how to say that it didn't matter, I hunched up my shoulders and turned up my palms in an American *I-don't-know* gesture that he had never seen before.

We entered the room on the left and he hung the lantern on a nail. The room was small and had a roof of corrugated tin that slanted down from seven to five feet high. Three walls were cement while the remaining one, which divided the two rooms that I had been offered, was a stack of unmortared bricks. The two windows had bars but no glass and were closed with simple wooden shutters. The plank floor was adorned with a plank bed. The room had no other furniture.

The young man sat down and patted the straw mat on the bed, "*Basnus*— Sit down."

I did, and I was overjoyed to have understood something. We were followed into the room by a score of giggling children.

"*Tapaailaai bhok laagyo?*—Are you hungry?" the man asked.

"I'm no hungry," I said.

"I'm *not* hungry," he corrected.

Stupid! The first thing I said and I said it wrong!

The children thought it was hilarious. They mimicked my mistake and grinned. A girl in a red frock balanced a baby on her hip with one hand and nonchalantly picked her nose with the other. A boy of about nine had his school English book with him, just in case. Altogether, the room held six children of various ages: four girls and two boys, including the baby.

I looked at the man sitting next to me and carefully thought out a question: "*Yi tapaaiko ketaaketiharu chhan?*—Are these your childrens?"

"No, they're my father's."

Double stupid! I had confused the son with the father. I decided that it was best to just sit quiet while they stared at me.

The boys asked me a few simple questions: my name, where I lived, my age. Nothing too hard; they had apparently concluded that I was feeble-minded. After that, the staring game resumed until I explained that I was tired and wanted to sleep.

They all filed out while the eldest son showed me in elaborate detail how to latch the door from the inside. I wondered who or what I needed to protect myself from.

I wasn't actually tired; I had only wanted to be alone. For an hour I lay on the bed and looked up into the dark. Was I truly there in the Himalayan foothills, smelling the smoke from a Nepali cooking fire? It had all happened so fast; none of it seemed quite real. Outside, crickets were chirping and their familiar song made me feel very far from home. I thought about Kay and felt doubts about my decision to leave her. I already missed her terribly and I had only been away for three weeks.

I woke in the morning with the uneasy feeling that I was being watched. I thought that I could see eyes peeking at me through the gaps in the brick wall, but I wasn't sure. I needed to relieve myself, and out in the yard the middle son asked me in honorific Nepali if I needed anything. He understood completely when I requested some water. He filled a rusted can from the irrigation canal that flowed behind the house and he led me back around two rice paddies to the *charpi*, the latrine.

The charpi was nothing more than a pit in the dirt with some tree branches laid parallel across the top. Some 4-foot-high poles were stuck into the ground around the hole, and pieces of burlap were draped over the poles to provide a screen of privacy. The charpi had been built solely for my benefit; the family would normally go out into the fields or among the bushes. I stepped out over the pit, stood precariously on two flexing sticks, dropped my pants, and squatted down to do my business. Toilet paper was not used in Nepal, so I followed the local custom and washed myself thoroughly with the water using my left hand. Perhaps this was crude, but it was certainly clean.

I returned to the house just as the clouds broke, revealing a pyramidal mountain that pierced the sky. From pictures, I recognized it as Machhapuchhare, The Fishtail. It rose to 23,000 feet in a smooth spire of rock and ice. It had never been climbed and it never would be; Machhapuchhare was considered sacred and the government prohibited climbers from attempting it.

The middle son came over to me as I scanned the mountains. He wanted to talk, and owing to his patience, I learned the family relations. The young man who had guided me to the house was his older brother, eighteen-year-old Megha Nath. He would soon be married. The other children were all his brothers and sisters; the Peace Corps census had classified only the baby as a child. The father was seldom home because he operated a trucking concern in the Terai, the Nepali lowlands adjacent to India. The middle son was called Ram Nath and he studied in the fourth class.

I sat on the veranda and watched the rice growing till Megha Nath called me down to eat. The kitchen door was only chest high and as I stooped through the entrance, my eyes began to sting from the smoke. By the door stood a small urn of water which I took outside to wash my hands. I left my shoes at the door when I went back in.

I had already learned much about the proper etiquette for living in a Hindu culture. Of utmost importance was the concept of *jutho*—ritual defilement. Feet, for example, were *jutho*, culturally unclean. Shoes were not to be worn in the house, and especially not in the kitchen. Pointing the bottoms of your feet at someone, or worse yet stepping over someone, was an insult. The left hand was also impure, *jutho*, and was not to be used to touch food or another person. Joining the fingers of either hand to form a circle, such as the American OK sign, was obscene. And on and on. It was a long list of things to remember.

Inside the kitchen, Megha Nath pointed to a 2-inch-high slab of wood which I sat on cross-legged. He had a higher seat and nine-year-old Ram Nath had a lower one. The baby sat on the floor of red mud, and the girls would all wait until the men and boys had finished eating. At the fire dishing out the rice was the mother, *Aamaa*. Her glass bangles jingled on her wrists as she worked. I was sitting further from the fire than the others, which forced Aamaa to get up to serve me. So to make it easier for her, I shifted my seat close enough for her to reach me. Megha Nath said, "No, no," and waved his hand sideways. I insisted on moving to help Aamaa, and their disapproval perplexed me. I assumed that a guest wasn't supposed to be so accommodating.

Aamaa gave me first a steel plate heaped with rice and then two brass bowls, one filled with lentil soup and the other holding some sort of dark vegetable. This was the invariable Nepali meal called *daal-bhaat*. Lentils were *daal* and rice was *bhaat*. I would eat essentially the same thing twice a day, every day, for my entire stay in Nepal.

I ate as I had been taught. I mixed some daal and vegetables into the rice and scooped it up with the fingers of my right hand. The day's vegetable was a mixture of bitter greens and pieces of potato, and it didn't exactly excite me. I ate till I was bursting but I managed to finish only half of the rice that I had been given. Meanwhile, the two boys were licking their plates clean. I felt ashamed; food that I had touched was jutho and could not be given to anyone else. They could only feed it to the chickens—a terrible waste.

"*Mitho bhayo. Malaai pugyo*—It was good. I'm full," I said apologetically and went out to wash my hands.

For the evening meal I was given a minuscule portion and Aamaa beamed when I quickly finished it and asked for more. Each meal we repeated the same confusing affair of me shifting my seat closer while Aamaa protested.

The language lessons continued, but now we had only four hours a day, and we were three trainees in a class instead of just two. The language teachers rotated groups every day. Each afternoon we received three hours of technical training, which included seminars on teaching methods, lesson planning, and student discipline.

Everything seemed to be going fine. I was doing well in class and the family could understand my broken Nepali—I just had difficulty comprehending their replies. Then one day Gopal, one of my favorite instructors, approached me with a grim look on his face.

"Phil-*ji*, we need to talk," he said in English.

"Sure. What is it?"

"It's your family. Aamaa asked me to talk to you about something."

"Really?" I didn't know what to say; I had thought we got along well together.

"You know they are *Braahman*?" It was more of a statement than a question.

"What! I was told they were *Kshetry*."

Braahman and Kshetry were two groups with greatly different status. Nepal was composed of a wide variety of ethnic groups and castes. The government made no official distinction between them, but each group maintained its own cultural practices and restrictions. Hindu tradition held the Braahman as the highest, purest caste while the Kshetry had a secondary ranking. A foreigner, such as a Peace Corps Volunteer, came from outside the system and was essentially out-caste. In practice, though, most Nepalis treated a foreigner equivalent to a Kshetry.

"They have a special part of the kitchen that is clean," explained Gopal, "where only a Braahman can go."

Triple stupid! I had learned this before, but I hadn't known that the family was Braahman, nor had I seen a raised part of the floor that would have shown me where it was clean and holy. At each meal I had moved into this clean section and had thus defiled it. Jutho! As well as being a terrible affront to Aamaa, I had caused her considerable work—having to scrub and re-sanctify the kitchen after each meal.

The next time we ate, I saw that the boundary of the clean area was just a beam in the roof. On the floor was no mark at all. I told Aamaa that I was very sorry, I hadn't known that I was sitting in the wrong place, from then on I would sit where I was, it was all my fault, and it wouldn't happen again. I was sure that she understood.

Later I talked with Gopal again—Aamaa had told him that I was very sorry about losing my place. She'd said that I was upset about having to sit in the back. She had gotten my meaning exactly backwards!

Gopal straightened the whole thing out, but from then on I was very careful about expressing my feelings in Nepali.

This reluctance was only one of my problems. Even though I was continually learning new Nepali words and new ways to communicate, I was still limited to very simple discourse: "I go now to class." "You like rice, because it tastes good." Nothing of what I said seemed significant. But besides this, I felt that my real concerns wouldn't interest a Nepali villager. I could speak with Megha Nath, but our worlds remained apart. I felt lonely even when surrounded by a crowd. The more people there were around me, the more isolated I felt. Some days were unbearably long, and dinner left me hungry even though I ate my fill. At night I would re-read letters from Kay:

Dearest Phil,

I have felt very in love with you this past week or so. I want to be able to write short notes to let you know specific feelings or moods when I don't have time to write more, but it seems I have so many things I want to tell you and so it's hard to sit myself down to write just a little. That usually means that I don't get around to it for a few days though.

Anyway, this will be fairly short. I mostly wanted to say that I love you. Honey, so much of the time you don't feel like you're far away at all! I've really been enjoying the picture of us at Lily Meadows and remembering those sweet days together. I'm getting choked up thinking how really neat and special you are. It feels really good to get choked up over you!!!

So, I hope to write you a longer letter in a day or two. Please take care of yourself, and stay happy, sweetheart.

Much love, Kay

Her letters made the evenings long and lonely. I always looked forward to the day's big escape—to sleep.

But there were fun times too. Just saying my name was good for a laugh. Nepali had no *f* sound, nor a short *i* sound, so the best that my name came out was something like *Peeleep*. If I said that I was called Phil, it was even worse for the *l* usually got lost.

Every morning when I was walking to school for my language lesson I was stopped by the same small boy pressing his hands together.

"*Namaste*," he would say.

"*Namaste*."

Then without exception he would ask, "*Tapaaiko naam ke ho?*—What is your name?"

"Phil."

He would then step back a pace, his face showing both shock and bewilderment, as though he hadn't heard me say my name countless times before. He'd pause a moment, then looking up at me with wide eyes, he would say with an air of absolute incredulousness, "*Peuw?*"

We played that scene every morning. It was much better to be called *Peeleep*.

Names. One day as I was looking at a picture of Kay in my room, Ram Nath, the nine-year-old, asked me who it was. It was a simple question except for the difficulty that the Nepali word for "what" was *ke*, pronounced the same as "Kay." Our Abbott and Costello exchange went like this:

"Who is that?" began Ram Nath.

"She is my friend, *What*," I answered.

"What? What is her name?"

"That's right. Her name is *What*."

"I don't know. What *is* her name?"

"Yes."

Klaus is luckier with his name. No one has trouble saying it nor understanding it. After browsing through Klaus's library, I find him at school as he ends his last class of the day.

He shows me around and we check on how the workmen are doing on the rabbit hutches. It's a three-section structure: one for males, one for females, and one for breeding. It won't be ready for another day. We help by cutting and splitting bamboo for the floor. The rest is made from hand-cut pine.

Walking back to the house, we pass a man with a limp. "See that man?" says Klaus. "He works for my neighbor, Bhim Bahadur. Last monsoon he was fixing some holes on Bhim Bahadur's roof and he fell off. He broke his leg and it looked pretty bad."

"They brought him to you?"

"Not really. I told them that they would have to carry him to the health post, a day and a half away."

"That's not too far."

"But that wasn't the problem. It was Bhim Bahadur. He kept insisting that if they took the man to the health post his leg would be cut off. He said that everyone taken to the health post had a leg cut off."

"Isn't that just because they wait until it's too late, until there's gangrene or they're about to die?" I ask.

"Yes. But I hadn't been here very long and they wouldn't listen to me. So they took care of him themselves and now he's walking around. Bhim Bahadur gloats about it, but I know if that leg had been properly set he wouldn't be limping, he..."

"Have you been doing much doctoring around here?"

"No, not after what happened in my first village."

"You never told me anything about that."

Klaus tells the story while we sit on the porch slurping Nepali tea: one part sugar, two parts milk, and three parts tea. Sweet and murky.

"There was no health post near the village," he begins, "so I tried to take care of anyone that came to me. The more I did that, the more people came. Fevers, cuts, diarrhea, all sorts of things. It got to be too much and the other teachers thought I was being taken advantage of.

"One night I was in my room talking with one of the other teachers when some men came to the door. The teacher went out to talk to them while I stayed inside. A man was sick and they wanted me to come and see him. The teacher told them that it was late and could wait until the morning. But what I didn't know, and what the teacher didn't tell me, was that they had carried the man on a litter for six hours. They had brought him to just outside my door. He lay there all night. I didn't find out till I got up in the morning."

Klaus pauses to gaze into his tea.

"Were you able to help him?" I ask.

"No," Klaus whispers. "He was dead. He died right outside my house, while I was sleeping and didn't even know about it."

"Oh God. I don't think I could have handled that. Did they blame you?"

"The man's family did, but no one else."

"How could that teacher have done nothing, said nothing?"

"I don't know."

The weather turns foul while we eat the evening's daal-bhaat. A fierce wind drives the rain against our faces as we rush back to Klaus's room. He shutters the windows and lights the lamp, while I take out my maps. He wants to know what my plans are. A detailed map of the Everest area covers the bed and the lamp casts golden light on our faces.

"First to Namche Bazaar," I say, pointing. "That'll probably take six days from here. I'll buy food and kerosene there and rest a few days. Then four or five days up to Lobuche. Some Sherpas cook food there, so I can afford to stay a while and acclimatize, making trips up these peaks here, both 18,000 footers, and to Everest Base Camp. I also want to try this one—Lobuche East, 20,075 feet." My words come very rapidly due to excitement mixed with fear.

"I think there's a route up this ridge here," I continue, "but it'll probably be extreme. I talked with the Nepal Mountaineering Association and they said that only two permits have ever been issued to climb Lobuche East. They said that it's a very difficult mountain, so I'll just have to go and see."

"Wait. You're going to do all this alone?"

"Yeah, unless I meet another climber up there. Why not?" Klaus shakes his head and studies the map.

"Then I'd like to go over this pass to Gokyo, but the snow may be too deep. I'll return to Namche, rest for a few days and get more food, before heading out this way."

"Out over the Tasi Lapcha pass?" asks Klaus. "And back to Kathmandu?"

"Yes. I'll take a porter as far as the pass. I hear it's almost impossible to find the way without one. I want to stay on the top at 19,000 feet for a few days. From there my ultimate goal is to climb Pharchamo, 20,580 feet."

"Solo?"

"It scares me too. Two Japanese climbers were killed on Pharchamo just a few weeks ago. I read the report the expedition leader filed, but his English wasn't the greatest. Apparently four climbers made it to the summit, but they got caught in a storm on the way down and were forced to spend the night out at about 20,000 feet. In the morning they continued climbing down, but they were about done in and the front pair fell into a crevasse. I don't know if they got the bodies out or if they're still up there on the mountain.

"So that's my trip. It should take about two months."

"Phil, are you crazy?"

"Yeah, sure," I say smiling. "Aren't you?"

Thoripaani 7,200 feet

ending under the tap, I rinse the soap from my hair. The cold water cuts
into my back and I grimace. A cloudy day is a poor one for bathing,
but at least it's a day with water. The village has had no water since I arrived.
According to Klaus, the farmers who live up the ridge periodically cut the
plastic pipe to get the water before it reaches the village. Thoripaani literally
means "Scarce Water." I'll be leaving tomorrow, so I don't know when I'll be
able to wash again. The villagers are accustomed to Klaus bathing here, and
no one comes to watch me.

As on the previous day, I meet Klaus at the school when his classes end.
The rabbit hutch is finished, so along with the two carpenters, we each take
a corner and lug it to the village. The cage is wider than the trail and we are
unable to see our feet as we grunt and stumble down the rocky path. Two
dozen students follow. They laugh at our curses and turn the procession
into a parade.

We make a place for the hutch beneath the stairs in the family's house,
and the rabbits are both happy and confused. I worry about security—the
rabbits could be stolen or they might escape if taken out. I fashion three
hasps from a tin can, but Klaus has no spare locks. So until he can get some,
we return the bunnies to their room.

It's a curious little room, made more curious from three days of the rabbits
and me living there. It's just about eight feet long and it tapers in width from
six feet down to four. No chair, table, nor bed of any kind grace the room,
though two straw mats cover the uneven floor. The mats are embellished with

three days' worth of black little rabbit turds. The low window has shutters that stay neither opened nor closed unless jammed with one of my stout climbing boots. The walls are partially mudded and partially whitewashed, and in one corner is a large hole that extends up into the stonework. This hole occasionally releases a flow of fine dirt that fills the air. Next to the hole is Klaus's homemade fireplace, with chimney. My mountaineering gear lies in a heap in the middle of the room and behind the door is a 20-pound chunk of limestone for whitewashing the house next year.

Klaus and I enter, push my stuff to one side, and let the rabbits free on the floor. They are more at home here. The ceiling is not quite high enough for us to stand, so we take places on the mats. Perched atop a metal trunk are two dusty long-stemmed wine glasses and a half-dozen old Christmas cards— Santa Claus and angels. From this trunk, Klaus pulls out two recorders and a collection of music: Telemann, Bach, and Vivaldi. We choose some pieces that won't be too hard, and the rabbits hop about excitedly.

"I hope that you won't have trouble with them," I say, gesturing toward the rabbits with my flute.

"What do you mean?"

"A lot of Nepalis won't eat rabbits. They think of them as rats. And the butcher may not want to kill them. It's hard to kill something that's so floppy and soft. Also you might get too attached to them."

One of the rabbits searches for a warm place up the leg of Klaus's pants. "I see what you mean," he says.

We tune up and play a duet while the bunnies keep sporadic time with their hopping. They have very distinct personalities. One is an explorer; she checks out every corner of the room. If the door is opened she immediately jumps out, then comes right back in to see what has happened while she was away. The fat one eats constantly; she now nibbles at a plate of day-old rice. If she can't find something to munch, she'll settle on licking your feet. What bliss to have that pink little tongue flicking between your toes! The scruffy male just sits all day in bewilderment; perhaps he was traumatized during his time in Kathmandu at the bottom of a three-tiered cage.

We are halfway through an interesting piece when I'm suddenly convulsed with mirth. I put down my recorder and laugh. "What's so funny?" asks Klaus.

"Aw, come on, look at this place. Look at us! This *beautiful* room of yours, with shit on the floor, rabbits hopping around, cobwebs up there, and we're playing Bach! What the *hell* are those wine glasses for?"

"Well, sometimes it's nice to be ah—elegant!" He sees the absurdity of it all, and we enjoy a melee of laughter as we point out the eccentric things in the room. The hole in the wall concurs by delivering us a cloud of dust.

We rock from side to side as we laugh, and the rabbits hop with increased excitement. We toast one another with the empty wine glasses, and Klaus checks a dirty sock for any long-lost Christmas presents.

As Peace Corps Volunteers we seldom get together and manage to push aside our troubles—the isolation, disease, and frustration—but when we do, it's always uproarious. In spasmodic relief, Klaus and I howl until our eyes water. It has been months since we laughed so hard.

"This looks like something from a movie by Fellini," I say as a rabbit licks my toes and Klaus wipes the dust off Santa Claus.

"But this is real!" says Klaus.

"Yeah, you're probably right."

Deuraauli 8,000 feet

The house is two storeys tall and the roof is adorned with newly printed prayer flags. Out front, four women and two men sit in a circle as they husk a pile of maize. Despite protests from Klaus, I have left Thoripaani without breakfast and now, after two hours of hiking, I'm hungry.

"*Khaanaa paauna sakinchha*—Is food available here?" I ask.

"What do you eat?" wonders a man who has a cap pulled down over his ears.

"*Daal-bhaat.*"

"*Basnus*—Sit down," he says.

Without the rabbits the pack is lighter, but not much, and I am glad to have it off. Normally I would help with the work while waiting to eat, but today I am content with just watching.

The people here are Sherpa. Of Nepal's myriad ethnic groups and tribes, the Sherpas are perhaps the most famous, having achieved worldwide acclaim as high-altitude porters and climbers on Himalayan expeditions. They are of Tibetan ancestry, as is evidenced by the Sherpa language. But like most people in Nepal, they can speak Nepali as well as their kindred tongue. Sherpa men and women traditionally wear heavy black felt robes and boots, though as in most of Asia, it's more popular for the men to dress in Western clothes.

The man in the cap takes me upstairs to the kitchen. I remove my boots at the door, but he keeps his on. Sherpas are Buddhist, not Hindu, and Himalayan Buddhists have no taboo against shoes in the kitchen; it's too cold to worry about such things.

We sit down to eat, but the main course isn't rice. It's *dhiro*, a thick paste made by mixing roasted flour into boiling water. Depending on the type of flour used, dhiro can range from incredibly bad to almost palatable. We have it made from corn flour, which is good enough. We mix the dhiro with a broth of sour vegetable leaves, and after eating a plateful, I'm more than satisfied.

I pay for the meal, and lastly before setting off again, I request water to fill my canteen. The Sherpas laugh. They think I'm foolish to carry water when streams are found along the way, but I know from experience to fill my canteen whenever I have a chance.

"Do you have *any* water left?" Jim asked despairingly.

"Just a bit," I answered as I took out my bottle. For psychological reasons I always kept at least a sip of water in my canteen. That way I was never *really* out of water.

Jim and I shared the last few drops, which reminded me of a cartoon I had once seen: The legionnaire in the Sahara pleads to his captain for some water. The captain relents and gives the soldier his day's ration—one drop, which he greedily drinks from his tin cup, complete with sounds of glug-glug, slurp-slurp, and smack-smack. The legionnaire finishes, and wipes his mouth with his sleeve saying, "*Whew!* I couldn't drink another drop."

"I imagine that there's water further up in the ravine," I said without conviction.

"I hope so," said Jim, humoring me.

The afternoon sun shone brightly, making it extremely hot for the middle of October. The top of the pass was another 2,000 feet up and we hadn't had much to eat or drink since the previous day. We looked at each other with tired eyes and continued upwards. Jim took the lead and I lagged behind.

It was Dasai, Nepal's biggest holiday, in honor of the Hindu god Durga. We had an eight-day break in training and most of the trainees had dispersed on various trips. Jim and I were on our way to Chitwan National Park in the Terai, the lowlands, where we might see rhinoceros and even tiger. I also hoped to travel to Lumbini, the place of Buddha's birth, but Jim was unenthused by the thought of making a religious pilgrimage.

Already the journey had taken twice as long as we had expected. A ride on a packed bus, a day's hiking, and a river crossing by dug-out canoe had brought us to the base of the pass. We hadn't eaten, and we had been sure that we would find water up the ravine.

But the ravine was dry, and we could only persist upwards. The climb seemed interminable, and my lips began to crack. I carried the heavier pack and Jim slowly left me behind. I sat down to rest and tried to lick some water from the canteen's cap.

Towards the end of the day, I heard Jim calling from above. He had found water and I quickened my pace. I came upon him sitting by a small spring, looking at his watch dejectedly.

"How much time left?" I asked.

"About five minutes."

We were under strict orders from the Peace Corps medical staff never to drink water that wasn't first sterilized, either with iodine or by boiling. The iodine needed a mere twenty minutes to be effective, but those twenty minutes could sometimes feel like twenty days.

On the top of the pass was a fifteen-house village where we could spend the night. Jim and I attempted to answer everyone's questions about us while we devoured heaping portions of pounded rice and curried vegetables. At nightfall I tried to write a letter to Kay, but I was hindered by the people watching. They repeatedly inched closer till they blocked the light of my candle. But the darkness and my sloppy writing didn't matter as it was one of the many letters that Kay never received. I had been told that people were stealing my letters to get the stamps. To send an airmail letter to America cost four rupees—almost fifty cents—the same as a laborer earned for a full day's work.

The following morning—with canteens full—we crossed the ridge for the long descent to the Terai. At one point Jim stopped abruptly and pointed to a tree that was bespeckled with a family of monkeys. They were covered in black fur, but their white faces flashed against the dark foliage as they scrambled from branch to branch. A mother with a baby clinging to her stomach paused to stare back at us. Neither of us had ever seen monkeys in the wild before. Jim spread his fingers and held them in front of his face. "Ah. That's more like I'm used to," he said, imitating the familiar sight of monkeys viewed through the bars of a cage.

The transition between hills and Terai was drastic. It was as though Brahma, the Creator, had drawn a line with His finger, proclaiming one side hilly and cold, and the other side flat and hot.

The trail to Narayangarh was as straight as a road and just as wide. We were surprised that the town's outlying houses were so flimsy compared to the thick-walled stone houses of the hills. They were made of wood or mudded wattle-work, and many of them sat on stilts. Since it was Dasai, the road was filled with families out visiting relatives. Everyone wore their finest clothes: mother wrapped in a bright red sari, father sporting a new cap, and the children wearing matching shirts and frocks. If they got new clothes once a year, it was on Dasai. Besides the new outfits, everyone was adorned with elaborate tikaa marks which covered their foreheads in color. Between the clusters of houses stood an occasional wooden Ferris wheel. They were turned by hand and had places for four shrieking children. Each wheel stood for just eight days before being dismantled and stored until next Dasai.

We reached Narayangarh, a hot dusty town crowded with shops and confusion, and found a cheap room for the night. In the evening we were visited by a black-skinned man who wore a flowing costume of white muslin. He entered without knocking and said, "*Tapaaiharulaai dastkhat garnu parchha.*" He looked at each of us, made a motion like he was writing, repeated himself, and left.

"Jim, do you know what he said?" I asked.

"No, but I guess he'll come back if it's important." Jim stretched out on his too-short bed and savored the slight breeze from an anemic ceiling fan. "Was he speaking Hindi or Nepali?"

"I'm not sure. They do speak a lot of Hindi down here," I said as I untangled the mosquito net. "And it's frustrating with our Nepali. We know so many words and structures that we could say a great deal if we could only put it all together."

"You're right," said Jim, sitting up now, "but it doesn't help much if we can't understand what *they* are saying. Don't you sometimes have doubts about this whole thing?"

"You mean the Peace Corps? I'm beginning to realize that you have to be a fool to really think you can do much here. We can barely speak, so how can we teach? And everything is decided by tradition or by the culture, so how can we change anything? I don't even know if we are *supposed* to change anything."

"But Phil, I'm worried about something more than that. What happens to someone who lives here for two years? I remember that Dan asked in Philadelphia if it was true that some volunteers had emotional problems during their time here. The staff acted like it was just an evil rumor. But now I've heard that several volunteers a year have to be sent home because they crack up."

"Are you serious?"

"Yes. There's one guy who's still in a sanitarium. He was in a very remote area and the villagers sent word to Kathmandu that he wouldn't eat and just stayed in his room all the time. Dr. Leslie and a couple others flew out there by helicopter and they found him sitting in his own shit. When they entered his room he went berserk. 'Bouncing off the walls,' they said. They couldn't control him at all. Then the doctor asked him, 'Don't you want to go to Washington and see the beautiful cherry blossoms?' That somehow calmed him a bit and they were able to tranquilize him. Medical records are all confidential, so no one hears about it."

The story sounded incredible, but I believed it to be true. Even during training I could see little quirks appearing in many of us. One guy locked himself in his room whenever he had a chance and played the flute for hours and hours. Another trainee wrote letters to her friends continuously. She had an immense correspondence and she kept a chart of when she wrote and received each letter. Two friends pulled out books at every opportunity, even during a five-minute break in class. A few drank heavily at each party, and several non-smokers, including Jim, had begun puffing a couple of packs a day. Then there was the wandering-eyed volunteer that Jim and I had first met in Kathmandu, and another who had told us that he knew of only three volunteers in Nepal who *didn't* use dope.

"I wonder," said Jim, "what sorts of changes we'll have to make in ourselves in order to survive here. I'm afraid that Nepal could put a twist in my personality that I don't want."

"I had a strange feeling the other day," I said. "It was as though I was a horse that had been broken. For so long I had been fighting against Nepal, trying to hold on to my old ways. But now I was speaking Nepali, wearing local clothes, and sitting on the floor while I ate with my hands. I felt broken from who I had been. I was something, someone new."

Jim looked at me evenly. "I think that's what I'm most afraid of."

The man in white reappeared, again without knocking, carrying a ledger. He wanted us to sign in.

The next morning we attempted to get transportation to the village of Chanuli Bazaar. A cousin of Jim's training family lived there and he had promised to show us around the national park. A tea seller told us that a bus went to Chanuli Bazaar, but it was actually a tractor which towed a flatbed wagon full of people. We asked him when it would go.

"*Ahile*—Now," was his reply.

We sat down with our packs, and after an hour we bought some tea and bread. Jim asked the tea-wallah about the "bus."

"It's coming, coming," he said.

After another hour, it was my turn to ask.

"Yes, it's coming," he answered. "First it brings people from Chanuli Bazaar here, then it goes back. It'll be here in four hours."

Jim and I were shocked. Four hours! Is that what *now* meant? What if he had said *soon* or worse yet *late*? Clearly the Nepali concept of time was different from ours. In Mexico they say *mañana, mañana*—tomorrow, tomorrow, but in Nepal it's *bholi, parsi*—tomorrow, or the next day. Eventually we would all call this Nepali time; things happened when they happened, not before and not after. We had to learn new ways to think, besides new ways to speak.

We were now unsure when, or even if, a bus went to Chanuli Bazaar, and we didn't really know if the cousin could help us once we got there. So we decided to salvage something of the trip by going to Lumbini instead.

First we had to cross the Narayani River to reach the road that led to Bhairawa, 80 miles to the west. There was no bridge, just a leaky ferryboat. It was paddled by three men and it had room for forty people plus all their baggage. The crossing was an adventure for Jim and me, and a prosaic trip for everyone else. In mid-river a woman pulled up her blouse to nurse her baby, and two men had a loud argument. The only words that we caught were "work," "holiday," and "money."

A garishly painted bus waited on the other side. The seats had been designed to hold two people each and they were already filled with three occupants apiece. The ceiling was too low for us to stand in the aisle, so we clambered up to the full-length baggage rack on the roof. This was the best place; we would get a grand view and plenty of air.

Before we left, another fifty people boarded the bus. Some came up to the roof, but most went inside, cramming into the aisle. The bus lurched uncertainly from the overloading and slowly plodded from one small village to the next. At each stop more people embarked. They sat on each other's laps inside, and up top I tried to cordon off a small space for myself—just enough room for my arms and legs. Someone kept pushing a basket up against me and I kept pushing it back. Another stop, and more people climbed in. It was incredible.

Jim and I were separated by a mass of humanity. Half of Nepal seemed to be on that bus: white-haired men holding canes, school girls braiding their hair, businessmen wearing sunglasses, and whole families carrying baskets of food. Some were well dressed and some were in rags, but everyone was in a happy, festive mood. It was Dasai and we were all on holiday. Most everyone carried presents with them: bolts of brightly patterned cloth, shiny new pans, chickens for a feast, and belligerent goats.

With each stop came more people. We pressed and squeezed to make room for everyone. Leaning over the side, I could see that the front and back doors would no longer close—a dozen men hung from them and they each had just a single hand and foot in actual contact with the bus. People sat in the windows with a leg or two dangling inside, while others stood on the window sills and clung to the luggage rack for balance. Viewed from a distance, the bus would have been totally concealed beneath the solid mound of people. As for me, the little area that I had tried to monopolize now contained five people besides myself: three adults and two children. I could no longer see nor feel my legs; a boy and an old man were sitting on them. I had to push the boy aside when I needed to scratch my nose. Jim wasn't doing any better. He was wedged next to a man with a tubercular cough who continually spat over him.

Then out of a window and up to the roof came a man crawling over everyone—the ticket teller! He collected fares and gave out bright yellow slips of paper. He mysteriously knew everyone who had yet to pay.

After five hours, we turned onto the road that connected Pokhara with the Terai and India. At the junction stood a bus headed south to Bhairawa.

Jim and I gratefully extracted our packs from the roof of one bus and transferred them to the roof of the other.

This new bus was far less crowded and we made good time, reaching Bhairawa in the late afternoon. Lumbini was only 15 miles west, so we decided to stay in Bhairawa and make just a day trip to Buddha's birthplace. Since we had been told that no vehicles went to Lumbini, we were surprised to find a tin shack with a sign advertising a bus service.

"Tomorrow, when goes bus to Lumbini?" we asked hopefully.

"No. It doesn't go. It only goes in the dry season."

The dry season? Jim and I were bewildered. The parched ground showed that it hadn't rained since the summer monsoon.

We put our things in a lodge and hunted for some other transport. Taxis and private cars wouldn't go, and a bicycle-rickshaw was too expensive. Unlike Kathmandu, bicycles were not for rent; they too easily disappeared across the border into India. After supper we continued our search and found a man with a soft spot for foreigners who rented out a friend's bike and his own for the trip.

We left at 7 a.m. in glorious sunshine. The road of packed dirt jostled our bikes, and the surrounding fields were carpets of green rice and yellow mustard. Gigantic white-backed vultures rode the thermals overhead, and far to the north glistened the Himalayan snows. We stopped for directions and I asked a man what mountains they were.

"Annapurna, Dhaulagiri, Everest," he replied with a sweep of his arm.

We smiled, realizing that the man had no idea what he was talking about. Everest lay way too far east to be seen from there. Those mountains were just names to him. It was one more thing to laugh about as we rode along on our creaking bikes.

We crossed two large streams on footbridges and then came to the river. A massive concrete bridge was being built, but it would require at least another year of work. Now we understood about the dry season. No vehicles could go to Lumbini until the river dried up in late winter.

We hoisted our bikes to our shoulders and waded across. Just short of the far side, I floundered in deep water, wetting our wallets and cameras. We dried them in the sun and were soon cycling again.

Our arrival in Lumbini was almost a letdown. Scattered about were crumbling temples, ruins that were mere piles of rubble, and little else. The government was developing the grounds into a park and was establishing a museum, but these were in their infancy. Only a handful of people strolled about and that seemed peculiar; Lumbini should certainly have ranked with Muhammad's Mecca and Jesus's Bethlehem. But Lumbini's disrepair was perhaps fitting, since Buddha scorned all acts of worship. He would be appalled at his own deification.

King Ashoka's 2,200-year-old pillar was the most impressive monument in Lumbini. I sat beneath a tree and contemplated the pillar, hoping to feel something of the sacredness of Buddha's birth, but I was unmoved. It was ironic to have our four-day journey by foot, boat, bus, and bike conclude in disappointment. We might have learned a philosophical lesson from this, but our biggest gain of the trip was an insight into Nepali travel. I rose from under the tree and Jim came over. He was bored and wanted to return to Bhairawa.

The following day, a long bus ride took us up to Pokhara, and the next morning we came home to Sisuwa. We were greeted with the news that one more of our group had decided that Nepal wasn't for him and had returned to the States. Homesickness for his friends and family was his compelling reason. I respected his decision. I felt that no one should stay who preferred to leave. So we were one fewer; we were nineteen.

Nineteen. There's not nineteen now, just one. Sometimes I feel like that's how it has always been. Alone I descend 2,000 feet to the bottom of a gorge, and alone I trudge up again to the ridge tops. I feel good to be on my own. That's how I accomplish the most.

The air cools as the sun slips behind the far ridge. If I sprint up the trail I can regain the sunshine. The race is a strange one, and I enjoy the feel of my legs working and pushing. I need to get into condition for the high climbing that I'll be doing further along. I look up the hillside and imagine it to be Pharchamo Peak—I suck air and push to the summit, higher than any mountain in North America or Europe. The race is a draw. The sun makes a hazy exit as I arrive at a cluster of thatched-roofed houses. I know from talking with Klaus that these are the first homes of Waakhu. A man stands at the edge of a terraced field and looks down at me. He seems puzzled by my sudden appearance.

"*Ma kahaa basna sakchhu?*—Where can I stay?" I call up to him.

He tilts his head to one side and points down to a house that has two crows perched on the roof.

I turn to study the house and I ask him, "Is that your house?" but it's too late; he's already gone.

I reach the house across dry fields. The crows don't budge and nobody's home. I drop my pack to the ground and put on my shirt for a possibly long wait. It doesn't matter when they return—I have nowhere else to go.

March 20

Waapsu 6,700 feet

"*Tapaailaai ke chaahiyo*—What more will you have?" asks the woman at the fire. Her ears are pierced by rods that support silver-dollar-sized disks of brass, and her nose is beautified with an ornament that dangles over her mouth like a small shield.

"Some more rice," I answer.

A morning of walking has brought me here from Waakhu and I'm hungry. The family is poor, and they replace the missing vegetables and lentils with thin onion soup and watered-down milk. The woman is impressed by the amount of rice I eat, and I stand to go. Without a Nepali word for "thank you", I merely nod my head and say, "*Mitho bhayo*—It was good."

I wash my hands outside and notice that the neighbors have gathered while I was eating. A dozen men squat or stand about the courtyard. They watch me critically as they smoke and gossip. I don't understand a word; they are *Rai* and they speak their own language. A dozen varieties of Rai language exist, and villagers who live just a valley apart may be unable to communicate. All the men wear large *kukuri* knives in their sashes and belts. They hold their heads erect, and everyone waits several minutes before switching languages to Nepali and beginning with the usual questions.

"Where are you coming from?" asks the man with the biggest kukuri.

"This morning I come from Waakhu," I say as the head of the household seats himself next to me on the house's stone foundation. "I'm going to Namche. How far can I get today?"

"Oh, maybe to Karikhola. It's about…"

"No, he can't," interrupts one of the younger men. "*We* could get to Karikhola, but not him."

The first man nods his head in agreement. "Why go to Namche? It's so cold there. *Brrr!* What do you do?"

"I'm a school teacher."

"In Namche?"

"No, in Sindhupalchowk District."

"*Ah, ah,*" they all say, but it's unlikely that they know where Sindhupalchowk is.

"Where's your porter?" wonders a man who puffs a cheroot by my pack.

"I don't have a porter. What for? I can carry my things myself. I don't need a porter."

They talk this over in Rai. An Englishman carrying a load like that! How strange. They continue in Rai and I'm forgotten.

Impatient to get started, I ask the house owner, "*Daaju*—Older Brother, how much for food?"

"Twenty," he says with no hesitation.

I laugh at his joke. That's four times the usual price. "Twenty what?" I say with a grin. "Twenty *paisaa?*"*

"Twenty rupees," he says in grim tones.

"That's too much," I say as I take out my cloth money pouch. "What's the right price?"

"I told you it's twenty rupees."

The men remain motionless, watching me through narrow eyes. "You know that's not right." I pull a bill from my pouch. "Here."

He refuses the five-rupee note that I offer him, saying, "Five rupees? What good is that? If you won't pay what's proper, then don't pay at all!"

I'm flabbergasted. "Five rupees is what I paid in Waakhu."

---

* One hundred *paisaa* equals one rupee.

"But you had milk!" He gestures wildly. "Do you know how much a *paathi* of rice costs here? Fifty rupees! And you'll pay even more in Namche." (A paathi of rice is about 8 pounds.)

"A paathi is thirty rupees in Waakhu," I say, correcting him.

He sets his teeth and shakes his head. His wife, with the baby on her hip, comes out to watch the commotion. I try to give her the five rupees, but after seeing the look on her husband's face, she refuses. I press the money into the baby's eager hand instead.

"What good is giving that to a baby?" he bellows. "A baby can't use money." The baby apparently understands him and lets the bill flutter to the ground.

I approach the surrounding men and ask, "What's the right price for food? Twenty rupees? You know that's not right."

They answer me with a stern silence and whiffs of exhaled smoke.

The situation is hopeless; we are both too proud to acquiesce. "*Hunchha—* So be it," I say and I put on my pack to leave.

They let me go without another word and the money remains on the ground untouched.

I stalk down the trail fuming. The uncompromising cheat! The thief.

Robbed! I couldn't believe it. I counted my money five times.

"Jim, Mary," I called. "Come here a second. Have you got all your money? I'm missing about 200 rupees."

"Are you sure?" they said. "Have you checked in your pack?"

"Yes. Yes. I looked there and I searched the room. And there was something strange—the sack for my sleeping bag was under the mattress, and some other things were stashed in the corner. It was as though someone had hidden them, hoping that I'd leave them behind."

Jim and Mary had no explanations. After two months of training, the three of us, plus Kabindra our language instructor, were completing a fortnight of practice teaching. Our particular village was five hours' walk from Sisuwa and the other trainees were also teaching at various schools in the area. During our stay we had been living with a Braahman named Bhoj Raaj who was the *Pradhaan Panch*, the head of the village council. This was our last day. All that remained was to pay for our food and give exams at the school.

"Everyone knew I had that money," I said. "When Indra came to pay us on Monday, he stopped me in the middle of class and counted out the money with everyone watching." Indra, we all knew, liked to be seen in a role of importance.

"But not everyone had a key to that room," said Jim. "Only someone from the family could have gotten in there."

"I don't know if this will help," offered Mary in her slight Bostonian accent. "But you know how the oldest daughter, Nirmila, has been asking me for money and gifts the whole time? Yesterday morning when I woke up, my watch was missing. Nirmila had taken it during the night and was wearing it. She wouldn't give it back. She demanded that I give it to her as a present, and I had to pull it off her wrist. She wouldn't think twice about taking someone's money."

We spoke with Kabindra and told him our suspicions.

"But Bhoj Raaj is the Pradhaan Panch," said Kabindra. "You can't say he's a thief. That would be a very bad thing. You just have to forget about it. There's nothing to do."

Bhoj Raaj the Pradhaan Panch. Bhoj Raaj the Pradhaan Panch. He had made us memorize his name and title the first day we had met him. He had always seemed a little too proud of himself, this high-caste Braahman. He acted as though we were there for his personal amusement, or as a means to enhance his status in the village, another feather in his cap. His children were the brattiest ones in our classes. And the previous day Bhoj Raaj had insisted that we take photographs of him, his children, and his two wives. The two wives were also a point of vanity for Bhoj Raaj. They lived in separate houses, and Bhoj Raaj lived with the newer, younger wife. At the photo session the older wife had refused to be photographed with the younger, and I had noticed that the children of the older wife were dressed in poorer clothes than the younger wife's kids. Bhoj Raaj's high position had bothered me from the start, and now it prevented me from inquiring about my stolen money.

"Can't we tell him that I've *lost* some money and that maybe he'll find it after we're gone?" I suggested to Kabindra.

Kabindra said nothing. Our language instructors were surrogate parents to us, teaching us how to speak and how to act, even how to think. We didn't argue with them; they were always right. So we paid for our meal— Jim loaned me some money—and we thanked Bhoj Raaj for the wonderful two weeks that we'd had there. Not a word was aired about my missing 200 rupees. Nirmila, I was convinced, had committed the perfect crime.

The school was thirty minutes away in the direction of Sisuwa, so we took our packs with us, and we wouldn't return to the house. We arrived early and Mary, who had neater handwriting than Jim or I, began copying our exam questions onto the movable blackboard.

She wrote slowly and carefully, with her left hand, checking that the spelling and strange Devanagri characters were correct. Her left-handedness had greatly amused the students at first. Mary always ate with her right hand, as was essential, but she wrote with her left. To Nepali children, this was as peculiar as walking backwards or standing on one's head. But by our second week, the students had stopped grinning and had accepted this as one more of our many oddities.

I watched Mary write while I reviewed my two weeks of practice teaching. I had been surprised to discover that I was indeed capable of teaching classes solely in Nepali. My language was mediocre, but the students truly learned from what I tried to say. To prepare myself for a single forty-five-minute lesson I needed a minimum of two hours. I thought out exactly what I wanted to say and looked up all the new words in the dictionary. I taught with a vocabulary list in my hand which included a copy of everything that I would write on the board; we became supreme fools when we misspelled words in class. Science classes were fun because we could do experiments and demonstrations, but they also had the disadvantage of requiring complicated explanations that were nearly impossible using our limited Nepali. Teaching mathematics was simpler. We could readily make up problems that would keep a class busy. We just had to be careful not to say a number wrong. Nepali numbers didn't follow a simple pattern like English numbers. For example: fifty is *pachaas* and two is *dui*, but fifty-two is *baaunna*. Clear as mud.

The ninth class was assembled, and we carried in the blackboard of questions. The students sat at long narrow tables, elbow to elbow, three to a bench. A din rose in the room the moment we set up the board.

"*Chup laaga. Chup laaga*—Shut up. Shut up," demanded Mary, but her effort was futile; Nepali students read aloud, and the students in the back rows needed their friends in the front to read them the questions.

I walked down the narrow aisle and found several students holding their science books open on their laps. I grabbed the books and flung them under their benches. One of these students was Bhoj Raaj's eldest son. The other boys pointed and grinned.

Worse than reading aloud, we learned that they also wrote aloud. They spoke their answers as they wrote them. With a sharp ear they could hear each other's responses. Persistent *chup laaga*'s quieted them slightly but it was pointless; sitting so close together, they could easily see one another's papers. We were infuriated. It was a slap in the face to us; they didn't even make a pretence at doing their own work.

As the minutes ticked by, Mary's face grew red with rage. She had been educated at parochial schools staffed by nuns and to her cheating on an exam was intolerable. She stormed around the room demanding that the students look at their own papers. She shouted "*Timi, timi*—You, you," and slapped her little hand on a desk. The students all looked up, for a large percentage of them were truly copying another's answers. They protested that they weren't doing anything and they returned to their papers snickering.

We were a pitiful sight as we tried to maintain order with the students stealing glances at their books, passing notes to each other, and calling answers across the room. They seemed puzzled as to why we were so upset about their cheating. They were just trying to help each other. What was wrong with that? They certainly realized that we were powerless to stop them. We weren't their regular teachers, we were leaving that day, and we could neither fail them nor lower their grades.

One boy stood up to consult with his friends behind him. I pushed him back into his seat and yelled, "*Basa!*—Sit!" He looked offended for a moment, then tilted his head to one side and smiled to his friends. Jim preferred the mean, silent look, which didn't work either.

The period mercifully came to an end, but the students bombarded us with complaints when we asked for their papers. "It wasn't enough time." "The test was very hard." "There were too many questions." The students clung to their exams, and we were forced to pull the papers from their hands as they tried to continue writing.

The second test went just as badly. The questions were in fact too hard, but we didn't feel that justified the students' actions, which we wrongly took as disrespect. We felt utterly defeated as we left for the hike down to Sisuwa. Both students and teachers had failed to meet the other's expectations.

Those two weeks gave me confidence in my teaching ability, but they also showed me an ugly side of Nepal which I had preferred to ignore. My long-held vision of Shangri-la was shattered; the Nepali people could be just as vain and greedy and dishonest as anyone in the corrupt Western world.

Back in Sisuwa, we learned that two more of the group had quit and were already headed back to America. One of them was the chronic flute player, who had been unable to cope with the singularities of Nepali culture. A friend who was with him during practice teaching said that the turning point came at a village festival. The spectacle of several dozen men all cavorting, singing, and playing drums as they advanced towards him across a flower-bedecked and swinging suspension bridge freaked him out. He realized then that he could never adapt to life in Nepal.

The other dropout had simply grown tired of being sick and eating poor food. Almost all of us had been ill with one thing or another. I'd had a persistent sore throat since coming to Sisuwa two months before, and almost everyone had developed stomach problems, including giardia and dysentery. Klaus was in the hospital for the second time and the doctors were unable to diagnose the cause of his continual diarrhea. As for poor food, I empathized with that too. Eating badly was as dispiriting as being sick. The food was definitely sub-standard at my own house and the language teachers took meticulous precautions against having to eat with me. Bitter greens and watery lentils, daal-bhaat twice a day, every day, including Thanksgiving. I was sick of it.

I ponder my present food situation. It's been bad these two days since leaving Klaus, but it should improve greatly from Karikhola onwards. At Karikhola, my route from the south will join the main trekking trail that winds from Kathmandu to Namche Bazaar. Each spring and autumn a parade of foreign hikers make the journey to view Mount Everest. These tourists bring their money with them wherever they go, causing resthouses and teashops to spring up along the trails. Such lodges always stock delicacies: beans, noodles, and even eggs.

The thought of a good meal spurs me on, and I hike without a break. The trail rounds a ridge high above the Dudh Kosi, the Milk River, and at dusk I descend a thousand feet to Karikhola. The Rais in Waapsu would be surprised.

Large houses stand on both sides of a tributary river and a field is dotted with a half-dozen tents of orange nylon—an organized trekking group, the

British on tour with Sherpa guides to point the way, porters to carry the gear, and cooks to make the tea.

Above a door, a hand-painted sign proclaims *Karikhola Lodge and Hotel*. "All full. No room anywhere," says a man with a goiter.

Another house is decorated with *hotEL* scrawled on the wall in charcoal. "*Namaste?*" I call in doubtfully. A Sherpa man comes around the corner. "Can I stay here?" I ask.

"How many are you?"

"Just me. I'm alone."

"Alone? Come in, come in." He leads me to a large room—empty but warm. "Are you hungry? What do you eat?" he asks.

"*Daal-bhaat*," I say enthusiastically.

"And tea?"

"Yes, some tea. A nice cup of tea."

March 21

Karikhola 6,800 feet

Toiling up the steep switchbacks are the sweating porters of the British trekking party. They press upwards, straining against their head straps. Some hike barefoot, while the majority of them wear rubber sandals or Chinese sneakers. They earn two and a half dollars a day, plus food, about the same as a teacher. On their backs they carry everything the trekkers might want: pots and pans, stoves, food for the entire trip, tents, sleeping bags, and even folding chairs and tables. I pass them one by one, with no feelings of guilt; I'm carrying as much as they.

An hour and a half of climbing brings me to Kharte, my breakfast stop. Three Americans sit airing their feet and boots. "Well, good morning," says the middle one as though we're old friends.

"How's it going?" I answer, trying to remember if I know him from somewhere.

Above Kharte, the trail continues climbing, but less steeply, working its way towards a 10,000-foot saddle. At noon I reach the top, where the view is obscured by a misty rhododendron forest. I feel fantastic, and am prompted to sing snatches of old campfire songs. The range of emotions I experience in Nepal can be phenomenal. The changes are often drastic and with no apparent cause, like riding a rollercoaster of the psyche. In an instant my mood can shift from the starriest high to the blackest low.

I lay in bed at Kathmandu's Inn Serenity. (Did the proprietor appreciate the pun?) I had a fever of 101.7°F, stomach cramps, and diarrhea. I felt miserable, and I had just decided to quit the Peace Corps.

We had completed our three months of training and the following night we were scheduled to swear in as Peace Corps Volunteers. A few days to a few weeks after that, the new volunteers would be heading off to their far-flung villages. I had been slated to go to a place called Nawalpur in the northern hills, and Jim was heading to the far west. He shared a room with a volunteer also going to his district, and I roomed with Rob, the entomologist. Klaus was in hospital for the third time. I waited for Rob to return from shopping to tell him my decision to quit, but I changed my mind before he arrived.

I tried to tell myself that I was just depressed from being sick, but that was only part of it; my disappointment had been growing since my arrival. Nepal hadn't matched my dreams, and I had yet to see that my work could be valuable. Training had exhausted me, for I had made the mistake of using all my free time to study word lists and to review grammar. The effort had helped my Nepali, but by the end of training I was worn out and fed up. Magnifying all of this was my desperate wish to be with Kay again.

Already I had written to my friends and family saying that I was unwilling to spend two years in Nepal. That had been a difficult admission for me. I had decided to join the Peace Corps while I still had two years left in college, and Nepal, specifically, had been my ideal choice. Asia had always intrigued me, and Nepal's isolated mountain villages had been irresistible. My wish had been to live in a world unspoiled by cars and consumerism.

I had been overjoyed on the day I was accepted to serve in Nepal, but now I was on the verge of giving up. We were not legally required to stay, and I knew of several trainees who were taking it a day at a time; they would go to their villages and see how it went. I felt that they were misleading the Peace Corps. I wanted to give it a try, but I couldn't conceive of two years here. I was an altruist, not a martyr.

The next morning I dragged myself out of bed and went to the Peace Corps office to talk with Virgil, the program officer overseeing the math/science volunteers. I found him working at his typewriter. He was clean shaven and he wore his blond hair cut shorter than necessary. He had a reputation of strict adherence to Peace Corps policies.

"Phil, what can I do for you?" he asked with a smile that belonged on a billboard for Crest toothpaste.

"I don't think there's anything you can really *do* for me," I answered. I wasn't sure what I wanted to say, but I eventually spoke for twenty minutes, expounding on the things that were troubling me. I concentrated on my belief that my work in Nepal would be almost futile, that almost any Nepali teacher could teach better than I.

Virgil felt my need to talk it all out. He didn't say much, though he prompted me with questions. "Didn't you have a girlfriend back home?" he asked.

"Yes, but everything with her is OK. We'd known for two years that I was leaving and we had pretty much accepted that." I looked at the ceiling and wished that it was true. I eventually came to my point. "I'm just not ready to commit myself to two years here. I can picture a shorter time, but it's dishonest for me to let you think that I'll stay the whole time when I know that I'm not willing to."

Virgil's smile had been waning from the start and now his face was somber. "How long a commitment are you willing to make?"

"If I go to my village," I said, "I would definitely stay for that full year. I think it would be very bad for the school if I left in the middle of the year."

"And what do you think your Headmaster will say?"

"I imagine that he'll be glad to have me no matter how long."

Virgil's smile returned to some degree; he had probably been worried that I would quit outright. "I don't see that this is a problem," he said.

He seemed certain that someone who would work for a year in good faith would also want to complete the full time. As for me, I'd been partially hoping that Virgil would take the decision out of my hands by sending me home. Now it was settled; I would stay for just one year.

That evening we recited an oath about upholding the ideals of the Peace Corps, and the U.S. Ambassador, Mr. Douglas Heck, christened us United States Peace Corps Volunteers. This amounted to 150 volunteers in Nepal, but that total soon dropped by three.

A week after swearing in, and before seeing their villages, my friend Jim and two other volunteers walked into Virgil's office and resigned. Their action was officially termed an "early termination." Jim was motivated by concerns for his health, both physical and emotional. He was truly scared of the long-term effects of living in Nepal. The other two terminees were tired, sick, and disillusioned.

Jim's departure hurt me. He was my best friend on that side of the world and with him gone I felt more isolated than before. I didn't have much time to dwell on it though; I was on my way to Nawalpur, my village.

I left Kathmandu at 6.30 a.m. on a cold foggy Sunday in the middle of December. Ambika, who was Virgil's assistant, and I drove north along a road that twisted up from the valley floor. My stomach churned with each turn. Three days before, a microscopic stool examination had revealed that I was suffering from amoebic dysentery. My guts were now as distressed by the cure as they had been by the disease.

Out of the valley, the road descended to the Indrawati River and Ambika showed me the village of Lamidada, the roadhead from which I would normally leave for the day-long hike to Nawalpur. Regular buses plied between Kathmandu and Lamidada, taking from two to four hours for the trip. With luck, I would be able to travel from my village to Kathmandu in a single day. But this trip, Ambika and I would hike to Nawalpur from the district center where I was to be introduced to the regional bigwigs.

The road was paved much of its length and it stretched from Kathmandu, Nepal to Lhasa, Tibet. It had been constructed by the Chinese and though the border was closed, rumors circulated that it would be opened to travelers within a few years. Other rumors hinted as to why the Chinese had built such a good road. It had bridges strong enough to support very heavy vehicles, such as tanks. Nepal has always been in a squeeze between the two Asian giants, India and China.

Halfway to the Tibetan border, Ambika turned the jeep onto a dirt road that shook my stomach for an hour and a half as we climbed up the hills to Chautara, the district center. The name meant "resting place," and the town had previously been an important stopover on the trans-Himalayan trade route. Now it was the center of Sindhupalchowk District. The town held dozens of tin-roofed government buildings and it was graced with electricity in the evenings.

Ambika met with some people at the District Education Office, and we were led to a large concrete house. We sat in steel chairs and we exchanged *Namastes* with men whom I assumed to be important. Ambika and the others fell into animated conversation, while I was generally ignored.

The only question they asked me was, "*Tapaai Nepali bolnuhunchha?*—Do you speak Nepali?"

Of course I spoke Nepali! Did they think I was going to teach in Chinese? "Yes, I can speak Nepali," I replied.

"*Raamro*—Very good."

They resumed their conversation. I sat in my chair feeling stupid and not saying a word, trying to pretend that I understood what they said. One hour and two glasses of sweet tea later, we left to eat a noon breakfast of daal-bhaat.

"The CDO and DEO aren't here," said Ambika during the meal, "so we don't need to stay. Do you want to hike to Nawalpur today?"

"Yeah, sure," I said as I searched my memory for the meanings of CDO and DEO. The one was District Education Officer, but the other escaped me.

Two porters were found who would carry my load of books, bedding, clothes, teaching supplies, and kitchen utensils. Ambika and I carried our own packs and sleeping bags. He had previously been to Nawalpur to check its suitability as a post, so he led the way. We hiked out of Chautara and across hillsides that had been stripped bare through overgrazing and clearcutting. The porters quickly dropped behind, causing us to wait for them to catch up. I was grateful for the forced stop, as I was still weak from the dysentery.

Past the bare hillsides, the trail followed the outer edges of dry, terraced fields and I carefully watched my footing—a slip could mean a crippling fall to a lower terrace. Ambika and the porters strolled along with perfect ease.

Next the trail dropped down a canyon to the tumbling Jhyanri River. It was already the middle of the afternoon and the porters were nowhere to be seen. Perhaps they wished to extend the trip to two days and thus double their wages.

Without waiting for the porters, we crossed the river and began the 3,500-foot ascent to the crest of the ridge. At dusk we reached the top, where the path leveled out and widened. Ambika steered us through two hours of darkness to the village of Nawalpur. I could hear dogs and I could smell smoke, but I couldn't see a thing; it reminded me of my arrival in Sisuwa.

We went to the Headmaster's house and his wife showed us a dusty storage room where we could put our things and sleep. The hour was too late for bhaat, so instead she brought us two plates of pounded rice and roasted corn kernels. Eating the corn was like munching on a handful of pebbles.

I woke before dawn, restless with excitement. While Ambika slept, I went out to tour my new home. A wide path served as the main street of town and was paved with large flagstones. On both sides of the "road" were several dozen large houses of unplastered stone. Some were two or more storeys high and all had slate roofs. The houses were close-set and many shared a common wall or had only a narrow passageway between them. The village seemed like something from the days of King Arthur. The central path had little visible life: some chickens pecked at the cracks between the paving stones, a goat scratched his side against a rough wall, and two women in shawls walked off with large jugs to fetch water.

I could see my breath in the cold air, so I buried my hands in my pockets and took a walk to keep warm. The village straddled a huge S-shaped ridge that curved to the south and west. I went out along the ridge hoping to get a view of the northern Himalayas, but the peaks were blocked by the upward sweep of the ridge. Just as spectacular, however, were the rows of lesser peaks sweeping far beyond the Indrawati River. The rising sun highlighted all the folds of the land in subtle shades of brown.

On one side of the ridge were two thatch-roofed cottages. Their walls were smeared with red mud and they were very different from the houses in the center of the village—apparently from a different caste or tribe. Further along, I came to a stand of pine trees and from there I looked down on a small temple surrounded by a walled-in courtyard. Across a parade ground from the temple stood a large whitewashed building which I guessed was a monastery.

I followed the ridge back to Nawalpur, and found more life there. A half-dozen of the houses had been transformed into shops. They had banks of doors that enabled their entire ground floors to be opened up, thereby exhibiting shelves and bins of merchandise. At the cloth shop, the owner sat on the floor and smoked a cheroot. The wall to his back was stacked high with brightly colored fabrics. Main Street was no more than 50 yards long, but compared to the empty countryside it gave the feeling of a large town. Every eye turned to watch me as I walked, and small excited faces appeared in all the upstairs windows. For most of the children I was the first *Angreji*, the first Englishman, they had ever seen.

At the far end of town, Ambika was drinking tea at the tea-stall by the Headmaster's house. A small crowd of people greeted me with enormous smiles. "*Namaste. Namaste. Namaste.*" A glass of tea was pressed into my hands and a man in a pointed cap cornered me to say, "If you need anything or want anything, you must come to me. If you have problems of any kind, you should trust me. I am the man to help you." He thumped his hand on his chest as he spoke and he repeated himself until he was sure that I understood. He left the shop, and I never saw him again—ever.

Ambika talked and flirted with three women who wore matching blue saris. The quality of their clothes made them look out of place in a small village, and I would later learn that they were college students from Kathmandu. Before they could begin their senior year of university, they were required to work a year with the National Development Service, the NDS. They were assigned to teach at the school and they had six long months left. They didn't like Nawalpur. They complained that there was "nothing available and nothing to do."

I could hardly understand a word that the women and Ambika were saying, which further depressed me about my bad Nepali. I had thought that I spoke fair enough, for at the end of training I had been awarded a score of two-plus on the five-point Foreign Service Institute scale of language competence. This meant that I had something better than a "limited working proficiency." But now, listening to the four of them talk, I realized how truly limited I was.

I slowly discerned that they weren't speaking Nepali at all, but Newari. The villagers were Newari, as were the NDS teachers, as was Ambika. The Newars are one of the many ethnic groups in Nepal, highly esteemed as merchants and artisans. They had built the city of Kathmandu and had invented the pagoda-style temple, which they had exported north to China.

Ambika explained to me in English that the two most important people that we needed to talk with—the Pradhaan Panch and the school Headmaster—were both in Kathmandu doing business. Their absence would make it difficult to get me settled in during the few days that Ambika would stay to help. Ambika kept referring to my two years in Nawalpur. Apparently Virgil had not told him of my decision to stay just one year. I didn't tell Ambika now, because I had noticed that the Nepalis on the Peace Corps staff took it as a personal rejection when a volunteer left early.

We searched for a room or a house where I could live, but we met with little luck. A number of people in the area had an empty room or could vacate a room for me to use, but I rejected them on account of Nepali architecture's greatest drawback—low ceilings. I was already tired of hitting my head on low wooden beams and getting lumps from shoulder-high stone doorways. The general shortness of the people combined with the difficult task of building houses completely by hand made high ceilings frivolous. What did it matter when you sat on the floor?

We went to see the school, and just outside Nawalpur we passed the only cement-walled and tin-roofed building in the region. The combination Health Post and Family Planning Center had been newly built with government funds, but they had yet to find trained people who were willing to come and work in Nawalpur. No one with an education wanted to live in a small village with "nothing to do."

The school, which I had thought to be a monastery, was a half-hour walk from Nawalpur. The January-to-December school year had not yet begun, and the school yard was empty. I poked around the vacant rooms and wondered where all the students would sit. The school consisted of all ten grades, primary school through high school, but I saw only six or seven classrooms. The building was two storeys high in the shape of a square-cornered C. Scarcely half of the rooms contained the requisite long, narrow benches and tables. Most of the furniture was up-ended and in bad repair, while the blackboards were almost unusable. They were made of rough-hewn wooden planks, pockmarked and only partially blackened with soot. The rooms had wooden doors, but less than half of the windows had shutters. This however was unimportant—during class, the doors and windows had to remain open to admit light. The existence of even decrepit blackboards made me glad; teaching without anything to write on would be miserable. The school supposedly had some science equipment, but the storage room was locked.

Overall, the decrepit state of the school put me at ease; perhaps the Headmaster would not expect too much of his American teacher.

The following day Ambika and I returned to the school and then continued a few minutes further to a tiny community called Aiselukharka. I was still searching for a place to live.

Aiselukharka consisted of five tight clusters of houses, one small shop, and a total population of 500. We were accompanied to the village by a tall, thin man who introduced himself as either the assistant or the former Pradhaan Panch—I wasn't sure which. He took us to his house, which was three storeys high and had a small two-storey extension. The surrounding houses formed the sides of a stone courtyard. Upstairs, he showed us a room already being used by one of the teachers, but he said that the teacher would move if I wanted to live there. I didn't like that idea.

We went back outside and entered the extension. The ground floor was filled with farming tools and hay, while the upstairs held bags of rice, stacks of firewood, and mounds of dirt. The walls were only 4 feet high, but the peaked roof made it possible for me to stand upright and even to stretch my arms over my head. Fantastic! The top floors of other houses were unavailable because Newars always used the top room for cooking. The room was about 10 feet by 15 feet, and had windows on three sides. I stepped over a basket of old pots and opened the heavy wooden shutters of the far window. I was awed. The Himalayas, bold and defiant, stood gleaming in the sun. Without knowing it, we had come so far around the ridge that the view was now exposed. I stood gazing at the peaks and Ambika was convinced that this was the reason that I chose that particular room. My landlord's name was, appropriately, Mr. Himalaya—Krishna Bhakta Himalaya.

We talked about the work that had to be done on the room. All the junk had to be taken out, the walls and floor needed to be smeared with fresh mud, and a wall with a lockable door would have to be built. The Nepalis were very security conscious of their guests. I looked at the roof and saw blue sky peeking through the gaps between the slate shingles.

"*Paani bhitra aaunchha holaa*—Water comes in maybe," I said as I pointed up.

Krishna Bhakta was puzzled. "What? You mean the roof leaks?" (I knew neither the word "roof" nor "leaks.") "No, no, no," he said. He smiled and gestured as he spoke.

"Did you understand what he said?" Ambika asked me in English. "He says that if the roof leaks he'll put up bamboo mats to stop it."

"You'll need a bed. I'll have a bed made for you," suggested Krishna Bhakta.

"No, I don't need a bed. I can sleep on the floor. I need a chair and a table. That is very important—*mahattwapurna*," I said with an exhibition of my longest Nepali word.

"What about his food? Is it possible for him to eat here?" asked Ambika.

"Eat here? I thought... Yeah, I guess so, for a while," he said.

He didn't sound pleased to have me eating there, but Ambika acted as though it was all settled. Krishna Bhakta and everyone else expected me to get a live-in student to do the cooking and cleaning.

We explained that the school was responsible for paying the rent of thirty rupees a month, and I would pay for the food from my quarterly living allowance. My stipend amounted to 900 rupees a month, or about $18 a week. Even though I was supposed to be a volunteer, I was actually receiving more pay than the Headmaster.

The next morning Ambika bade me "*Namaste*" and "good luck," and left for Kathmandu. When he was gone, I stood at my window and looked toward the high Himalayas. I felt lost and insecure, but the snowy peaks calmed me. I had experienced the same sensation during training; when I had been troubled or lonely, looking up at the mountains had always relaxed me. Sometimes just knowing that they were there made everything seem all right. Perhaps that was why high mountains were so often worshipped as gods.

I watched the sun warm the fallow land as two men walked along the trail below my window. "*Namaste*," they called up to me, and I was lifted by their greeting. I was already more at home here than I had ever been in

Sisuwa. The people in Aiselukharka stared at me and laughed when I spoke, as the villagers had in Sisuwa, but here it was a good-natured laughter. They laughed with their eyes, as they might laugh at themselves; they didn't laugh down from the lofty stance of Braahmans. But maybe I was imagining all of this. The past week had zipped by too quickly for me to clarify anything's importance. My bout with dysentery, my decision to stay just a year, Jim's departure, and my arrival in Aiselukharka had all left me in a swirl of confusion. Even now I hadn't the time to stop and think.

I had my books and clothes moved to Krishna Bhakta's house, and contrary to Nepali custom, the work on my room was being done immediately. I tried to tell Krishna Bhakta that I was impressed and happy, but all that came out was, "*Raamro, ekdam raamro*—Good, extremely good." Ambika had done most all the talking while he was there, but now I was completely on my own—sink or swim. I wasn't scheduled to go to Kathmandu till April, and until then I would speak nothing but Nepali.

The Headmaster arrived in Nawalpur the same day that Ambika had left, and he came immediately to the school. He was overwhelmingly happy that I had come, and he didn't care that I would only stay a year. Besides bringing prestige to the school, I was greatly needed; fewer than half of the high schools in the Nepali hill regions had qualified teachers of science and mathematics. I explained to him that because I would need so long to make lesson plans, I preferred to start with only three classes. He readily agreed to this and even let me choose the classes I wanted.

His name was Shyama Nanda Misra, but he was always referred to as just Headmaster or Headsir. He was a handsome man with brilliant teeth that shone when he smiled. His skin was much darker than anyone's I had seen in Nepal. He wasn't actually Nepali; he and his young wife were from a Nepali-speaking section of Calcutta. They had lived in Nawalpur for only a few months, but they were already highly respected. Esteem was inherent according to one's position, and he was both the school principal and a Braahman priest.

Later that same day, I sat outside with some of the other teachers while the Headmaster did paperwork in the office. Five of us kneeled, reclined, or sat cross-legged in various positions on a straw mat. We tried to get some warmth from the low afternoon sun and we ate roasted corn that threatened to break our teeth. A single communal plate was used, and the procedure for eating was important. First take a handful from the plate with your right hand. Then pour it into your left hand. (Note: the left hand doesn't contaminate dry or uncooked food, unlike boiled rice, but you can't eat directly with that hand nor touch another's food with it.) Pass a few kernels back into your right hand and pop them into your mouth, being extremely careful to not touch your fingers to your lips. If you do touch your lips, your fingers become jutho, and then the entire plate becomes jutho when you reach in for more. You would then have the whole plateful for yourself. I watched the others closely to make certain that I did everything right.

The teachers asked me various questions: my full name, if I was married, if my parents were alive, where they lived, what they did, my age, where my brothers were, how I liked Nepal, and whether I had chosen to come there or had I been required to come by my government. I answered their questions and asked them about the school and the village. They were generally amazed at how much Nepali I spoke after just three months of training. Most of them had studied English in school, but they couldn't begin to speak it. As the conversation slowly developed, I was gradually left out. I spoke well enough for questions and answers, but I couldn't take part in a real discussion. I was a foreign expert who was limited to one-line statements. I felt like a child in a forced masquerade as an adult.

At the end of the day, they all goodbyed me with, "*Namaste*, Philipsir." That would be my new name. Philipsir.

I walked hurriedly back to my home in Aiselukharka. The clouds were gathering overhead, and I wondered if it would soon rain.

The sky is almost solid gray as I descend to the small village of Surkya. This is the last descent. From here on, the route is a continual upward plod towards Everest. I look forward to reaching the high mountains, and thus to matching my emotional displacement with a physical one.

The three American trekkers from Kharte are here to spend the night. The next village, Chaurikharka, is another two hours further on. It's late afternoon, rain or snow is imminent, and this is a good place to stay—to go further would be pointless. But from Chaurikharka I could hike to Namche Bazaar in a single day, putting me two days ahead of schedule. Without much thought, I continue towards Chaurikharka, reaching shelter at dusk as a sleety drizzle begins.

March 22
Chaurikharka 8,500 feet

I wake to the low rumbling of Buddhist chanting. Peeking out of my sleeping bag, I see a wrinkled old woman standing in front of the household shrine: The sound comes from the back of her throat in a deep murmuring. She squats down, prostrates herself in front of the shrine, returns to a squat, and stands back up. She repeats this again and again, reciting verses with the pitch of her voice rising and falling like waves of the sea. She stops and reverently sets her hands on the sacred objects of the shrine: a carved image of the Buddha, a faded photograph of an incarnate lama, and a row of small brass bowls filled with water. She extinguishes the butter lamp and stands motionless, her face calm and young.

The young girl placed the two red and yellow flowers on the head of the stone deity. In her left hand she held a small steel plate of the materials needed to perform her *pujaa*, her daily worship. This was a modest pujaa. Large ones could last a day or more and might require animal sacrifices, bushels of flowers, and an assemblage of chanting priests. Next, she smeared a red tikaa of vermilion powder on the Hindu idol's forehead, and quietly sprinkled grains of rice over His body. The girl was nine-year-old Nilam, the youngest of Krishna Bhakta's four children, and the waist-high sanctum was in the far corner of the square enclosed by the neighboring houses. I leaned out of my upstairs window as I watched Nilam light a strip of twisted rope incense. She put the incense and a five-paisaa coin at the idol's feet.

A chicken also watched the pujaa, waiting for a chance to hop up and eat the rice. Later that day, one of the poorer children would come by and snatch away the money—enough to buy a small sweet. The god, after all, took only the essence of the giving, not the objects themselves. For performing the pujaa, the family received religious merit and a divine blessing. Lastly, Nilam jangled a bell that hung by the shrine. That ringing would become as familiar to me as a friendly "Good morning."

Two weeks had passed since I had first come to Aiselukharka and I had yet to teach a class. I decided that today would be the day. My lessons had been prepared the previous week and they lay on the floor along with my other assorted papers, including a twenty-page letter to Kay. She had met a guy named John, but she was reluctant to get involved with him. She knew that I would be back in a year. I wrote to tell her that it was all right with me and that I wasn't hurt, but instead I used page after page to describe how much I loved her and how important she was to me. I had begun to feel desperately alone, and the days dragged by, one by one. I had no one to really talk to and no one to do things with. As the first weeks slowly passed, my need to be with someone focused exclusively on Kay. She was my lifeline to a distant world of familiarity and I burdened her with ponderous letters of love.

Krishna Bhakta's second son, sixteen-year-old Mahendra, brought morning daal-bhaat to my room. My first meal in the village had been served in my room and from then on that was the routine we followed. Mahendra put the dishes on the floor while I washed my hands. They had made me a trough-like sink that drained through a hole in the wall, so I was able to wash my hands and brush my teeth without going outside or spitting out the window.

Mahendra squatted down to watch me as I ate. He looked much like his father, tall (by Nepali standards) and thin, with a longish nose. His mouth and teeth protruded just slightly. Both he and his father were very social and vocal, and they had many friends. They were fun-loving

Aiselukharka

and sometimes mischievous, and neither of them seemed enthusiastic about manual labor. The younger son, Surendra, was more serious and hard-working. He was shorter and stockier, like his mother, and was more handsome. Only a year separated Mahendra and Surendra, and they both studied in seventh class. They were both athletic, but the younger Surendra was a bit faster and stronger. He also got the higher grades, which would have been uncomfortable for Mahendra if it had not been for Surendra's natural modesty and the overriding importance of age. The first son was married and living in Kathmandu, which left Mahendra in the dominant position as the eldest. All of Surendra's higher scores and faster running could never change that. They would always treat one another as big brother and little brother.

Strangely enough, I never saw any real rivalry between Mahendra and Surendra. Each member of the family had a well-defined role, with certain privileges and responsibilities. Arguments were prevented by their natural adherence to the pecking order. Krishna Bhakta was at the top, followed by his wife, Mohan Devi, who was never called by name. To Krishna Bhakta she was "Nilam's Mother," and to her children she was "Aamaa." Following her in the hierarchy was Mahendra, then Surendra, and lastly little Nilam. Aamaa's only daughter was adorable and spoiled.

Mahendra waited until I assured him that I had enough rice before he went back to the main house to eat with the others in the top-floor kitchen. Aamaa was a good cook, and I especially appreciated her meals after the third-rate food that I had received during training. Fortunately Newars put more importance on eating well than did Braahmans. Still Aamaa was limited by the materials she had to work with. The rice and lentils were generally good, but today's vegetable was the same as we'd had every day of the past week—*seto mulaa*. It was a type of edible horseradish that was cut into chips, had the consistency of rubber, and was spiced with burning chillis. Many months would pass before I would learn to appreciate its merits. But one thing that I had already gotten accustomed to was eating with my fingers. It had become second nature, and to eat with a spoon would have seemed ridiculous, if not crude.

As I ate, I heard footsteps on the wooden stairs, and I immediately recognized the sound of Tauni, the family's yellow dog. Her curled tail wagged in a circle as she waited for me to finish. She had lately developed a special fondness for seto mulaa. This was the big advantage of eating alone in my room; if I had too much food, or something that I particularly disliked, I could get rid of it with no embarrassment to the family or to myself. In the process, Tauni became my closest friend.

I was accepted into the family as a paying guest, and the children called me Philipsir, not big brother. They openly received me as a resident in the family, but not as an actual member of it. This was fine with me, for I preferred to spend much of my free time alone, and the family protected my privacy. But I could also feel the understanding and the affection that the five of them had for one another, and this stirred longings deep within me.

Krishna Bhakta and Aamaa seemed perfectly suited to one another. Krishna Bhakta would one day tell me that their marriage had been arranged for them and that prior to the wedding they had been virtual strangers. They married for life without exception. They accepted that, and thus each other, totally. From this absolute acceptance, their love had grown as naturally as corn in the fields. They were now in their mid-forties and they had a good, assured life together, raising the sons who would be their security in old age.

As Tauni cleaned my dishes, I began the short walk to school. Surendra and two other students followed just behind me. They carried their hand-me-down textbooks in ragged cloth shoulder bags, and they talked happily as they walked. The trail passed a group of nearby houses and skirted the narrow outer edge of the terraces.

"*Padhaai kahile shuruhunchha?*—When will teaching begin?" I asked Surendra. For a week, most of the students and teachers had been coming to school, but no classes had been held.

"I don't know," said Surendra. "It's when the Sirs, the Teachers, decide. Will you teach us?"

"No, I won't be teaching the seventh class. I have eighth science, and ninth mathematics, and sixth English. Nothing with seventh."

"Awww." He actually sounded disappointed.

"*Namaste.*" "*Namaste,* Philipsir." "*Namaste.*" "*Namaste.*" Scores of students stopped to greet me as I stepped onto the playing field. I *Namaste*-ed to them and also to the teachers as they arrived. The students lined up in columns, grades one through ten. According to the roll book, the first class had about seventy-five students while the upper grades decreased in size to about twenty, making a total of 500 students in the school. They came from miles around, and some walked as much as two hours one way to school each day. If they lived further from school than that, they tried to get a place to stay in the village. If that wasn't possible, they didn't go to school. The classes shrank in size as students failed or as parents kept their children home to work. One of the teachers called them to attention and we all sang the national anthem:

All of us Nepalis
Pray lovingly to our fortunate, serious, glorious,
King of the Kings of Nepal.
God bless Him.
Long live His Majesty the King,
And let His subjects prosper.

Each class sang at its own tempo, except the primary grades that couldn't remember the words. Afterwards they filed off to their classrooms, and the three lowest grades ran over to play in the courtyard around the temple. That was the only classroom they had.

I retreated upstairs to the storage room where the science equipment was kept. A table was strewn with rusted magnets in wooden boxes, a few assorted lenses, some wire, lots of dusty glass tubing, two boxes of test tubes, a supply of chemicals with the labels peeling off the bottles, a set of gram weights, but no balance, a huge bag of corks, and a rock collection. It was a standardized kit provided to rural high schools by UNICEF. Much of it had been damaged by misuse and disuse, and the things of obvious utility, such as the petrol lamps, had been pilfered by the students, the teachers, and even by the Pradhaan Panch. The other table was stacked high with textbooks that the government provided free to the three primary grades, while on the floor were heaps of old exams and record books. After spending an hour making new labels for the bottles of chemicals, I took my lesson plans, chalk, and teaching aids down to the eighth grade's empty room.

"*Kakshaa aath! Kakshaa aath!* Class eight! Class eight!" yelled a boy, and the students came running from all directions. They hurried into the room and stood at their places with their eyes gleaming.

"*Basa*—Sit down," I said, motioning with my hands. I disliked the old British custom that required students to stand until the teacher gave them permission to be seated.

One last boy, coming late, came to attention at the door. In unintelligible

English he asked, "May Aai kam een?" This was more British etiquette that had trickled north from the Indian school system.

"*Aaau*—Come in," I said with a wave. Of the twenty-four students registered in the roll book, only a few more than half were there that day—thirteen boys and two girls.

I erased the scribbles from the blackboard as the children outside crowded around the open window to watch. I put on my angry face and stomped over to them. "What do you all want?" I demanded, which in Nepali carried the added connotation, *You have no business here. Get lost!* They scurried away in alarm, for they had yet to learn that I was harmless. My first try at discipline was also aided by one of the teachers who came from behind and smacked the students' heads as they ran off. This type of help I didn't need. I thought that the worst thing that a teacher could do was to hit a student. The teacher, who was called Durga after the "inaccessible" Mother Goddess, was oblivious to my irritation and proceeded to stare through the window for a while before he moved on.

I waited until the whole class was quiet and attentive before I began. "*Ek mitar kati laamo ho?*—How long is a meter?" I said slowly.

The students looked at me as though I had two heads.

"Show me with your hands how long is a meter," I repeated.

They all just sat there with their brimless cloth caps perched on their heads. They looked completely baffled.

"Is a meter this long?" I said holding my hands apart the size of a cooking pot, "Or this long?" stretching my arms wide, "Or this long?" pinching my fingers to acorn size. "How long is a meter? Show me."

Now they got the idea and they held out their hands at every imaginable size.

"That long?" I asked, going around the room questioning how long each of them thought a meter was. The girls were shy and would take a guess only after some coaxing. I was disappointed that they were guessing; they should have learned the basic measurements in the fourth grade.

I showed the class a meter-stick that I had made from a piece of split bamboo, and I went around the room again so that everyone could adjust their hands to the right size.

"Now, can you show me how big is a centimeter?" I talked slowly and simply, being sure that I made no mistakes. I didn't want to begin with a demonstration of my poor Nepali.

After establishing the size of a centimeter, I tried to relate the two. "How many centimeters in a meter? Who knows? Do this," I said as I put up my hand. The idea of raising a hand to answer a question was new to them, and I didn't know how to explain it except by example. "No, don't talk. How many centimeters in a meter? If you know, then do this." I raised my hand again.

Three or four students put their hands up, and I pointed to a boy who had caught my attention. He was blind in his left eye, the iris of which was obscured by a monstrous white cataract. He stood up and said with confidence, "One hundred centimeters are in a meter, Sir."

"*Thik bhayo?*—Is that correct?" I asked the class, which caused a general stir of uncertainty. "A hundred centimeters in a meter? Right or not right?" I wanted them to think, to be sure.

"That's right," whispered two boys without conviction.

"Yes, that is right," I said, and reassured them by writing it on the spotted blackboard in Nepali:

100 centimeters = 1 meter

Turning around I saw that the boy with the blind eye was still standing. "Sit down," I said. "That was good. Very good."

The students seemed astonished by the fact that I was there speaking to them. They sat in bewilderment and I often repeated myself to help them catch my accent and to convince them that I was truly speaking a language that they could understand. I moved around the room nervously as I spoke, and I tried to get all the students involved.

Next, I handed out short sticks with centimeter marks on them and had the students measure the lengths of various objects: their books, fountain pens, and benches. Some of them had never used a measuring scale before, but I could easily show them how without a difficult oral explanation.

At one point I tried to say that the width of a table was twenty-seven centimeters, but it came out as *twenty-eleven*. The whole class—except me—laughed merrily. I should have joined them and laughed at my own mistake, but I was neither secure nor strong enough. My ears were stung by their mirth, and I tried to go on as though nothing had happened.

I ended the class by establishing that the meter was the *unit* for measuring length. In the next few days I planned to cover the units for measuring area, volume, time, and temperature.

As I left the room, the students all stood up. I felt fantastic. I had survived my first lesson and it seemed that the students had really learned something. They had gotten an understanding of the meter and centimeter, and not just a textbook definition. I bounced as I walked out of the room, and despite my one error, I felt almost proud.

I also taught ninth mathematics that day. They were an extremely active class and several times I had to ask them to be quiet. I tried to review the algebra that they should have learned the previous year, but the material was new to most of them. A few of the students had a grasp of the subject, while the majority of them were three or more years behind. That put me in a quandary of not knowing to whom to gear the class. Should I teach at the level of the better students and leave the rest of them both confused and unruly? Or should I teach for the average student and thus forfeit the top students' slim chances of passing the national examination? I had the impression that most Nepali teachers avoided the dilemma altogether by lecturing directly from the textbook regardless of the students' actual understanding. I had only just begun teaching and I was already finding it difficult to compromise my educational ideals to the realities of a Nepali school.

That evening I sat in my room and made a list of the prerequisite math concepts that the ninth grade would need to learn before they could understand the year's new material. I heard footsteps on the stairs and I knew that it wasn't Tauni. Krishna Bhakta was making a habit of coming to see me each evening. In particular, he liked to hear the news that was broadcast over Radio Nepal at 7.30. I had brought a $30 shortwave radio with me from the States, and it had the unfortunate effect of confirming my image as a rich foreigner. The villagers were quite familiar with radios, but to actually own one was a sign of great wealth.

During those first months I didn't exactly enjoy Krishna Bhakta's nightly visits. The loneliness was hard on me, but I also felt stupid when I spoke Nepali without a lesson plan, and I didn't like situations in which I was forced to speak. I lacked things to say and we had long—and for me uncomfortable—periods of silence. But Krishna Bhakta still came every night and tried to talk with me. Perhaps he understood even more than I how horrible it was to be alone. To a Nepali, one's family was as important as one's self, so for me to be without friends or family had to be true misery.

As he stooped through the door, I pulled my down sleeping bag off my lap and pushed it against the wall. I didn't like to be seen using things that were so luxurious. Leaving his shoes at the door, Krishna Bhakta came over and squatted in the circle of light that shone from my hurricane lamp. He sat back on his heels and wrapped his heavy white blanket around him. He pulled it up to cover the back of his head and drew it across his nose and mouth. He resembled a miniature snow mountain with eyes.

"*Ah, ma ma ma...*" he shivered. "*Katiko jaardo bhayo!*—How cold it is!"

"*Derai jaardo chha*—Very cold," I said and wrote *multiplication of polynomials* on my list for ninth class, letting Krishna Bhakta see that I had been busy working. I put down my papers and waited.

"Is it this cold there?" he asked finally.

"Huh, *there?* Where?"

"There," he nodded vaguely towards the window, "in Amaarika."

"Ah— America is very big. Cold in the north and warm in the south."

"So it's cold at your home, because you live in the north."

"Not. I live in the south and it's warm."

Krishna Bhakta wrinkled his brow and tilted his head to the side. Much later I would learn that he was confused because he knew that I lived in North America, but now I was telling him that I lived in the South.

After a pause, it was my turn to say something. "Does it snow here?" I asked.

"Not usually, but sometimes. Fifteen years ago a very bad snow fell. It snowed this deep." He stuck a hand out from under the blanket and indicated thigh-deep snow. "Many people died and we all stayed inside by the fire for six days."

He looked at his watch and pulled the radio towards him. He tuned out the static and turned up the volume to listen to a radio play involving a woman and a doctor talking about some disease that I didn't understand. The government was wisely using the radio for both education and entertainment.

I tried to pay attention to the news when it came on, but my head felt too foggy. I often experienced this when I used a great deal of Nepali. As I spoke, my thoughts as well as my words were in Nepali, and I would actually think in Nepali. But with my limited vocabulary, only simple thoughts could materialize clearly. To think of anything complicated stuffed up my head. It was as though my ears hadn't popped after coming down from the mountains. It gave me a sluggish, buzzing sensation.

At the end of the news, Krishna Bhakta turned off the radio and asked, "Could you understand it?"

"Not all. I understand half." I omitted telling him that the words I didn't understand were the ones that carried all the meaning.

Krishna Bhakta looked at me a while. "It's hard for you here, isn't it?"

"What? Nepali? No, it's an easy language," I said. "It's easier than English."

Krishna Bhakta said nothing more and his expression was masked by the blanket.

After a few minutes of silence, I yawned and stretched. "*Malaai nindra laagyo*—I'm tired."

He rose to go, and the sweep of his blanket made a gust that almost put out the lamp. "*Raamro sanga sutnus*—Sleep well," he said.

"*Namaste.*"

I profer a *Namaste* to the Sherpa boy coming down the trail. He drives two goats ahead of him and he looks at me wide-eyed. It's midday and despite the 9,000-foot elevation it's warm enough to hike in shorts. The canyon of the Dudh Kosi is narrow here and the trail crosses the river three times in 2 miles. The bridges are sturdy wooden affairs made with cantilevered supports and hand-rails. They're built by the local people and are strong enough to hold yaks, the all-purpose pack animals of the Himalaya.

After a last bridge, the switchbacking climb to Namche begins. Dozens of porters with empty baskets come bouncing down the trail. Today, Saturday, is market day and the porters have carried goods from up to a week's walk away to be haggled for in Namche. Their wares now sold, they hurry back to their home villages.

Clouds still linger from the previous night's storm and the sky darkens as I push up the steep slope. I pause to take out my sweater and windbreaker. The snow begins to fall shortly before I reach Namche. The large flakes swirl heavily in the wind, and my ungloved hands turn white from the cold.

For a quarter of a century, Namche Bazaar had been the starting point of expeditions leaving to climb Everest, and the sight of the sprawling town-sized village brings images of Tenzing Norgay and Sir Edmund Hillary. I am intrigued by how these two men are viewed locally where their fame should be the greatest. Tenzing, the Sherpa, is almost forgotten; he now lives in

India, where he operates a mountaineering school. While Hillary, the New Zealander, has become a local hero—not for being one of the first two men on the summit of Everest, but for the work he has done since then, returning again and again to build schools and hospitals in the Everest region.*

I make my way through the narrow stone alleyways of Namche Bazaar, asking directions to a certain warm lodge that Klaus has recommended. I hope the food will be good.

---

* Tenzing died in 1986, Hillary in 2008.

March 23 & 24

Namche Bazaar 11,286 feet

The Trekker's Inn is run by a friendly Sherpa family. The Aamaa cooks while a servant girl cleans. Three Germans are also staying here, and that's unfortunate. With hopes of talking with other trekkers, I'm disappointed that they speak nothing but German. And the family also alienates me with the Sherpa language they speak to each other. But they are good people and the hired girl is pretty—long dark hair in braids always reminds me of Kay. The twin boys run about getting into everything. They each wear a bright green badge which proclaims "Honorary Irishman." These were probably presents from an Irish trekking party. The baby is dressed in a full-length, one-piece knit suit that has a handy window in the seat. He can squat down and defecate anywhere, anytime without messing his clothes. Aamaa then wipes him clean with a blanket, which she tosses back on the bed. Besides that, she blows her nose into her own wool skirt and uses her *left* hand to scrape the remaining rice from the pot. I'm only mildly disgusted.

Of the many things that I need to do here, the most important is to rest. My calves ache from carrying a 60-pound pack, and I must ascend slowly so that the rest of my body can acclimatize to the altitude.

The houses of Namche lie arranged in a huge horseshoe, built against the inside curve of the mountainside. The roofs are covered in wooden shingles and the outside walls look newly whitewashed. Traditionally, the large second-storey room is for people while the yaks are kept below. But with new-found affluence due to the influx of trekkers, many yaks have been evicted to make room for shops.

Namche has about a dozen stores, some specializing in cloth and tailoring, while others offer antiques and novelties: Tibetan masks, kukuri knives, and Buddhist ornaments of brass. The majority of the shops are more like country general stores and are stocked with an amazing assortment of items: canned goods, hand-knit sweaters, Indian chocolate, surplus climbing gear and dehydrated food from expeditions, slabs of old yak meat, and even (is it for sale?) a fiberglass skateboard.

I examine all the shops, comparing prices and buying the extra food that I'll need for up high. The Tibetan and Sherpa shopkeepers are not surprised that I speak Nepali; they remember many Peace Corps Volunteers and other foreign workers who have visited Namche. Only someone exceptional could surprise shopkeepers who sell goods to such a menagerie of customers: rich Europeans wearing knee socks and knickerbockers, Americans sporting new jeans, Japanese clomping about in gigantic mountaineering boots, and international hippies shivering in baggy purple pants and bought-in-desperation sweaters. In addition to the foreigners, the merchants cater to the bored civil servants from Kathmandu who strut about proudly in their moon-boots and ski jackets. Mixed in with everyone else are the maroon-robed monks who ceaselessly twirl their hand-held prayer wheels as they mumble chants over their rosaries.

The local people take us all in stride, charging prices as high as we'll pay and secretly laughing at our peculiar costumes. The main occupation of outsiders is to keep warm. We sit inside by the fires, drinking hot Sherpa tea. It's colder than I had expected and I worry about the temperature at 20,000 feet. The daily weather follows a pattern of clear in the morning, then increasingly cloudy and windy, turning to snow by mid-afternoon, and clearing again during the night. Such a weather cycle can be dangerous for climbers. The morning clear beguiles one to climb high, and then turns bad when you are high and exposed, both tired and prone to mistakes. Most climbing accidents occur on the descent, and I brood over the specter of the two Japanese frozen on Pharchamo.

In two leisure days, I get myself ready to leave. I wash my clothes, have my shirt and the backpad of my pack repaired by a tailor, and spend 450 rupees on food. Some of the food I will leave behind for my return prior to tackling the Tasi Lapcha Pass and Pharchamo.

This last night before leaving Namche, I sit by the fire and write to a friend about the trip so far and my future plans. Aamaa makes tea, Tibetan style. First she pours the steaming tea, along with some chunks of rock salt and a glob of yak butter, into a long wooden cylinder that looks like a cross between an old-fashioned butter churn and a bicycle pump. Then she holds the base of the tea churn to the floor with her feet, and she pumps the piston, making a wooshing-sucking sound. The frothy gray tea is kept hot in a flowered Chinese thermos. It tastes bitter, salty, and greasy all at the same time. Sherpa tea is wonderful if you're used to it, and it keeps you warm even if you're not.

I finish my writing with an elaboration of the fears I'm having about solo climbing. I wrap the letter with my exposed film, which I'll leave behind in Namche. The packet is plainly marked with the Peace Corps address in Kathmandu. I hope someone will carry it out of the mountains if anything should happen to me up high.

Namche Bazaar 11,286 feet

I wait while Aamaa prepares breakfast. I have asked her to cook some porridge, hoping that it would be done quickly and thus give me an early start. She makes it by adding four times as much water as is needed and then boiling it down to the right thickness. So much for an early start, but *Ke garne?*—What to do?

By ten o'clock, I have eaten and paid my bill for the past two days. We trade *Namastes* and I start the climb away from Namche. From the ridge overlooking the village, I can see far up the canyon of the Thame Khola to a peak that might be Pharchamo. It's a mountain of solid white with a sheer east face and a climbable north ridge. I reluctantly turn my back to it and head toward my more immediate goal, toward Everest and Lobuche East.

I'm happy to be moving up again. The pain in my legs is gone and the day is beautiful and clear. The wide trail traverses the mountainside high above the river, and around each bend I expect a view to the north. I round a corner and suddenly it's there—Mount Everest. I shed my pack and take out my camera and mini-binoculars. Everest's black pyramid juts up from behind the Nuptse-Lhotse ridge and the intense wind on the summit blows a plume of snow and vapor which stretches far over Tibet. Many mountains are more beautiful and more awesome than Everest, but having read countless reports of climbers struggling against the thin air and the arctic cold, risking their lives to stand atop that dark summit, Everest is more to me than just a mountain. It's a symbol of the power that can be generated when we strive for a goal.

I sit on the ground, leaning against my pack in the warm sunshine. Everest looks down on me as I slip into a half-sleep.

After a series of bizarre dreams, I woke from another long night. The vivid dreams were habitual. They would come for a week or so and would stop as inexplicably as they had begun. This night's dreams were forgotten as I awoke; I remembered only that the main character was someone I had not seen since grade school.

Light shone through the gaps in the roof, making a pattern on the wall. After a month and a half in Aiselukharka, those spots told me the time as accurately as my watch. I filled an urn from the water bucket by my "sink," and outside someone rang the shrine bell—*Good morning.*

I took the water down the stairs and through the backyard vegetable garden to the charpi. My family's outhouse was probably unique in all of Nepal. A wooden frame the size and shape of a phone booth was covered with flattened Nebiko biscuit tins, and a rusted metal door completed the structure. A gap between the floorboards created a bombsight and the whole thing sat over a deep pit. When the hole was full, another was dug next to it, and the charpi was shifted to the new location. It had handles on the sides to make it easy to lift.

I poured the water from my urn into the old can that sat on a nearby stone. I took the can into the latrine with me and left my empty urn on the stone outside. This announced to the rest of the family that the charpi was occupied.

Back in my room I sat on the thin pad that I used for a bed, and with my sleeping bag wrapped around me I graded the previous day's math homework. The papers lay on the floor, for no progress had been made on the table I had requested. I gave my classes as much homework as I could find time to correct and they were amazed that I read it all. I believed that schooling had to be an active process on the part of the students, that they wouldn't learn anything by just sitting in class. This was doubly important in mathematics. Math involved a skill which could only be learned through practice. Their practice was their homework, and reading it was a drag, especially when I realized that half the students were copying. I hoped that even from copying they were learning something. Perhaps they would eventually learn enough to be able to do the work themselves.

As I scribbled corrections with my red pen, little Nilam crept into the room carrying a glass of sweet milk tea. She timidly set it down in front of me and then zipped out of the room only to reappear at the door a minute later.

"*Tapaaiko jastaa...*" she whispered, her voice trailing off to nothing. *Jastaa* meant zinc, but it was also the word that the family used for my galvanized washbasin. They used my basin more than I did.

"I'm not washing clothes. You can take it," I said, and Nilam was down the stairs with the washbasin almost before I had finished speaking. She slapped it with her hand outside, making a sound like an oriental gong.

I was hungry, but the tea would have to tide me over until daal-bhaat came at ten o'clock. The timing of the two meals left me hungry in the early mornings and in the late afternoons. I spent much of each day feeling hungry.

I finished grading the homework and rewarded myself with a walk around the room to warm up. Next I began to pre-read the upcoming science chapter, underlining the words that I didn't know and looking up their meanings in my assorted dictionaries. I spent over twelve hours a day doing schoolwork, and even when I was free, I felt that there was something more that I should have been doing. This kept me exhausted, and with classes held six days a week, I really looked forward to Saturday, the single day of the Nepali weekend. But when Saturday came, I was often more depressed than usual. I felt best when I was busy.

Daal-bhaat arrived late and the rice was undercooked. I wondered how Aamaa, who had cooked rice every day for the past twenty-five years, could sometimes do a bad job of it.

The anthem was sung at the school at 10.30, but I missed it. Since I had no class the first period, being late didn't much matter. I entered the office and performed a general *Namaste*. Apparently a half-dozen of the other teachers also had the first period free. Three of the older students were in the office paying their school fees and they watched me as I wrote my name in the teachers' attendance book. Like everyone else, I signed that I came to school at ten and left at four. This had no correlation with the actual times that we were at school. I set my watch according to the alarm clock that sat on a shelf, and as I left I read the temperature from the laboratory thermometer that hung by the door. It was 9°C, or about 48°F. That was the *inside* temperature, and it was certainly too cold for a student to want to sit still on a wooden bench all day. But what to do? *Ke garne?*

I prepared science equipment until two loud rings announced the beginning of the second period. A pancake-sized disk of brass hung by the storage room to ring the periods, and the man who rang it was a big white-haired Braahman who sported a droopy mustache and was missing his lower front teeth. He was paid to do assorted jobs around the school, but since he could also read and write, he doubled as a teacher for the primary grades. This seemed appropriate for a man named Guru.

My morning science class went well, as it most often did. I never went to class without a prop; I needed objects to touch to compensate for my mediocre language. Today, I brought in the lenses and the students had the entire period to handle them and to learn whatever they could. It was mainly play, but I felt that it was time well spent. It generated interest and allowed the students to discover some things on their own before we discussed the textbook's dogma. I, too, made a discovery during the class: Nepali children couldn't wink. I asked some of the students to look through two stacked lenses, but they had trouble seeing clearly. "Look with one eye," I said. "Close the other." But they couldn't do it. They covered an eye with their hands instead. Nepali women evidently played no winking games with their children.

My next class was ninth mathematics and I returned their homework. Two of the students worked a problem on the blackboard, and I did the rest. The board was only big enough to hold one example at a time, so we used too much time when students worked in front of the class. I preferred to have them work at their seats while I went around helping the less capable students. They were slowly learning the material, but they were the class that I least enjoyed. They were generally noisy and rude, even to each other. I rationalized that it was their age, but I still found myself becoming impatient with them.

Besides that, I saw no reason for them to learn complex mathematics when they would all be farmers. A few might use some math if they became shopkeepers, but for everyone else the math seemed a frustrating waste of enegy. The curriculum for the rural high schools was identical to that used in the big cities like Kathmandu, Biratnagar, and Pokhara, and the ultimate goal was to pass the nationally standardized examination granting them a School Leaving Certificate. The SLC exam was another British-Indian invention. The previous year not one student from Sindhupalchowk District had passed the exam. What was the point of it all?

We had three books to cover in ninth math: algebra, geometry, and arithmetic. I put the emphasis on the arithmetic, which they could best understand and which included such quasi-practical topics as interest rates and proportional prices. In addition, I told myself that *how* a subject was taught was more important than the subject itself. Perhaps through the guise of mathematics, my students might learn to think and to reason. That was valuable even if the ability to solve equations wasn't. Learning to think was an admirable goal, but I sometimes believed that I was fooling myself, that my efforts were futile.

After finishing the homework, I demonstrated the use of *pi* (π) to calculate the area of a circle. It was a simple matter of plugging numbers into a formula and I hoped that the class would find it easy and would feel successful. I assigned no additional homework, and as I left the room, I took the extra chalk with me. When chalk was left in a classroom, the students used it to write on everything in sight. The teachers weren't bothered by the graffiti on the walls and tables; we only wished to conserve valuable chalk that had to be carried in from Kathmandu.

The fourth period was also free for me, so I continued to pre-read the science book. I worked alone in the dirty storage room, because I didn't want the other teachers to see how many simple words I needed to look up. It was embarrassing. I was supposed to be the science expert! As I toiled, Guru came in carrying an armful of old exams. He stood on a chair and haphazardly stuffed the tests into spaces in the rafters next to other hoards of yellowed papers. This was a miserable place to put it all; whenever the wind blew, pieces of paper rained down in the room.

"Why put that *uh*... Why put it there?" I said without substance. Nepali had no words for trash or garbage, and to "throw away" meant the same as to "waste." "The papers fall again," I clarified with a gesture toward the scraps of paper that littered everything in the room.

"*Ke garne?*" said Guru with a shrug. His voice carried a slight whistle caused by his missing teeth. "Where should I put it?"

"Can it be put in the flame?" I suggested.

"Burn it!" said Guru. No one had thought of that before. Nepalis had no understanding of waste disposal, and this was a major problem in the large towns. The streets of Kathmandu were filthy.

Between fourth and fifth periods came the midday recess, which I spent sitting on the temple wall reading a book. A dozen of the younger children stood around to watch. I was still a great novelty—the tall white-skinned teacher from *Amaarika*. Sometimes I joked with the little ones, but sometimes they disturbed me and I shooed them away. Today I was indifferent to their gawking and I ignored them except when they blocked my sunshine. Just glancing up was then enough to make the offender move.

Ding-Ding-Ding-Ding-Ding-Clang! Guru hit the bell till it shook loose and fell to the ground. This happened a lot. My sixth grade English class came running to their room and I had a mock race with two boys to see if either of them would arrive after me and thus be tardy.

"Open your books to page thirty-six," I said in English, and then I repeated the instructions in Nepali; I clearly remembered how it felt to be totally lost during a language class.

"One... day... Ram... caught... a... spider. One... day... Ram... caught... a... spider." I read the new lesson from the book at an agonizingly slow pace; I had forgotten that I should have first reviewed the previous day's material. Of my three classes, I put the least amount of time into teaching English, and the lessons sometimes suffered as a result. I was needed as a math/science teacher, and I was only doing an English class because it was easy. It was the one class that could boost my confidence.

"He... put... it... in... a... matchbox... and... took... it... to... school."The class repeated after me, and I wrote the sentences on the blackboard for the benefit of those who had no books. To aid them in understanding it, I drew pictures on the board and acted out the story. I also translated it all into Nepali. The ideal would have been to speak only English during the class, but I felt that this was impractical since some of the students knew no English at all.

We were halfway through the story when Guru rang the next period. As I collected my things to leave, one of the boys said, "*Sir, haamro hajur bhayena*—Sir, we haven't had roll taken."

"OK," I said. "Go get the roll book." He hurried out the door and up the steps to the office.

"*Ek, dui, tin, chaar,...* One, two, three, four,..." I found it easier to call out their roll numbers than to read their names; they laughed too much when I said someone's name wrong. When their numbers were called, they stood and answered, "*Hajur.*" Of the forty-five students enrolled, thirty-two were present that day, which included four girls.

"Why hadn't roll been taken?" I asked. It was normally done first period, but for the past week they had been asking me to do it in the afternoon.

"Sir?"

"Why don't you have roll first period?" I repeated.

"We have no first period."

"No first period? Then your second period teacher..."

"Sir, he isn't here."

"What? Who isn't here? Say that again." All the students began talking at once, and I couldn't understand a word. "Haven't you had *any* of your classes today?"

"No, Sir, not just today..."

"What! You've *never* had a class in the morning? None at all?" I had been too busy with my own classes to notice what was happening or not happening in the others.

"The teachers don't come," said a boy in the front. "They aren't here, only sometimes..." Everyone started speaking again and the room became a chaos of voices. The students kept explaining, but I couldn't listen any more.

I just couldn't believe it. No classes, and the school had been in session for six weeks!

I went to the office and studied the posted schedule of classes. The teachers of the sixth grade's morning subjects were four men whom I had never heard of. While I examined the chart, Durga, the teacher who had hit away the spectators from my first lesson, came over to help.

"Who is this?" I asked, pointing to the name of the sixth grade's math teacher.

"He's not here now. He's gone to his family in Nuwakot District, but he'll be back." Durga also had excuses for the other missing teachers. He thought that their absences were nothing to be concerned about.

This was incredible to me. The teachers didn't even care enough to come to school. I looked again at the schedule and saw that the teachers who had been lounging in the office that morning were supposed to have been in class. What sort of school was this? More classrooms were being built, a student hostel was under construction, some science equipment was on its way, but it wasn't considered necessary for the teachers to conduct classes.

I was in a daze for the rest of the day. My first reaction was to teach as many of the vacant classes as I could, but I realized that this would only hurt the classes that I already had. Then I felt disappointed with myself for my unwillingness to take on extra work.

When the day's classes ended, instead of going home I took a walk up to the small forest which covered the hill behind the school. I often went there to watch the birds, but now I just wanted to think. I remembered that I had once thought that any Nepali teacher could do a better job than I. It was probably true that they *could*; the point was that they *didn't*. Teachers who didn't teach. Students who didn't come to class. The school was a farce, and I saw nothing that I could do about it. I didn't even have the words to tell anyone how I felt.

I walked round and round, not caring where I went. As the sky began to darken, Tauni came running from out of nowhere. Her tail wagged in that funny way, and I knelt down to ruffle her fur and to push her around, something I usually avoided doing for fear of getting fleas. She responded by attacking my face with her tongue, slobbering all over me, and trying to push me to the ground with her paws. It was good to have a friend.

She walked with me back home. I lit the lamp in my room and looked at the calendar hanging on the wall. Each evening I crossed off one day. In three days was a Sunday that I had marked "⅓," meaning that one third of my time in Nepal was over. I had just ten months left.

I took the lamp over to the sink and scooped out a cup of water to wash the dog slime from my face.

The cold water freezes my cheeks and nose, and I decide to search for a better spot to bathe. Between the boulders of the streambed are a number of semi-stagnant pools, and I eventually find one that has been partially warmed by the sun. I wash my hair, but I only sponge off the rest of me; it's too cold for a real bath.

Two more hours up a steep dusty trail bring me to the Buddhist monastery of Thyangboche. The newly built lodge has expensive dormitory accommodation, at six rupees a night. However, this includes a foam-rubber mattress, a wood-burning stove, and even glass in the windows.

My supper is a heaping plate of boiled potatoes garnished with salt. I get a cot by two large windows in the far corner of the room. The stove gives more smoke than warmth, and in the other beds a half-dozen trekkers fall fitfully asleep. The weather has been strangely clear today, and the absence of evening clouds grants me magnificent picture-window views of Everest and Ama Dablam. It's a beautiful night and I stay awake watching the moonlight play across the face of Everest.

Thyangboche 12,687 feet

Today is for rest and acclimatization. The view is too fabulous to leave behind. The altitude seems to draw a tight strap around my head, and if I ascend too fast now the chances of developing altitude sickness later will increase. So be it; Thyangboche is a good place to squander a day.

Out in the sunshine, I sketch the peaks and talk with the other trekkers. Two of the three Americans that I first met in Kharte have arrived; the third stayed in Namche to convalesce after a cyst was removed from the bottom of his foot. To pass the time, Dan bets Jeff dinner at a restaurant in their hometown Seattle that he can't write the names of all fifty states. They agree on a one-hour time limit.

While Jeff labors on his list of states, I make a startling calculation—if someone made a beachball-sized replica of the world, Mount Everest would be only one hundredth of an inch high; rubbing your hand across the Himalayas would give the feel of a smooth surface. Even the world's highest mountains are just a thin film in relation to the vastness of the earth. Dan is intrigued by this comparison, but Jeff is unimpressed; he has left out Rhode Island and Wisconsin. The day passes.

The midday clouds seal off the sun and we retreat indoors to eat potatoes. The cooking, washing, wood chopping, and water carrying are all done by three young Sherpa men. This contrasts greatly with the rest of Nepal where the majority of these tasks are done by women.

The women in Aiselukharka worked non-stop. In the morning Aamaa ground daal on the hand mill, while Nilam cut grass for the water buffalo. Other women and girls lugged water up the trail or laid out their washing on the rooftops. From my back window, I watched a lady drive her five goats down the trail while another woman climbed the terraces to begin work in the fields.

From my front window was a different view. Krishna Bhakta and other neighbor men sat in the morning sunshine, enjoying a smoke and talking over the latest news. The men worked too, but if a family was prosperous enough to afford any leisure time, it was the men who enjoyed it all.

Now, at the end of February, the weather had been warming up, and the women were just starting to prepare the fields for the planting of corn. Aamaa, though, did only minor work in the fields; Krishna Bhakta owned enough land that he could afford to hire the poorer people from neighboring villages to come and do the dirtier jobs.

Another woman who was exempt from field work was Renuka, the Headmaster's wife. Nevertheless, Renuka rarely had a free moment. First of all, she had the twenty-four-hour task of caring for her husband and their three-year-old son. Then at school she was in charge of collecting the students' monthly fees, recording the amount paid, and filling out receipts. To help relieve the shortage of teachers, she also taught some classes, and she kept her son with her constantly. She had only a grade-school education, so she was additionally studying to take exams that would give her a secondary diploma. And recently she had begun a laundry business, organizing some of the women in Nawalpur to do the washing for teachers and other men who were living without a family. If for some reason she had a moment's pause, she would take out her knitting. Renuka always spoke to her husband using the honorific *tapaai* form, whereas he talked to her in the informal *timi* form, as if speaking to an inferior or a child. Life was rough for ladies in Nepal, and the country would have collapsed if not for the work of the women. Now, with the warmer days coming, they had even more to do.

For me, the rising temperature brightened my spirits more than anything else could have done. To arrive in Aiselukharka during the lifeless winter had depressed me, but now, with the tiny green buds appearing on the trees, I felt good for the first time in months. I was slowly adapting to my new existence, and the tranquility of life in the hills was gradually seeping into me. My classes were going well enough, and my Nepali was improving by leaps and bounds. The pitiful state of the school made me feel vitally needed, and I began to consider staying for the full two years.

One major thing was troubling me: no letters had come from Kay for the past month. My mail was sent care of the Peace Corps in Kathmandu, and once a week Sudharshan, the mail clerk, wrapped up my personal mail, the week's Peace Corps memos, a summary of Nepali news, and a copy of *Newsweek* magazine. He would send the packet by registered local mail to the Nawalpur Post Office, and I would sit in my room, counting the days, waiting for it to arrive. Receiving a letter or two, no matter who from, made me jubilant, while opening a mail packet containing nothing but official bulletins dropped me into an emotional funk. The scarcity of letters from Kay actually helped me in a way. It forced me to concentrate on my life in the village rather than dreaming of being with her again. My love for her hadn't changed, though, and I was sure that it never would. She continued to receive long letters from the far side of the world.

The warmer weather also coincided with a good time for getting married. The date of a wedding was determined by the positions of the stars, so many marriages were conducted on the same auspicious days of the year. A girl from Aiselukharka was to be married to a boy from Nawalpur, and though everyone else must have known about it for weeks, I found out only a couple of hours before the evening wedding feast. An invitation came to the school addressed to "All the Honorable Teachers, and Philipsir."

A feast was given by the girl's parents and the square in front of her house was packed with people. A few lamps illuminated a flurry of chaotic activity. The teachers, along with the Pradhaan Panch, Krishna Bhakta, and other men of position were taken to the top floor. The house was filled with people waiting to eat. Straw mats covered the floor and we were seated in two long lines facing the center. In front of each of us was placed a brass or stainless steel plate. The family had borrowed plates from every house in Aiselukharka.

First a man served each of us a heap of dry pounded rice called *chiuraa*. This was a food indigenous to the Newars, and it was particularly well suited to feasts. It could be prepared weeks in advance and it had no caste restrictions against it—a Braahman, for example, couldn't eat boiled rice prepared by a non-Braahman. Next, a half-dozen women came up the stairs and spooned side dishes onto our chiuraa: stewed buffalo meat, boiled potatoes, beans, mashed pumpkin, fried potatoes, and bitter greens. In addition, we were given servings of red chillis and gooey sour chutney.

"Do you eat garlic?" the lady who dished out the chillis asked me. I said that I did and she hurried down the stairs.

As I ate, I concentrated on the potatoes and avoided the chutney. Kedar, the geography-history-government teacher, watched how I ate and asked, "Philipsir, how do you like Nepali food?"

"Ah, well, it's very good here, but when I first came to Nepal I didn't like it at all."

"Yes, you must become accustomed to it," said Kedar. "The food from one's own home is the best." To this everyone nodded in agreement.

The mashed pumpkin and bitter greens were unappetizing, but I did like the beans and chiuraa. The buffalo, I didn't try, and I was highly respected in the village for my refusal to eat any meat. Besides not robbing the children of their protein, vegetarianism was also a good choice on my part, for only half a serving of meat was actually digestible. Nepali-style butchering was a simple process of randomly hacking with a kukuri until the buffalo, goat, or chicken was in bite-size pieces. A portion of meat, therefore, usually contained 50 percent bone and gristle.

The lady who had served the chillis came back up the stairs and dumped a half-dozen garlic cloves onto my plate. They were fried but otherwise whole. *Ughh!* I wasn't accustomed to having my garlic in such large doses. The first two seared my tongue as I bit into them, but I had no choice—everyone was watching me.

One of the lady NDS teachers began to speak and when attention shifted to her, I flicked two of the garlics off my plate and hid them in the cuff of my pants. "Does the bride cry at her wedding in Amaarika?" she asked me.

"Cry? The what?" I didn't understand.

"The bride," she repeated, "does she cry?"

"She cries? Who?"

"The bride is the girl who gets married," said Krishna Bhakta, coming to my rescue. "Bride" was a new word for me, and Krishna Bhakta best perceived the limitations of my vocabulary.

"Yes, very often she does cry," I said.

"Ah, just like here then," said the NDS ladies to each other, and I slipped a garlic clove under the edge of my plate.

After second and third helpings, we covered our plates with our hands and declared that we couldn't possibly eat any more. We joined the milling crowd outside, and a family member led me through the confusion to the porch where the bride sat amid a jabbering pack of the village girls. She was dressed in a scarlet sari that had a metallic luster. With her head down, I couldn't see her face; the only thing I could see of her was her sari. She must have been one of the young women that I saw carrying water every morning, but I didn't know who. After she was bustled inside, I stood in the press of people for an hour before I realized that there was nothing more to see. I went home and Krishna Bhakta soon found me in my room.

"Is it over?" I asked.

"No, this is only the second day," he said. "Tomorrow they take her to her husband—to her man in Nawalpur."

"And the parents always arrange the marriage here?"

"Yes, but one of the boy's relatives actually talks with the girl's parents. He checks that it's all right with everyone before the fathers meet."

"What if the boy or girl don't like it?"

"Oh, they're asked about it before the village is told. If they don't like it, someone else is chosen."

"Can a boy and girl choose each other?"

"Like a love-marriage in Amaarika? Sure, if their parents agree. The fathers then arrange the marriage. First the boy's uncle..." Krishna Bhakta gave me a full description of the marriage process for Newars: a mediator makes the negotiations; gifts are exchanged between the families; the girl's parents give a feast for friends and family (this was the part that I had just attended); the following morning the girl is taken to her husband's home where private ceremonies are performed for two days; the girl's mother-in-law ritually washes the bride's feet; the couple makes a final visit to the girl's home for a meal; and most importantly, vermilion powder, called *sindur*, is poured along the part of the bride's hair. For as long as her husband lives, she will put this red powder in her hair to display her status as a married woman.

I saw the bride again the following morning as the wedding procession passed by the school on its way to Nawalpur. First came a band consisting of a dozen men and boys playing drums, cymbals, horns akin to trumpets, and a clarinet that sounded like an asthmatic oboe. At the end of the column came men carrying the bride's dowry: new brass pots and water jugs, large cloth-wrapped packages, a window-sized mirror, and a wooden cabinet with various doors resembling a turn-of-the-century icebox. The body of the procession consisted of perhaps fifty people, almost all men, parading happily. Amongst them was the bride herself, carried in an open palanquin constructed from a cane seat slung between two poles. She was wrapped head-to-toe in bright red cloth like the other dowry gifts. As she came closer I could hear that she was indeed crying. Closer and louder, her cries grew into a wail.

"*Aamaa! Aaamaaaa! Aaamaaaaiiiyeee!*" She was pleading for help from her mother and crying in panic. Her face was covered and only her hands were visible. Her knuckles turned white as she clung to the sides of the swinging chair. Nearer now, I could see her hands clearly. They were tiny and smooth. She was *not* one of the young women who carried water; she was one of the village girls who played with little Nilam!

"*Aamaa! Aaamaaaa! Aaamaaaaiiiyeee!*"

She was just a child, but her childhood was now over. She was being snatched from the only home she had ever known and was being given over, body and soul, to strangers—to her husband, to his parents, and to the whole of his extended family. In a traditional Hindu household the new bride would be a virtual slave to the whims of her mother-in-law and would have to work doggedly to win her new family's acceptance. Among Newars, the transition was said to be easier, but this girl seemed unconvinced.

"*Aamaa! Aaamaaaa! Aaamaaaaiiiyeee!*"

The girl's cries of despair hung in the air as she was carried up the trail to her new home in Nawalpur. I stood on the school ground and thought back on the previous night's wedding feast. I had told the NDS ladies that the bride often cried at American weddings, but this wasn't the type of crying that I had meant. We had spoken the same language, and we had understood one another's words, but we hadn't communicated at all. They would not have believed that brides in Amaarika cried for joy, not sorrow.

The men in Thyangboche continue to wash, and chop, and cook. Among the Buddhists in Nepal, the male and female roles are much more equitable than among the Hindus. But on this trip I'm not concerned with the cultural roles of men and women. My attention is focused on the mountains.

I listen attentively as a British trekker details the troubles that his party had at high elevation: the intense cold, the steep icy slopes, and the weakness inherent from the altitude.

"It's not worth it," he says, not understanding that his very complaints are the things that fire my enthusiasm. "We tried the Chikim La pass to Gokyo, but couldn't get through the snow. It was up to my waist. Some blokes came over from the other side, but they had a Sherpa with two yaks to plow the way. Only a yak could get through there."

I think to myself: *I can't wait to try.*

I join Dan and Jeff for a dinner of boiled potatoes. They peel the skins off theirs, but I eat mine intact—skin, dirt, and all.

"How can you eat so many potatoes?" Dan asks me as I consume my own plateful and then finish half of his portion too.

"Well, I like potatoes. There are things a lot worse. In my village I was once asked if I ate garlic..." Jeff and Dan laugh at the story of the garlics and I omit the truth of how sad it actually was. *Aaamaaaaiiiyeee!*

March 27
Pangboche 13,074 feet

"The famous monastery is uphill to the northwest of cultivated terraces," reads Dan from the guidebook. "It houses what are reputed to be the scalp and the hand of a yeti. They can be inspected and the monastery can be toured for the price of a small donation."

Jeff, Dan, and I look up the hillside, seeing nothing. We have only come an hour from Thyangboche, but the altitude is already taking its toll. We feel lethargic. The yeti relics interest us, but we are not enthusiastic about the extra climb to the monastery and back.

"I wonder if they really have parts of a yeti?" Jeff ponders aloud.

"Oh, they're real all right," I say. "I've seen pictures of the hand and the scalp, but who knows if they're from a yeti, or from a bear, or a large monkey?"

"Well, they'll still be here on our way back," reasons Jeff, and so it's settled. When in doubt, procrastinate!

A Sherpa woman digs in a field for potatoes, the only crop that grows in this cold rocky soil. She glances up as we walk by and then returns to her work. We touch her world like a passing cloud.

Just outside her village, a spring trickles from the mountainside. A tin can, opened at both ends, has been stuck in the rock and it directs the water into a convenient spout.

"Technology," says Jeff.

As I laugh at his joke, I miss my step and knock my foot against a boulder. This time, the ache is only momentary.

The throbbing in my toe made it impossible to sleep. The pain grew, and I thrashed and moaned in the dark of my sleeping bag. Periodically I lay quiet, trying to relax, attempting to convince myself that everything was fine, that I felt no pain. Then the throbbing sent me turning and groaning again.

A few days previously, I had stubbed that toe. I didn't even remember how I had done it, but it had festered, like every injury in Nepal. The infection had spread under the toenail, and it now pushed up with incredible pressure. The ceaseless throbbing coincided with my heartbeat, and I felt that I would soon go insane.

By 3.45 a. m. I still hadn't slept. The pounding throbs had grown worse and I'd had enough. My toe was only one problem. For the past week and a half, I'd had diarrhea and fevers with no apparent cause. The nearest doctor was in Kathmandu, so the Peace Corps had provided me with a quantity of MIF kits. These were packages consisting of preservation solutions and a glass vial for mailing stool samples to Kathmandu for analysis and diagnosis. I had sent in a MIF kit, but the results wouldn't come for another two weeks: *No parasites seen. Submit another sample if symptoms persist.* Meanwhile I was exhausting my water supply with repeated trips to the charpi. Everyone in Aiselukharka knew about my excursions to the outhouse; *nothing* about me was a secret. The worst part was that I had missed three days of school.

The right side of my face had also begun troubling me. My hearing in that ear was fuzzy, I couldn't open my mouth all the way, my right eye was irritated, and my nose was stuffed up. My body felt like it was falling apart.

The toe worsened until I had to do something about it. Groping in the dark, I found some matches and lit the lamp; I no longer had a working flashlight. I had smashed it against the wall a few days before. I drew the last of my water and stuck my foot in the cup. My plan was to relieve the swelling with the cold water, but it didn't help at all and I only succeeded in knocking over the water. *Damn!*

The toe was much worse now that I was standing. All the blood pressed down into my foot, making the pressure unbearable. *God, please, no more!* I got out a pin and heated it red hot over the lamp. I wanted to let the pus out, so I stuck the pin under the edge of the nail. Slowly and deeply, I pushed it in. I clenched my teeth and pushed, but no pus came out. I pulled the pin out and tried another spot, going even deeper, down to a half an inch. All that came was a little blood, and now it hurt even worse. *Oh God!* I felt tears in my eyes.

I threw the pin across the room. Then, infuriated with the futility of that, I kicked over the bucket and knocked a stack of books across the floor. *GOD DAMN IT ALL!!* I let out a scream, and that felt good. Damn toe, damn textbooks and exams, damn shitty food, damn it all! I yelled again and turned over a broken stool that held a pile of dirty clothes. I kicked my papers around and put my open hands against the wall. I pushed and I hollered. Then I pressed my hands against the floor, pushing and pushing, trying to push out all the frustrations that I felt inside: frustration at not having anyone I could really talk with, frustration at being unable to teach as well as I wanted, and frustration at no longer being the *me* that I had been in America.

Finally, I crawled back into my sleeping bag and lay down exhausted. The pain in my toe had gone beyond my threshold of sensation. My nose began to run, and I let it flow freely down my face and onto the bedding.

At first light, someone began to pound at my door. It was latched from the inside, so I pretended to be asleep and hoped that they would go away. Then a window was pushed open with a pole and Mahendra was boosted up into the room. With the light from the open window, I saw that my nose had been *bleeding*, not running. Blood covered my face and hands. Mahendra unlatched the door while I tried to wipe the blood off my face.

In came Krishna Bhakta, Durga-sir, Surendra, and a couple other men, all looking apprehensive. "We heard the screams." "What happened?" "Are you all right?" "Was it a witch that came?" "What was it?"

I sat up and looked around the room. Books and clothes were scattered over the floor, the lamp was overturned in a pool of kerosene, and the bucket lay on its side in the far corner. Nothing but me was in its proper place. I didn't know what to say, so I acted as though I was waking up and seeing the carnage for the first time.

"Was it *you* screaming?" asked Krishna Bhakta. "We were very frightened. Did you have some drugs?"

"Was it a spirit that entered your body? A demon?" queried Durga-sir.

"Did you take some medicine for your illness? Was the medicine bad?"

I shook my head to all their questions. I was dazed and embarrassed. They looked at the mess in the room with expressions of deep concern, and I was fortunate that they didn't notice the traces of blood on my face.

"Are you better now?"

"Was it a dream? Can we…"

"Yes, yes, a dream," I said as though I was beginning to remember. "It was a bad dream. A nightmare. It was very, very bad." I turned to and fro, showing them how I must have thrashed about knocking things over.

They could understand this, and they accepted my explanation, though they undoubtedly believed that the nightmare had been caused by a demon. I was touched by how worried they were. They kept asking if I was all right and if there was anything that they could do to help.

When the others left, Krishna Bhakta and his sons began to clean up the room. We picked up the clothing and re-stacked the books. Mahendra pulled up the straw mats and began to sweep the floor. When Krishna Bhakta left, I followed him out and took a walk to clear my head. The infected cyst had finally burst. My foot dripped blood and pus with each step.

I took the path that circled the house and then zigzagged through the terraces towards my little stand of trees. The new shoots of corn were coming up and the odor of their greenness was calming.

I limped slightly as I walked up the trail. That afternoon I would make a self-diagnosis and begin a course of antibiotics. My infections would soon be healed, but I knew of no medicine that would heal my frustrations. I just had to accept and adapt. The night's rampage had been a catharsis that had released my stored-up tensions. Perhaps I should have screamed more often.

As I passed through the fields toward my grove of trees, several of the villagers whom I recognized watched me without interest; I was becoming a common sight. They nodded at me and resumed their work. From the beginning I had been accepted for what I was—a foreign teacher at the school—but after three weeks came an event that marked a change in my status. I was being welcomed as a full member of the community.

The occasion was New Year's Day. The Nepali year began in the middle of April, at a time of birth and growing. This seemed a much more appropriate time for celebrating New Year than in the middle of winter, as the Western world did.

Throughout the previous week, Krishna Bhakta had been brewing prodigious amounts of *raksi*, the local liquor made from fermented rye. The still was located downstairs of the extension and it had daily filled my room with pungent smoke. The raksi was an important part of the celebration. Krishna Bhakta was expected to provide an ample supply, for this was his year as bursar of Aiselukharka's *guthi*. The guthi was a collective trust that conducted festivals, religious ceremonies, pujaas, and cremations. The bursar was responsible for collecting the rent on the common land that provided the guthi with funds to pay the musicians, priests, and others who were hired by the guthi. Any surplus of funds was kept by the bursar and any deficit was paid by him, so Krishna Bhakta wisely saved money by making the raksi himself.

The afternoon before New Year's, several hundred of us assembled in a clearing outside the village to raise a huge pole called a *lingu*. The pole was the trunk of a large pine tree which had been stripped of its bark and branches. No leader coordinated us in erecting the lingu; anyone who felt like shouting orders did so, and a general consensus was reached with much reference to past years of experience.

A hole was dug and boards were angled in to accommodate the bottom of the six-storey spar. Then with much hollering and grunting, several dozen men used crossed poles to push from beneath while the majority of us pulled on the ropes. The lazy ones just watched and the even lazier ones yelled contradictory commands.

"*Haainse!*" a man bellowed.

"*Honse!*" we called as we pulled on the ropes.

"*Haainse!!*" he shouted again.

"*Honse!!*" we replied in unison, and we heaved together.

We raised the lingu to about twenty-five degrees and it began to swing to the left, forcing the pullers on the other rope to run to one side to compensate. They overdid it, and the lingu swung the other way, giving our side a turn to run and stumble across the uneven ground, trying to keep the spar from sweeping down on the people below.

We tried again.

"*Haainse!!*"

"*Honse!!*" And on and on.

As we heaved and hollered, I could feel an occasional eye on me. For four months the men and women of Aiselukharka had watched me walking to school, fetching my own water, washing my clothes, and otherwise living as simply as any of them. I hadn't acted the part of the rich important man, and here I was, barefoot and sweating, working along with everyone else. No other school teachers or men of influence were there; it was just those of us who had dirt between our toes. And I was the only non-Newar. As such, I couldn't understand what anyone said, but *haainse-honse*, heave-ho, was clear enough.

The assemblage of villagers was fantastic—the women squatted and watched at a safe distance, the men pushed, pulled, and bellowed in unison, and the small children ran about trying to help but only getting in the way.

Expectation rose for the moment that the lingu would stand erect and I knew that the roar of joy would be deafening. But no matter how hard we tried, we couldn't get it up. The ropes were re-tied at different angles and the positions of the poles underneath were rearranged, but it still wouldn't go up.

As evening approached, people began to desert, and those of us who remained gave it a final try. The tallest people were needed to push on the struts from below, so I moved over to help there. *"Haainse!" "Honse!"* The lingu reared up and seemed on the verge of standing upright when one of the bamboo struts broke, setting the whole thing off balance. Other supports then snapped, and the people on the ropes lost their footing and were pulled down. A dozen men screamed as the lingu began to fall. We all tried to leap out of the way as the breaking supports knocked people over and the lingu came crashing down. I managed to jump clear, though many of the others were hit by the spar. Dozens of men groaned in the wreckage, but miraculously no one was badly hurt. That night the New Year arrived with the lingu lying impotently on the ground.

In the morning we all tried once more. A foolproof solution had been found; the village carpenter sawed off the lingu's lower 20 feet. It then went up amid cheers, and two red banners were unfurled from the top. It was an impressive sight.

The real celebration to welcome the Nepali year 2035 was held that afternoon. A litter bearing a statue of the Hindu goddess Mahadev was covered with a pile of leafy branches and carried to each stone shrine in the area. Most of the villagers followed and at each stop the band of drums, cymbals, and a nasal-sounding oboe played with abandon. A few men of the throng danced, and the women either watched or performed a pujaa.

A man wearing patched pants and holding a bottle in his hand accompanied me. *"Raksi khaanus*—Have a drink," he insisted.

"No, I don't drink," I answered.

"Here, just a little little bit," and he tried to put the bottle in my hand.

A couple of the other men explained to him that I didn't drink, that I *never* drank, but he couldn't understand that. "You're drunk," I told him and everyone laughed and stomped.

"OK, so you have to dance instead," he compromised, and his mouth dropped open when I agreed.

A circle was cleared amidst the crowd and only a few men danced at a time. Everyone was in a joyous mood, but when I stepped into the circle they became delirious. Their shouts echoed off the far mountains. The music had a strange rhythm, and at first I followed the lead of the other dancers: holding their arms straight, they swung their hands up and down, and took rapid little steps with their feet propelling them in small circles, or they stood almost stationary with their knees together and with their hands placed on their oscillating hips. There were many variations, and as I gained confidence, I added steps of my own—jumping on one foot and clapping behind my back. Whenever a dancer stopped to rest, I pulled someone new into the ring so that I never danced alone.

We had an uproarious time, and if anyone harbored any doubts about me, they were now broken. They wouldn't let me stop dancing, but I finally demanded a rest.

As the procession moved to the next idol, two of my neighbors walked with their arms around me. We laughed and smiled, and they spoke to me in Nepali.

"You've become our brother now. We're like one family."

"Yes, you're our brother. How old are you?"

"Ah, twenty-four." My birthday would come at the end of the month.

"So! I'm older than you are and he's younger. I'm your Big Brother and he's your Little Brother!"

The crowd jostled us down a particularly narrow part of the trail and I switched partners; I walked hand-in-hand with a man who had once been described to me as the best card player in Aiselukharka. He complimented my dancing. Then with a lot of laughing and joking, he and two friends explained that I danced very well, which was especially good since I was so very tall. All the crops, the corn and the rye, the wheat and the rice, would also grow tall, and for this they were grateful. All was good and they were very happy. *Raamro.*

The day progressed like this, with much dancing and laughter and touching. Toward evening, as we walked in a mass, something inside of me seemed to float up and view myself from above—one man in light skin among a hundred men in brown. As I watched from above, it became a difference without distinction and I blended into the crowd. I became the whole village's brother that day. They had accepted me without reservation, but I wasn't as accepting as they were. I was still adapting to both the Nepali people and to Nepali Philipsir.

At 14,000 feet, my acclimatization is far from complete. I need more time to adapt fully. We've reached Pheriche and my breathing is much too rapid. The wind blows as if from a frozen hell, turning my fingers to ice. Jeff and Dan warm themselves in the sod and stone hut, while I stay outside studying Lobuche East and making sketches.

Using binoculars, I search for a safe route up the peak. At about 18,000 feet is a possible spot for a high camp, but the route there is anything but clear. The lower part of the mountain is all rock cliffs and hanging glaciers. Above 18,000 feet the route is obvious enough, but it looks very dangerous, especially the last bit which is honeycombed with crevasses. I'm worried. To see myself planning a climb like this scares me. I scan the peak again and again, and my eyes water and ice over from the wind blasting my face. Darkness forces me inside, where the evening's potatoes are cooking.

"Are you really going to climb that mountain?" ask Jeff and Dan, but I have no answers, only hopes.

March 28

Pheriche almost 14,000 feet

The three of us get a late start, for we have no reason to rush. Lobuche village is not far, but the trip involves a 2,000-foot ascent. We'll take it slow.

The trail angles along the slope far above the iced-over stream, and we hike in silence. The altitude slows us and we move forward inch by inch. I feel a tightness in my head that I pretend isn't there. I wonder how Jeff and Dan are feeling. Dan has previously climbed Kilimanjaro, but for Jeff each step is the highest he has ever taken.

We stop often and long, and by midday we are somewhat above 15,000 feet with only a mile or so left to go. The vista is breathtaking; we're surrounded by peaks over 20,000 feet. Taboche Himal seems to hang over the valley, and Ama Dablam is a magnificent spear point covered in glaciers. The landscape is all rock and ice, snow and scree, with nothing green in sight. A silence surrounds us that's so deep it rings in our ears.

We rouse ourselves and continue leadenly upward and on. We skirt the edge of the Khumbu Glacier, which flows from Everest itself, and at this point the trail peters out to nothing. Another couple of hours further, just as we decide that there's no such place, we come to the three squat huts of Lobuche. We've reached 16,000 feet.

Scattered about Lobuche are a few yaks, a dozen half-frozen hikers, and an equal number of Sherpas. As we look for places to sleep, Jeff realizes that his sunglasses are gone. He thinks they've slipped from his shirt pocket when he stooped into one of the huts. We search everywhere and find nothing;

someone must have picked them up. I am convinced that the Sherpas know where the glasses are—no secrets can exist in such a small group—but they won't tell. I talk with a group of Sherpa women who refuse to look at me. This upsets me and the more irritated I become, the faster flows my Nepali.

"He has to have those glasses," I plead. "They're essential; he needs them to see. He has walked three weeks from Kathmandu and he must walk back. How can he do that without his glasses? He has to have them. Someone must have seen them."

They give me no answer. No one is willing to help.

Jeff eventually decides to offer a fifty-rupee reward with no questions asked. This is much less than what the glasses are worth, but it greatly disturbs me. What about integrity and honesty? Apparently honesty costs fifty rupees, for the sunglasses soon reappear and the thief makes a tidy profit.

The huts have space for only one of us, so Dan (who snores) will sleep inside, while Jeff and I will share my tent. Dinner is no surprise—potatoes. The meal is hot and filling but unappetizing. At this elevation nothing tastes very good. Jeff and I both have trouble sleeping, so we're awake until late—till nine or ten o'clock. We shiver in the darkness, and we recite the epicurean delights of Kathmandu: Pie. Chop Suey. Vegetable Soup. Spaghetti. Cake and Ice Cream. Chocolate. Pancakes. French Fries...

Visions of food urged me up the last rise to the road at Lamidada. I was on my way to Kathmandu, where I would eat familiar foods and speak English for the first time in four months. The time had not gone quickly. Often it had lumbered along, a day or an hour at a time, like a prison sentence. I had been looking forward to this trip since January. I would enjoy the food, and I would do some shopping and business, but most incredibly, Kay and I had agreed by mail that I would telephone her the following morning. I also needed my next gamma globulin injection.

The bus chugged in. It was too full to get a seat, but not yet full enough for me to be allowed onto the roof. I took a place in the rear door's stairwell, the only place that I could stand upright. At each stop, people pushed and elbowed me, but *Ke garne?* The bus was a good one, and we reached Kathmandu in just three hours.

Coming the last few miles into the city, I began to feel heady, like my brain was filled with fog. The streets and cars, glass-windowed buildings, shops, markets, and people rushing about were all too much for me. When I had first been in Kathmandu I had thought that it was a small town, but now it seemed like a huge metropolis. I'd become accustomed to a simpler life, in a world apart from electricity, piped water, and the wheel.

I went first to the Peace Corps office to check my mail. Nothing. A fisheries volunteer that I knew talked with me for a bit, but I had trouble speaking. Nepali words came easier than English words, and many words didn't come at all, making me st-st-stutter. In addition, I often verbs at the end of the sentence put, and my eyes wandered as I spoke. I felt no connection between myself and my surroundings.

Next I went to the toilet which was shiny, white, and Western. I was inclined to wash my rear before sitting so that I wouldn't soil the seat. And when I did sit, it felt so funny and cold that I almost fell off laughing.

I talked with Virgil and Ambika, and they told me that two other volunteers from my group were in Kathmandu. Greg had lost a filling, so he had flown in to have it replaced by the dentist. And James Pesout walked in the door as we spoke. He had lost weight since I had last seen him, but he still wore his orange hunting cap and black goatee. He reminded me of a fifties beatnik, deeply sincere and slightly crazy. He was in town with a class of his students for a five-day field trip to the capital. The office was closing so he walked with me to the center of town.

"Where are you staying, Phil?"

"I don't know. Do you know a cheap place with a hot shower?"

"Sure. The Monumental Lodge. It's on Freak Street."

"Where?"

"Come. I'll show you." He led me to a dirty narrow street that was lined with small hotels, noisy bistros, and cheap shops. "Here it is."

The Monumental Lodge was wall-to-wall with two other buildings, one room wide and four storeys high. The hallway had probably never been washed. "And there's hot water?"

"The hottest in town." Pesout left to go eat with his students and we agreed to meet later.

Before my own grandiose meal, I toured Freak Street and discovered the aptness of its name—they were everywhere, in beads and long hair, sandals and flowing oriental trousers. The hippies and world travelers sat in the tea and pie shops, sauntered about, mumbled in many languages, and smoked their chillums of hashish. I wondered where they all came from and what they did in Kathmandu.

That evening I met Pesout at one of the freak-filled teashops. We talked about our villages, our schools, and our illnesses.

"Do they teach in your school?" Pesout asked me.

"Not very much, it seems. This past month we had the quarter exams, and then an athletic competition, and then New Year's, so all in all we had no classes for over two weeks. I don't know what to do when there's only a few students. Should I continue teaching and forget about the students who are missing class or should I wait until all the students come back?"

Pesout, too, had stories of teachers who were never in class and holidays that were extended almost indefinitely. He was very concerned about how much his students were learning, but he was also worried about himself. He said that he sometimes felt so lonely that he thought he was going crazy. I knew exactly how he felt.

We talked about the freaks for a while, and then I went off to bed. My mind was in a buzz from speaking English and being in the city, so this, combined with my excitement over the coming phone call to Kay, made it hard to sleep. Pesout, I imagined, stayed up talking with some travelers, and perhaps making contact with a pretty lady tourist.

I was up at first light and I walked the grotty, reeking streets until a shop opened for breakfast. I had toast, eggs, and pancakes, then more toast and an order of fried potatoes. The Central Telegraph Office opened at ten o'clock, but I was there a half-hour early. For Kay in California, the time would be around nine at night. I paid in advance for four minutes and I began the long wait. I could neither stand, nor sit, nor relax. My head was ready to burst. After three hours they called my name and I ran to booth number two. My hands were trembling.

"Hello? Hello?" came her voice.

"Kay?"

"Hi, honey!" she said, and my heart seemed to melt.

"Hi!" I jammed a finger in my free ear to block out the office noise. "You sound like you're down a well."

She laughed. "*You* sound like you're in a tin can." Her voice was the best thing I had heard in seven months.

"So, honey, how have you been?" I asked.

"Oh, pretty good. I feel better this quarter, but it's hard." She seemed to be crying.

"Yeah, I know. Are you getting choked up?"

"Hm-hm," she sobbed. "It's pretty misty here."

"Yeah, here too." Tears came to my eyes, but at the same time my soul was soaring. To hear her voice and to feel her so close! I wanted to reach through the wires to hold her and to kiss her.

We talked about little things: the time difference, her classes at school, and my knees. We had a couple of long pauses with the time ticking by at over a rupee a second, but this didn't matter. We basked in the love and the personal contact.

Finally I had something important to ask. "This guy, ah—John, that you wrote about, what's going on with him?"

"He's just a good friend, nothing more."

"But you know if you want to get involved with him or maybe with someone else, it's OK."

"I don't think that I could find anyone like you," she said.

I felt the tears come to my eyes again. The time was nearly up, but one last thing had to be said. I wanted Kay to say it first. There was a pause, and then another, and I couldn't wait longer. "Kay, I love you."

"I love you, too," she said.

"Say hello to everyone for me, and to your folks when you see them."

"All right. Do you need anything?"

"No, I have all I need. I think the time's up."

"Take care of yourself, honey," she said.

"Yeah, I'll try. Bye."

"Bye..."

Bzzz.

I walked away with my feet hardly touching the ground. I had forgotten how good it felt to be in love. When I met Pesout later, he could see that I glowed.

"I guess it was a good phone call," he said as we walked to a restaurant.

I closed my eyes and just sighed.

"But you've still decided to stay for the two years? I thought you were quitting after just one."

"Yes, but that wasn't because of Kay. Training did me in, and I had amoebic dysentery. I couldn't imagine two years like that. But now, in my village, I'm settled in, and I can't see quitting."

"Good," said Pesout. "You have to take it slow. Being here is like being a child again. You've got to learn everything anew. A baby never rushes."

As he spoke, two men squatted in the road to have a chat and a Brahman bull fell asleep at the corner.

"See," he said, "everyone takes it slow in Nepal."

This meandering pace kept me in the capital longer than I had planned. I needed five full days to do my business, and during that time I learned much about Kathmandu.

Of my fellow volunteers, fewer than a half-dozen had their principal jobs in Kathmandu, but many other volunteers were in or out for some reason: builders of bridges or water systems who were arranging for materials, new volunteers arriving, old volunteers leaving, and current volunteers who were sick, or needed supplies, or were on vacation. We all stayed in cheap dingy hotels and followed the same general schedule. Each day began with a sizeable breakfast—consuming enormous amounts of food was the essence of being in K'du. From ten to four we endeavored to do our business at various offices, shops, or government ministries. Most of us took a break for lunch. Then at four we converged at the Peace Corps office, for this was when the mail arrived. Sudharshan distributed the letters and the occasion became a cross between Christmas Day and a state lottery. The winners gleefully tore open their mail, while the losers were only consoled by Sudharshan's assurances that they would get a letter the following day. Evenings consisted of long talks over big dinners. I found myself hungry for any kind of meat—in the village I was developing ridges on my fingers from protein deficiency. Dinner was followed by more conversation and then dessert at one of the pie shops. Finally we would mount our rented Chinese bicycles and ride back to our grimy beds.

Saturdays were for lounging around Phora Durbar. This was a small country club situated just opposite King Birendra's royal palace in the center of Kathmandu. The complex contained a swimming pool, basketball and tennis courts, a small theater, and a snack bar. It was owned and operated by the US Embassy and it was restricted to Americans who had official business in Nepal. The various patrons of Phora Durbar fell into unstated levels of status, with the Peace Corps Volunteers at the bottom. Privileges such as bringing in guests (especially Nepali guests) and reserving tennis courts were denied us, but we didn't complain. We were grateful for the chance to take a swim and to see an English movie.

Besides learning the volunteers' routine when in the capital, I had a chance to watch the activities of the foreign tourists: Frenchmen with cameras gave money to children who pretended to be lame, Australians in mountaineering boots signed up for organized treks, and hippies from around the world bought hashish. I was distressed by the impact of all these tourists. The Nepali people were emulating the foreigners by degrees. Western clothes and music had become marks of prestige, and wearing spectacles—even ones made of plain glass—was considered high class. Everywhere I turned, I met someone trying to buy my clothes or offering to sell me some drugs. It made me sick.

One night on Freak Street, Pesout showed me how easily the freaks got their drugs.

"Walk slow and watch what happens," he whispered. Almost immediately we heard a voice murmuring in the darkness. "Hashish? Hashish? Hashish?"

"One," said Pesout with a grin.

A few steps later came another appeal. "You wanna buy some hash? Smack? Anything..."

"Two!"

"Hash. Dope. Smack."

"Three!" hooted Pesout. He thought it was great fun.

Then a man stepped forward and blocked our way. He spoke fast in a Bengali accent. "You wanting some hash? Yes? I have the best I'm thinking. You come with me. I show you..."

"You want to go to jail?" Pesout asked.

"What? I've *been* to jail."

"Four," I said, and we continued.

Next a child's voice beckoned, "Hey, you want some dope? Hashish, hashish, hashish..." He sounded like he was calling a cat to get its supper.

"Five!" laughed Pesout.

We had come less than 60 yards.

This decadence was in response to the influx of travelers, and throughout Kathmandu were signs that foreign influence was undermining traditional Nepali values. As I finished my last dinner in Kathmandu, I overheard a conversation between a European traveler and a Nepali/Tibetan seller of brass ornaments and jewelry. They spoke in broken English and they both sounded stoned.

"No, not nothing I want," said the European as he looked over the curios spread across the table.

"Tomorrow maybe," said the Nepali nodding his head. "You have something to selling? I buy your jeans. Levi very good." The status of denim was more important than the size.

"No, man, I don't sell them," drawled the European. "Can't sell mine clothes. I need them. I sold already everything else." As he spoke, he slowly swung his head from side to side.

"You people have very good way to living," said the curio dealer. "No working. Some dope. Some eating. Some tea." He raised his open hands to his shoulders and leaned back in the Nepali gesture of relaxation. "Ahh... You have good life. Very good."

While the curio dealer extolled the virtues of a doper's lifestyle, the European put his head on the table and slipped into insensibility.

The percentage of Nepalis who wanted their country to be Westernized was steadily growing, and I wondered if the Nepali way of life would survive. Cultures didn't mix like colors or flavors. The stronger, more abrasive, culture would drown out and supersede the milder. The process was well underway in Kathmandu. A man's career was becoming as important as his family, and to own a motorcycle or a car was unquestioned proof of an individual's superiority. I was already tired of it, and I was eager to return to the purity of Aiselukharka.

On the bus back to Lamidada, I thought about the destruction of cultures. The insensitivity of tourists was not the real cause; their mere presence was enough to instill their foreign principles into the society. And I was as much to blame as anyone. Rich tourists, long-haired freaks, and Peace Corps Volunteers. Who was I to be so self-righteous? No matter how Nepali I became and regardless of how accepted I was, the villagers would see through me. They would inevitably be affected by the basic Western values within me. I felt like the carrier of a crippling disease. And I was spreading that disease among the people I most cared for, among the villagers of my adopted home, Aiselukharka.

Lobuche 16,175 feet

Snow! The large flakes drop fast and heavy, covering the ground in a white blanket. I sit on the edge of a crate, drinking Sherpa tea in one of the huts. Periodically I get up to check the weather. No change. I chalk it up as a day of acclimatization. I take aspirin for the drumming in my head, and persist in pretending that I feel fine. Jeff does no pretending, and he's glad that I have codeine for him. I read a book, *Soldiers on Everest*, which I carry for days like this. Slowly the time passes.

I formulate a plan for the week: today, for resting; tomorrow, up to 18,000 feet on Kala Pattar; Monday, another rest day; Tuesday, a reconnaissance of Lobuche East; Wednesday, a hike to Everest Base Camp; Thursday, a final rest; and then Friday, off to climb Lobuche East. I hope that this easy schedule will let me acclimatize so well that the altitude will not be a problem.

The Didi warms our bellies with alternating batches of fried potatoes and boiled porridge. At dusk, after a final plate of spuds, Jeff and I wade through the snow to my ice-bound tent. A candle gives erratic light as I dig in my medical kit after more codeine.

"I have some valium too, if you don't think you can sleep," I suggest.

Jeff shakes his head. "It looks like you're ready for anything," he says as he peers into my kit of bandages, salves, and pills. "Did the Peace Corps give you a medical course or something like that?"

"No, but they're starting one for new volunteers. We're not supposed to be doctors, but we can hardly say 'no' when someone sick comes to us."

"I know what you mean," says Jeff, as he burrows deeper into his sleeping bag. "People always ask me for medicine as I hike around, but I don't carry any at all. To the Nepalis every foreigner is a doctor."

"No, that's not completely true, but there were plenty of people in my village who wanted medicine from me: students with colds or the runs, women with sick babies, and everyone with infected cuts. I did what I could and gave them long talks about improving hygiene, giving babies only clean water, and washing cuts with soap."

"But I thought there was a medical center near your village."

"You mean the Health Post? The villagers came to me saying that I had more medicine than the Health Post."

"You should have sent them to a shaman. I hear those guys know everything about health and have a lot of good cures."

"I don't know how good they are. I was once at a friend's village where a woman kept pleading for medicine for her cold. Her whole head was stuffed up, so my friend finally gave her some tablets he had. They must've not worked, because the next morning she had the *jhaakri* there. He's like a medicine man, and his cure was to have her pull up her shirt and then he began hitting her on the back with a hand broom, hoping to whisk away the disease."

"Did it work?" Jeff wonders.

"I don't know. I guess so, if she believed in it enough. I heard of a jhaakri in the east who goes through his whole routine with chanting and drums and dancing, and then at the end he takes out a hypodermic and gives the patient a shot of penicillin."

"You saw him do that?"

"No. A friend told me about it. In my village if someone was very sick, they carried them to Kathmandu, that is, if they weren't already dead. When someone was so sick that they couldn't walk they usually figured that they would die."

They carried the boy across the playing field and towards the school. Guru, the school helper with the droopy mustache, had the boy on his back while another man shaded them with a black umbrella. Viewed from the window of the second-storey storage room, he looked like a small boy of about five years old, probably with a hurt leg. I didn't stop to think what they would do with him; I'd had no free time since my trip to Kathmandu three weeks before. I was organizing a science fair and a half-dozen students were in the room preparing their equipment. Two of them asked me questions while I tried to grade a stack of exams. The door creaked and we all turned as Guru carried the boy inside.

He spread out an old shawl and set the boy on the floor. The boy lay motionless, like a sack of bones. He had a large open sore on the top of one foot, but that wasn't his major problem. He was so thin that he hardly seemed to be there at all. His arms and legs were without flesh and his ribs protruded like rafters. I looked at Guru, who squatted by the boy. Over a week before, Guru had come to me wanting medicine for his nine-year-old son. I hadn't seen the boy, but the symptoms of diarrhea, cramps, and blood in the stool sounded like amoebic dysentery. I had told Guru what medicine he should get from the Health Post and I had heard nothing more about it. Now here was Guru's son, emaciated and lifeless. He was much too small to be nine years old.

"*Dherai biraami bhayo*—He's become very sick," said Guru, looking at his son. He held the boy's shoulder as though afraid that he would blow away.

"Didn't the Health Post medicine help?" I asked.

"They didn't have it. They don't have anything."

"He still has diarrhea?"

"Yes, just like water, many times a day."

"And the blood?"

"No more blood comes, but he doesn't eat. He hasn't eaten a thing for five days."

"Five days?!" I knelt down to look him over. Every bone and joint was visible. He wore only a short shirt, fully exposing his shriveled body. He seemed too gaunt to be alive. He made no sound and his breathing was shallow. As I looked at him I felt a growing fear, the fear of imminent death.

I touched his arm, but he made no response. His skin looked and felt like clay; he was badly dehydrated. "Does he drink?"

"No, only a little water sometimes."

This was exactly what Guru had told me over a week before. It was a wonder that the boy was still alive; he was suffering from a disease-treatment combination that was the number one killer of Nepali children. First, a baby gets an intestinal parasite causing diarrhea. Then, the Nepali cure is to deny the child fluids. It's simple and effective. Nothing in, nothing out—no more diarrhea. But this in turn causes severe dehydration. Some children recover, but just as likely they die from fluid loss or are so weakened that they catch some other fatal disease. The government was attempting to educate people about the dangers of diarrhea and dehydration, but new ideas were accepted slowly.

The boy lay with his back to me and as I stepped around him I was shocked by my first look at his face. It was the face of a corpse, a skeleton. His eyes were half open, but they were rolled up into his head so that only the whites showed. My hand trembled as I felt his forehead. He had a slight fever. I took his wrist and felt for his pulse. At first I could find none, but probing deeper with my fingers I discovered it—so very faint, though hysterically fast. It was more like a vibration than a pulse, and was much too fast to count.

His pulse, more than his appearance, terrified me. What if he died right there? My hands began to sweat. "Relax," I told myself. I took a few breaths and tried to speak to the boy with my thoughts: "You *will* live. You *will* be OK."

I went straight home, half running, half walking, and I fumbled through my medicine chest for the things I needed: tetracycline to kill the parasites, lomotil to stop him up long enough to absorb some fluids, and vitamin-mineral tablets to combat his anemia. Rehydration drink would also help, so I needed some sugar, salt, and soda. Snatching up the medicines and my container of

129

sterilized water, I went down to Shyam Krishna's shop. He had sugar, but no soda, and I already had enough salt at the school. In addition to the sugar, I bought a packet of sweet crackers. My stomach had been feeling bottomless, and I would be glad that I had eaten something if it was to be a long ordeal.

Up in the storage room, a student fanned the boy to keep the flies off. He still hadn't moved. While I mixed the sugar and salt into the water, I explained to Guru what I was doing. Next, I cut the tablets in half to make proper dosages for a child. When I was ready, Guru attempted to arouse his son. He tried to sit the boy up, but he was utterly limp. "He's sleepy," explained Guru, but it was more than that. He was unconscious. Guru spoke into the boy's ear and held him in his lap. Slowly he began to come around and his eyes rolled back into place. We propped him upright and I put my arm around his shoulders to keep him from falling to the side. Guru held the glass of rehydration drink and I had the tablets. He had absolute faith in me and my American medicine.

"Here, this is for you to drink," coaxed Guru.

"Naaaa," whined the boy. He closed his eyes.

"You must drink this and take the medicine."

The boy made noises that were only vaguely human.

"This is sweet-water. Drink some sweet-water and take the medicine."

The boy would not.

"After you've drunk the sweet-water and taken the medicine we'll go home, but first you must drink the sweet-water..." Guru talked and talked until the boy's resistance slackened.

He accepted a sip from the glass, and I got the smallest pill ready—half a lomotil tablet. He took a second sip, but immediately spat it out. He refused to have any more and Guru resumed the coaxing. He pleaded and reasoned, but it was hopeless. He absolutely would not accept the medicine. I wanted to suggest forcing the boy to take it, but I didn't know the Nepali words to explain that.

The boy whimpered his first intelligible sounds, "*Aamaa, Aamaa—* Mother, Mother."

"His mother is able to get him to eat," said Guru. "Perhaps at home he'll take the medicine."

We tried time and again, and after two hours we realized it was futile. In desperation, I asked Guru and the others to leave me alone with him.

The boy began to cry and call for his mother the moment they were out of the room. I put my arms around him, cradling him and rocking him until he quieted down. "*Ma timro saathi ho*—I'm your friend. I'm your friend. You're going to get well. This is something good for you. You should eat this and get well." I tried putting the tablet into his mouth, but he began to scream. I rocked him more, and talked and coaxed. He relaxed, but would cry whenever I tried giving him the medicine. Eventually I laid him down on the shawl and he seemed grateful. He didn't go to sleep or pass out. He just lay still and looked up at me. I began talking to him again. "You're going to be fine. I'm your friend. You should take this medicine. Look how small it is. So very tiny. Isn't it very small?" Finally, he agreed that it was small, but he was still unwilling to swallow it. He no longer cried, though; he was probably worn out. My last attempts to drop the pill into his half-open mouth also failed. I too was exhausted.

I sat for a while looking at his cadaverous little face. His eyes gazed straight ahead and were filled with terror—not terror of me, but terror of his own disease. He knew how deathly ill he was, and he no doubt understood how little time he had left. The longer I watched him, the more worthless I felt.

I opened the door and the others came in. Guru squatted down and the boy used inconceivable willpower to crawl onto his father's back. He had more strength than I had thought, but I had little hope that he would live. They wrapped the medicines carefully and, taking the sweet-water with them, they set out on the hour's walk home.

I decided that I would never ask Guru if his son had survived. I was too afraid of the answer. It was better to hear nothing and to know nothing.

I came to the school the next day and taught my classes and tried not to notice Guru's absence. He was a Braahman and the death of a son would necessitate a period of absolution. As the days passed, I pushed the boy's ravaged face further from my thoughts.

Then on the fifth morning, Guru arrived at the school and came walking to where I stood on the playing field.

"No, no. Oh, no!" I pleaded inside. My hands were in my pockets and they formed into fists. I didn't want to hear it.

"He ate rice today," was all Guru said.

March 30
Lobuche 16,175 feet

Aand still more snow—a day identical to yesterday. We sit and talk. We eat and watch the weather. In *Soldiers on Everest* I read of two mountaineers who attempted Lobuche East. They got "close" to the summit. The book says no more, and I'm troubled. Why would Lobuche East defeat climbers who successfully climbed Everest? I consider the last part of the peak, which is honeycombed with crevasses, and I seriously doubt that I'll have a chance. The weather depresses me.

The tedium is broken by occasional episodes of excitement. Sooner or later, we must all dash outside to relieve ourselves. It can be done amazingly fast when your behind is being blasted with pellets of ice.

Nightfall finds Jeff and me back in the tent, which is now covered in snow like an igloo. As we settle into our sleeping bags, our breathing slips into a familiar pattern. First comes an almost imperceptible breath, followed by a slightly deeper one, then come gradually deeper and deeper breaths until the full lungs are used. Suddenly the breathing stops altogether, and it begins again with a shallow breath. The cycle is called Cheyne-Stokes breathing and it is so common at high altitudes that I would be surprised if we *didn't* breathe like this.

Sleep comes lazily. We talk of Jeff's travels in South America and I recount my journeys in Nepal. I describe one of my first treks in Nepal, a hike that involved a certain dog...

The dog seemed to be following me as I hiked out of Shermatang Village. I stopped and so did he, a hundred paces behind. It was a large dog of a disagreeable Tibetan breed, having coarse black hair, an oversized square head, and massive jaws well suited for continual snarling and fighting. This particular dog was shedding his winter coat and his ugly fur stuck up in ragged tufts of dusty brown. I wanted nothing to do with him; one of my Peace Corps friends had recently been in Kathmandu for two weeks to get rabies shots after being bitten by a stray dog.

I was headed home from a four-day excursion to Helambu, a Sherpa region situated one ridge west of Aiselukharka. One of the days had been a holiday (on the occasion of King Birendra's visit to China) and another had been a Saturday, so altogether I had missed only a day and a half of school. If not for Vishnu, the assistant Headmaster, I would not have chosen to miss any school at all. We had planned the trip together, but he had opted out when one of his sons had become ill. By then I'd felt committed to the trip and I'd gone alone, which Krishna Bhakta and Vishnu had said was a dangerous thing to do. Bears and snakes would attack me and road bandits would rob me. I would fall and become lost. And worst of all, I would be without a friend. How could I possibly enjoy the trip alone?

Krishna Bhakta and the others would be surprised when I returned with stories of friendly people and bear-free trails. I had encountered none of their dangers, that is, none until the appearance of the dog.

He continued to pursue me and he came closer each time I halted. I carried my binoculars in my shirt pocket and I stopped often to study the birds along the sides of the trail. I spotted one with a crested head and a blue tail that I had never seen before. As I brought it into focus, the dog barked and charged past me, intent on catching an avian breakfast. I cursed the dog and I hurled a stone at him, which unfortunately missed. The damn dog seemed accustomed to such treatment and he followed me like an evil spectre.

Seeing him closer, I realized that he was an exceptionally bad dog. He had a large gash across his forehead, the skin was missing off one side of his face, and an abscess grew above his left eye. Wounds covered his body, and I preferred that he keep his distance.

An hour past Shermatang, the trail started downhill. I would have to descend 6,000 feet to the river and then climb 4,000 feet back up to Aiselukharka. The day was hot and sunny, but the previous three days of rain (the faint beginnings of the summer monsoon) had made the trail slippery. The sections with reddish soil were particularly bad, verifying the Nepali adage: *Raato maato, chiplo baato*—Red mud, slippery road.

The dog tagged along. He flopped on his side and panted whenever I stopped to rest, but he was up again the moment I began to move. He looked extremely thin and quite old. I couldn't understand why he followed me. I had shown him no kindness—unless not kicking him was a kindness—and I had no food to give him. As we walked, he occasionally scavenged some nasty-looking things to eat along the side of the trail. By and by, I got used to having him along, but I was glad that he would have to halt at the river. Most animals, and many people, were afraid to cross the suspension bridges.

At the bottom of the trail, we reached the confluence of the Melemchi and Indrawati Rivers. First I had to cross the Melemchi on a simple wooden bridge and then the Indrawati on the big suspension bridge. Just one thing stopped me—the wooden bridge was gone! The recent rains had swelled the river and washed the bridge away. The map showed other bridges up both of the rivers, but they were a couple of hours away, which would put me in Aiselukharka after dark. No houses were in sight for me to ask about a closer bridge.

I decided to ford the river, so I bade farewell to the dog and set off with my shoes hung around my neck. The current was stronger than I had expected. As I went further out, the river became too deep and I had to retreat to shore.

I tried again further upstream, and the dog came to watch. Once more I went as far as I could, but I got stuck in the middle. I could neither continue nor return. The swift current swept the rocks from under my feet and brought stones smashing against my legs. I needed all my strength just to stay upright and I was gradually drawn into deeper water, where I would certainly be pulled under.

I looked across at the dog and hoped that he would recognize the danger I was in and go for help—like a scene from a *Rin Tin Tin* film—but he only sat in a pool of water and cooled himself. I dug my feet down among the rocks and told myself that I *would* make it back. Eventually I cleared all the loose stones from beneath my feet and slowly worked myself ashore. The dog seemed unimpressed.

I put on my boots, and the dog tailed me as I started up the Melemchi River to the next bridge. No trail existed on that side of the river and before long I was forced to climb a bluff of unused terraces. I followed one terrace that traversed a cliff high above the river. The narrow terrace slowly tapered to a 6-inch catwalk, and then it ended altogether. On the left was a 200-foot vertical drop and on the right was a chest-high ledge leading to an upper terrace. I should have retraced my steps, but I chose to climb the ledge instead. I kicked out a toe hold, dug my fingers into the soil above, and carefully hoisted myself up. I made it OK, and I was now free of the dog; he couldn't possibly climb that ledge.

I started to leave, but I turned around when I heard an unexpected noise behind me. The dog had somehow jumped up and he was hanging by his paws on the edge of the shelf. His big ugly head strained forward, but he couldn't get his hind legs up and he was slowly slipping back to what would be a fatal fall. I dove for his front paws, but the sudden movement scared him and he let go—falling down and down to the rocks and the river.

My stomach felt like lead and I slumped to the ground. It made no sense—that dog, so unaccountably devoted to me, was now dead. I forced myself to look over the side at where his body might have landed. But I saw no body—he stood on that narrow catwalk, wagging his tail! I was stupefied. It was a miracle that he had landed on that ledge and had kept his balance. This was a dog that I had underestimated.

I guided the dog around the other way so that he would not attempt more heroics. Further up the terraces, we met a boy who spoke of a bridge across the river. He took us back in the direction that we had come and led us to his home.

"It's easy to cross the river. It's only so deep," said the boy's father as he gestured to a height just above the boy's knees.

"No, look!" I showed him how far up my clothes were wet. "It's been raining. See how the water is brown, not green."

"I'll take you across by the hand," offered the father. Even the boy said he could cross. They ignored my description of how deep the river was; they said that I should use the bridge if I was scared of the water. When I explained that the bridge was gone, they smiled as though I was a fool.

I rebuffed the father's kind offer and I walked back to the confluence where they had insisted the bridge still stood. A hundred yards past the site of the washed-out bridge, the dog and I rounded a bend and saw, just *above* the confluence, a second bridge spanning the Indrawati. The boy and his father had been right to treat me like a fool.

I walked across the swaying bridge clutching the upper cables with my hands. As I had expected, the dog refused to follow, and I was almost sad to say goodbye. By this time I had even given him a name—Sherman, as derived from Shermatang.

The dog, however, had no plans for saying goodbye. He went down to the river, looked straight at me on the far bank, and plunged into the water. This section of the river was a crashing mass of white water, and Sherman was immediately dashed against a boulder. He swam and was swept onto a large rock where he stood for a moment before jumping in again. He was knocked against rocks and pulled under by the current as he tried to swim. With a struggle, he reached the center of the river where he got a stance on a large boulder. Here he realized that he was unable to go further and he did the most amazing thing of all. He began to yelp and whine like a puppy crying for its mother.

After listening to his pitiful cries for five minutes, I re-crossed the bridge and called him back to that side. He reversed his river crossing, but he would not venture onto the bridge. I had to carry him! He was a heavy, foul-smelling heap, dripping dirty water and muddy fur. Fortunately he moved not a muscle as I carried him over. Our balance was precarious and I couldn't hold him tightly with my left hand; I had recently jammed a finger in a school volleyball game.

Safely on the Aiselukharka side of the rivers, Sherman and I hiked past the confluence to the lower bridge. I wanted to get something to eat on the other side, and knowing that the dog would not follow me across, I told him that if he was still waiting there when I came back I would take him to Aiselukharka and find him a home. But as I started onto the bridge, he followed eagerly. His fear of bridges had vanished.

As I ate, Sherman was chased across town by the half-wild local dogs. When I was ready to go, he was nowhere to be seen. I searched the village and the surroundings, but he just wasn't there. I didn't want to believe that he was gone, but finally, dejectedly, I crossed back over the bridge and continued home.

For the first mile past the village, I kept looking back to see if he had spotted me from a distance and was coming along. The images I had of him hanging on the ledge and swimming the river were very strong. Now he was gone. Though he had been so dedicated to me, I had done nothing for him, and I felt ashamed.

The route up to Aiselukharka was steep and the mountainside was a labyrinth of narrow paths and small villages. I stopped frequently to drink water, to cool off in the shade, and to ask if I was on the right trail. About three-quarters of the way up, I came to a stone resting place, a *chautara*, which was shaded by a sacred pipal tree. Beneath it sat a single man and with him was a dog of that same Tibetan breed. I slipped off my pack and sat down to rest. I looked again at the man's dog. Across its forehead was a large gash. Sherman!

"Did this dog come with you?" I asked the man

"No, I've never seen it before."

Sherman gave me no sign of recognition. He lay motionless as though asleep. I couldn't understand it. He had been walking *ahead* of me. How had he known to re-cross the bridge and to come this way? From the village at the confluence I could have chosen a dozen equally possible directions. Could he have tracked my scent from my outward journey three days before? No. That was impossible; the rain would have washed my smell away. Perhaps he was just psychic.

We continued to Aiselukharka, but we walked slowly because Sherman was so weak. As we neared the village, though, he began to high-step and to prance. He knew we were home.

Sherman got a terrible reception. Krishna Bhakta wanted to know why I had brought home a dog, and if I wanted a dog, why a dog like *that*? "He followed me," was my only defense. The family dog, Tauni, barked and snarled at the intruder, but Sherman just tucked his tail between his legs and cowered. Krishna Bhakta left immediately to find the dog a home.

Within three hours, a man from a nearby village had agreed to take him. Sherman, however, refused to leave my side, and they had to drag him away on a chain, yipping and barking.

I couldn't keep him myself for two reasons. First, was the disapproval of my family and their dog, Tauni. The second, and greater, problem was that I would soon be leaving for the summer. In just two weeks school would close for the monsoon break and I would be going to Kathmandu. If

Sherman remained attached to me, he would certainly attempt to follow me and I would have to abandon him at the road in Lamidada, a town already overcrowded with starving dogs. The best would be if he was taken in by a family that wanted him.

But Sherman rejected the family that took him. Three days after he had first been taken away, he arrived at my door with a broken chain hanging around his neck. His new owner came to fetch him that evening. He told me that the dog refused to eat. He had tried everything: rice, potatoes, and even old meat. This was the opposite of my own experience. With me, Sherman had eaten anything he could find, including decomposed rodents and cow droppings. The man apparently treated him well, but Sherman began making daily escapes and returning to Aiselukharka.

This continued for about a week. I tried to discourage him, but I nevertheless felt good inside each time he came shuffling through the door dragging that futile chain. For the children of Aiselukharka, a strange and ugly dog was something to pelt with stones and to kick with all their might. I tried to stop them, but they were probably the most vicious when I was away.

One day I spied a boy hurling a brick-size stone at him. The rock hit Sherman's side with a deep thud and he limped down the trail to get out of range. He almost certainly came looking for me again, but I never saw him. The last image I had was of him limping away before the next stone could be thrown.

March 31
Lobuche 16,175 feet to
Kala Pattar 18,192 feet

I awake in the dark and poke my head out of the tent to see stars—a clear day! I dress awkwardly in the cramped space of my sleeping bag and I leave as the day begins to lighten. I carry only a day pack, but the fresh snow makes it hard going. No one has passed this way for two days, leaving the snow clean and virgin. I feel like the first man on earth.

Without a trail, I make my way along the moraines that border the Khumbu Glacier. In four hours of steady snow trudging, I reach the frozen lake of Gorak Shep at about 17, 000 feet. From here begins the climb of Kala Pattar. The name means black rock, but "brown lump" would be more descriptive. It's no peak at all, just a spur on a ridge of Pumori. Kala Pattar is famous because it offers the world's best view of Everest. From nearly all points (except the Thangboche monastery) the sight of Everest is blocked by the colossal Nuptse-Lhotse ridge. Now as I move up Kala Pattar, Everest's summit inches into view.

The sight is spectacular, but my eyes stay fixed on the ground. I labor up the slope, stopping frequently to suck in the thin air. The grade is not steep; it's only the altitude that slows me to a crawl. I puff upward, and a half-dozen brown-and-white striped Himalayan pheasants join me as they forage for food. They make *peep peep* noises when I come close, but they are otherwise unafraid of me. They look foreign in this lifeless world of rock and snow.

After an eternity, I reach the rocky crest where I sit down in a fissure blocked from the wind. The ice-clad peaks are limitless, and above them all stands Everest. I take photographs, draw sketches, and most of all I daydream. There she is, the highest mountain on earth, and beneath Everest sleeps the entire world—countries, seas, and people. I haven't seen that much of the world, but I've certainly seen more than I would have expected. Much more.

The monsoon rain poured down on me, and I felt deliriously free. I had finished my first half-year of teaching, all my exams were graded and submitted, and I was on my way to Kathmandu. For the first time in years, I had no commitments to school and no commitments to work. Free!

School would be closed from mid-June to mid-August—the children would be out working in the fields—and I had already formulated a plan for the summer. First I would enjoy a couple of days in K'du, then I would take a ten-day hike to a group of sacred lakes called Gosaikund. My group's in-service training would be held in town for two weeks, and after that I was looking south towards Sri Lanka or maybe west to Kashmir. The various possibilities were all tantalizing.

My first full day in Kathmandu I had the Peace Corps doctor examine the finger that I had jammed a month before. The X-rays showed that it was broken.

"Why didn't you come sooner?" asked the doctor.

"I thought it was only sprained or something," I replied. "I couldn't leave school for something like this. It's only my left pinky."

"Hmff," he grunted as he consulted a volume of orthopedics. "You're going to Washington for this," he said.

"W-w-what!" I was incredulous.

The doctor looked me straight in the eye. "You *don't* want to have this done in Bangkok." He explained that it required a delicate operation. A surgeon would need to drill tiny holes in the broken fragment of bone so that it could be wired back in place. I would have to wear a finger cast for six weeks before the wire could be removed.

I was in a state of shock and disbelief. For medical problems that were untreatable in Kathmandu, the doctor had the power to evacuate volunteers to Bangkok and even to Washington, but I hadn't dreamed that it could happen to me—not for a broken pinky!

I had a few days to talk with my friends as they trickled into the capital. Many of them envied me. A trip to America was what we had been dreaming of—to be with friends and family, speaking English and enjoying all that good food, feeling really at home and not being stared at. These things would be nice, but I was reluctant to go. I felt like I was stopping in the middle of something that would be difficult to resume. On the way to the airport, I nearly called the trip off. I could live with a crooked pinky. Just one thing made me go—the thought of seeing Kay again.

The journey to Washington was blurry. I had hardly slept in Kathmandu and on the plane I couldn't sleep at all. I had a half-night layover in New Delhi where I was put up in a five-star hotel. The doorman wanted to carry my luggage and all I had was a plastic bag of clothes. In Tehran, security had been tightened and we were required to stay on the plane. In Frankfurt, the connecting flight to Washington was delayed and the airline staff escorted the passengers to the VIP lounge. They supplied us with free drinks while a multi-lingual public relations man came around to cool our tempers. Everyone was upset by the delay, and they demanded an explanation of the problem. I couldn't understand why they were so riled up. We couldn't go anywhere until the plane came, so what did the reasons matter? We only had to sit back and wait. I was still on Nepali time.

In the evening, I arrived in Washington and checked into a no-star hotel. I sat on the bed and looked at the floor. The room seemed to spin around my head, so I left to find something to eat. Out on the street, where I had thought it was night, lights shone everywhere. Street lamps and car headlights, lights in the shops and lights in the sky. The lights told you when to stop and when to go. Signs said to turn right, turn left, eat here, eat there, buy this, do that.

Many of the signs were made of light and others were painted on the street. The street was infinite. First came the road, then sidewalk, then vertical street up the side of the building, and then more sidewalk. Macadam, concrete, asphalt, and blacktop. Pavement on pavement. Atop it all and through it all snaked the cars of steel and glass. Their eyes lit the way as they raced about in intricate circles. They made an awful noise and stink, and the ground beneath my feet seemed to rumble of machinery. The sound of it went through my ears and into my brain. After two blocks, I staggered into a fast-food restaurant.

The woman behind the counter smiled mechanically as she wrapped my order in wax paper, placed it inside a foam box, and slipped it into a paper bag. She had change to the penny. I watched the other people eating—some of them ate using their left hands, and I tried to contain my disgust. "This is not Nepal," I told myself. Black people ate together, and white people ate together, but nowhere did black and white people eat together. And everyone was fat. How could they get so heavy? They tossed out as much food as they ate. In the plastic trash cans were enough half-eaten French fries and unwanted burgers to have fed entire families in Nepal. The food itself tasted good, and the milkshake was sublime. There was just one problem—I was up half the night with diarrhea.

In the morning I went to the Peace Corps office. A secretary gave me four days' per diem and told me that I had an appointment with a hand-wrist-and-finger specialist. My appointment wasn't till that afternoon, so I had a few hours to get my head into place. I still felt dizzy.

When the specialist examined my finger and heard my description of how it had happened, he said, "Ah-ha! I don't need to look at your X-rays. I know exactly what's wrong." He crossed his arms, hooked his thumbs under his armpits, and leaned back. "What do you want to do with your life?" he asked.

"Huh? What do you mean?"

"Well, do you want to be a concert pianist or anything like that?"

"No," I shook my head, "I hadn't exactly planned on it..."

144

"OK, then I suggest we just splint the finger and it should be fine."

He got out a piece of aluminum and a roll of surgical tape. He was done in five minutes, and he gave me the extra tape so that I could periodically redo it. Finished. Now I was truly in a daze.

I rushed back to the Peace Corps office, checked out with them, and received a Government Travel Request good for a return ticket to Nepal.

That night I took a Greyhound bus to see my mother in Pennsylvania. The bus was half-empty and the seats were padded and reclining. I remembered my bus rides in Nepal—packed like cattle or standing the whole trip.

Two middle-aged women sat just ahead of me and I could hear every word they said. "No, she just doesn't get enough money. She'll have to see her lawyer. If she doesn't..."

I was embarrassed to find myself eavesdropping. I was accustomed to living in a partially understood fog of language, so I was now shocked to understand everything that I heard. I felt like people were calling in my ear.

At 2 a.m. my mother met me at the bus terminal and we talked until dawn. After an hour's sleep, I went to visit my Grandmother Rose.

"How is it with the cannibals over there?" she asked me with a wink.

I gave her a woodblock print of a Hindu goddess and she insisted that I write down the meanings of all the arms and faces. She told me the names of the different birds that came to feed at her window. She was dying of bone cancer. Recently she had been in and out of the hospital and when I hugged her I felt only her bones. She wasn't afraid of dying; her solitary fear was of being put in a nursing home. "They give you just a single drawer for everything you own," she said. "And they don't let you hang pictures on the wall." The thought of being a forgotten number in a nursing home terrified her and she began to cry. "The staff is only concerned about you when you're dead and must be swept away."

This was so different from the treatment given to old people in Nepal. Elderly parents and grandparents in Asia were respected and cared for by their children and grandchildren. They stayed in the security of their homes, and as they aged they could work as much or as little as they wished. To have your old relations living with you was an honor, not a burden.

Fortunately for Grandmother Rose, she would never have to endure the horror of a nursing home. A few days after my visit she would be returning to the hospital for the last time. Sleep well, Grandma.

That afternoon, my mother generously paid for me to fly to Los Angeles. I wanted some private time with Kay and in just two days she would begin her summer job as a camp cook. As the plane landed I felt apprehension holding me in my seat. I knew that she would be there to meet me, but I was the last one off the plane.

I stepped into the arrival hall and Kay was suddenly in my arms, her warmth pressing against me and her hair flowing through my fingers. A year of loneliness seemed to melt away with that first embrace. I covered her face with tiny kisses and we held each other tight. Was this all a fantasy? Just days before, I had been in Aiselukharka sitting on a mud floor and eating with my fingers.

We went to her parents' house in Burbank and we looked at the slides that I had been sending home to be developed. I talked of Nepal and the words flooded out of me. For too long my experiences had been unshared and my emotions had been unexpressed. Descriptions of the things I had seen burst forth in spasms that caused my eyes to dart about as I spoke. The night ended beautifully. I had expected to sleep alone, but Kay wanted us to be together. We made love and this convinced me that our relationship was unchanged.

The following day we journeyed to her camp in the San Bernardino Mountains, but now our time together would be very limited. I knew that her mind would be filled with the burden of cooking for 200 children. From Nepal I had sent a message asking her to get a replacement for a week. She hadn't found a substitute, and I felt that she hadn't tried very hard. The best we could do was to have a friend of ours, Sandy, come take Kay's place for a weekend. We met with the camp director to explain who I was and Kay failed to mention the weekend that she wanted free. I had to ask the director myself. Kay told me later that she had forgotten about it.

The camp was a beautiful place. It was surrounded by pine forests, contained a small lake, and had a stable of horses. The first few days I still had trouble sleeping, but as I caught up with the time lag I was able to relax. Walks among the trees revived me, and I was glad to be out of the city. I had some experience with camp cooking, so I busied myself organizing the stockroom and making pancakes.

Kay and I slept together nights and had short conversations during the day. Everything triggered recollections of Nepal. Kay told one of her kitchen staff, "Please keep the door closed. We don't want flies in here." And I reminisced, "Yeah, flies. In my village the flies were getting so bad that when I sat still literally hundreds would land on my arms and on my face. I had to eat with one hand and wave the flies off the food with the other. And then the mosquitoes..." Kay could only reply, "Oh. I think we need more flour." I lived in Nepal and Kay lived in the kitchen.

Sandy came, but the free weekend had already been reduced to a single day. She loaned us her orange Volkswagen, named Ichabod, so that we could go home, but Ichabod refused to start. Somehow I felt that if Kay had truly wished to leave, the car would have started. When it did start, we had only time enough to sleep a couple of hours and to see a movie before returning to camp. I was deeply frustrated. Kay seemed unmoved by my presence. Something was missing. One day she said to me, "I don't understand why I don't act like I love you." The answer was obvious, but we weren't strong enough to face it.

After a week and a half at the camp, I needed to go. Even with the difficulties, we wanted more time together. Kay felt sorry for me. She didn't fully understand what my life was like in Nepal, but she did realize that it was very hard on me.

As we stood on the empty road outside the camp, she asked, "Will you be very lonely?"

"I hope not," I answered, and we kissed away each other's salty tears.

It was on the Fourth of July that I left the camp and hitchhiked back to Burbank. I kept thinking of Phora Durbar in Kathmandu. The embassy staff, the Peace Corps, and other official Americans would be having a party. They would have a tug-of-war and a pie-eating contest. Ten thousand miles away, I stood at the side of the road and waited for rides.

In the San Fernando Valley I saw some friends and got my climbing gear out of storage to take with me to Nepal. Everyone I saw expressed polite interest in Nepal. They asked me superficial questions: "What's it like?" "Do you like it?" "Are you glad you went?" I couldn't answer their questions with anything that made sense, but that was immaterial; few of them were truly interested in Nepal. My friends could have better related to me if I had just come back from Canada rather than returning from another century.

I hitchhiked north to see my brother in Sacramento. We had some good talks but these were mostly about Kay, and I was soon anxious to return to Nepal. America had not been dreamland, and I was getting hungry for daal-bhaat.

I phoned Kay for a last goodbye, but she said that she wanted to see me again. In a week she would have four days off. We arranged for her to fly up to Sacramento and we would take a canoe trip down the Feather River.

During the week that I waited, I received a letter saying that another volunteer from my group had left Nepal. Debbie had been medically terminated. Her back was broken and she would have to wear a body cast for six months. She had done it by falling off the swings at Phora Durbar. Our group had shrunk by one more, down to thirteen.

Throughout the four days that Kay and I spent on the Feather River, we treated each other more like we had during our previous years together. She relinquished her worries of the kitchen and I put aside thoughts of Nepal. We focused on each other and we talked easily as we drifted with the gentle current. Together we explored the river's tiny inlets and counted the great blue herons.

The days passed quickly, and with a final I-will-love-you-always goodbye, she left. I felt empty inside and cheated in a way; I had only gotten a taste of being with her before she had gone. I would later get a letter from her saying that during our canoe trip she had fallen in love with me again. I would be puzzled by that—she had never said that she had fallen *out* of love with me.

The following day, I took a bus to San Francisco and changed my Government Travel Request for a ticket to Kathmandu via Hawaii, Hong Kong, and Bangkok. By flying in this direction I was actually saving the Peace Corps some money. Twenty-seven hours after Kay had left, I was sleeping in a field just outside Honolulu.

Oahu was lush beyond imagining. For five days I sunned myself on the beaches, snorkeled among the iridescent Pacific fishes, and looked for people to talk to. One night the police caught me sleeping in a park. They accused me of being a thief, a pusher, and a pimp. They searched my pack for drugs and weapons before they let me go. Other nights I slept on the beach or in the bushes and I was all right. I also had problems with the young descendants of the original Hawaiians. They threw curses at me, calling me a "fuckin' white boy," and tried to provoke me into a fight. My refusals to fight only confirmed their superiority.

One evening I went to one of the Waikiki hotels to meet a pair of vacationers I had met on the beach. I waited for them in vain and a security guard eventually forced me to leave. He said that if I wouldn't go he would take me to the cellar to be photographed, fingerprinted, and given a "physical reminder" never to come there again. *Aloha!*

On the flight to Hong Kong, I sat next to a young Chinese-American named Tom. He was initially reticent, but by and by, he told me his story. He was traveling to Taipei to be married. He had never seen his future bride, but that was unimportant. The marriage had been arranged as a family obligation, the sole purpose being for her to obtain an American residence permit. Tom refused to say how he felt about it.

During the night we crossed the International Date Line, and this left a mysterious blank space in my datebook.

Hong Kong was full of surprises. It was clean and organized, with signs in both English and Chinese, and the water was safe to drink. Hong Kong, after all, was still a British colony. I stayed in the cheapest hostel I could find and I explored everywhere, mostly on foot. Even late at night I felt safe on the streets. The colony was larger than I had expected, and the New Territories contained large tracks of rice paddies and ancient walled cities. Old wrinkled men charged tourists a Hong Kong dollar to take their picture. The New Territories had escaped development because the land was under lease from mainland China. The lease would expire in 1997 and Hong Kong would then revert to Chinese sovereignty.

I ate in minuscule restaurants and I happened into one that was wholly Chinese. With great confusion I managed to order peas and prawns, which I assumed came with rice. I sat at a large round table with nine Chinese men, and they watched discreetly as my food came—peas and prawns, but no rice, and only chopsticks to eat it with. I washed my chopsticks with the hot tea in the center of the table, as I had seen everyone else do, and I began to labor through my meal. I needed five or six tries to grasp each pea, but then it usually slipped free before reaching my mouth. I pretended that I was purposely eating slow in order to savor each morsel. The Chinese men closely followed my efforts, and none of them laughed. Their faces showed signs of relief each time I got one of those elusive peas into my expectant mouth. The food was cold long before I had finished.

My next flight put me in Bangkok in the middle of the night. I had very little money left so I needed a cheap place to stay. The Peace Corps had given me a ticket back to Nepal but not money for sightseeing along the way. A guidebook mentioned that the Thai National Scout Headquarters operated a hostel near the National Stadium. I took a bus (which the taxi drivers had said did not run so late at night) to the vicinity of the stadium and I began wandering the streets. The signs were all in Thai and no one I met spoke any English. Eventually a taxi driver stopped to help. He couldn't understand a word I said, but I had an idea. I took out my bandanna and wrapped it around my neck like a scout neckerchief. I repeated "scout" and I did a little pantomime. With a look of glee, the taxi driver deciphered my message and pointed to the building I wanted—just across the street.

The city's heat and noise made sleeping difficult. I lay atop the sheets and I periodically sprinkled myself with water. This reduced the heat, but nothing stopped the noise. The gargantuan streets had four or more lanes going in each direction and the traffic flowed twenty-four hours a day. Loud cars seemed to be the height of fashion. When I explored the city, I crossed the street only when I had a few Thais on each side of me for protection.

Bangkok is a city full of Buddhas. I visited the Golden Buddha (10 feet high, 5½ tons of solid gold), the Emerald Buddha (actually jasper), and the Reclining Buddha (with mother-of-pearl on the bottoms of His feet—the sign of a true Buddha). The whores were as conspicuous as the Buddhas. One lady wrapped her arms around me as I walked down the street and she held on until I protested that I had no money. During the Vietnam War, Bangkok had been the U.S. military's center for "rest and relaxation," and the end of the war had brought great unemployment and misfortune to Bangkok's ladies of the night.

During four days in Bangkok, I learned to speak enough Thai to live very cheaply. I spent a total of only ten dollars. But that afforded me little to eat and I eagerly awaited my flight to Kathmandu; I knew that they would give me a meal on the plane. Unfortunately I was flying on Royal Nepal Airlines. The *Yeti* was ill, forcing a delay of four and a half hours. Once in the air and well fed, I watched the ground as we passed over Burma, Bangladesh, and India *en route* to Kathmandu. My left pinky was still safely clad in its metal and tape—a little souvenir of my fifty-two-day round-the-world tour. I had done better than Phileas Fogg, but for the Peace Corps the money had been wasted. The doctor who had sent me to Washington gained a poor reputation and the Peace Corps administration eventually got rid of him.

The landing at Tribhuvan Airport felt like a homecoming, and I was impatient to use my Nepali again. I walked to the terminal alongside a man who was obviously Nepali.

"*Tapaai kahaa baata aaunubheyeko chha?* Where are you coming from?" I asked him.

He looked at me with a startled expression and replied in perfect English, "I don't understand what you're trying to say."

I wake from my reveries and shiver. Everest is hidden by the clouds and I must start back. Halfway down Kala Pattar, I meet Dan and a Dutchman slowly hiking up. Jeff had set out with them, but he gave up when his feet began to freeze. Now Dan and the Dutchman turn back too. The route I came up has become a clear trail and we reach Lobuche in two hours.

As I warm my hands around a mug of Sherpa tea, a tall young man with curly hair comes into the hut. He wears down pants and double mountaineering boots. The Dutchman has told me about him. He's a Swiss mountaineer named Thomas, who's looking for a climbing partner for an attempt on 20,300-foot Island Peak. He has climbed the Matterhorn, and now he wants to climb a peak over 6,000 meters (19,685 feet). We talk about climbing in the Himalayas, and we seem to get along fine. "I'm interested in Island Peak," I tell him, "but only if Lobuche East looks too bad. I'll let you know tomorrow." He nods his head as he eats a can of fruit cocktail. "Nepali food—it is not very good," he says with a grin.

April 1

Lobuche Village to Lobuche East

I start at first light. The cold air stings my lungs with each breath, while my hands and feet go numb. The new snow makes the going hard, but despite this, I feel tops. I'm moving over new ground, alone—free and unrestrained. And it's April! My birthday comes at the end of the month.

Today's goal is to reach my proposed high camp on Lobuche East and to get a better look at the final section of the peak. My route crosses three low ridges and then ascends a large boulder field. This section is a pain in the ass. I sink into the deep snow between two boulders, climb onto the next rock, and sink in again on the far side. Two hours of this, accented by my curses, puts me at the top of the boulder field. Here the route to the upper glaciers is blocked by a cirque of cliffs. Passing the cliffs will be the crux.

A steep, snow-filled groove leads to the left. I grunt up, taking in great draughts of air. I reach 17,000 feet and the bottom is a long way down. My legs feel lighter than they did on Kala Pattar and this is a good sign of acclimatization.

The weather is already turning bad. Clouds form on the peaks across the Khumbu Glacier and the temperature stays below freezing.

The groove ends. On the right is an icy rock wall, to the left is a doubtful snow ramp, and straight ahead is a rock overhang. After a short rest and a drink of water, I start to the right. I take off my gloves and overmittens the better to feel the rock. My fingers soon turn to ice. The moves are dicey, and I feel unsure. Retreating, I turn my attention to the snow ramp. It angles up at 45 degrees and its surface is featureless. This worries me. What's beneath the snow? Perhaps there's nothing and I'll fall through, or maybe it's iced rock and I'll slip off. First I must scale a short rock pitch before I can reach the ramp. One move requires me to step up using a ledge that accommodates only one foot and offers no handholds. I chicken out and down-climb the short distance I had gained. Damn.

Back to the rock. I reach my previous high point and advance a few moves higher. The holds shrink with each step, and my throat tightens with fear. The wall above is featureless and everything is covered with slick ice. I am losing my nerve, which I can't afford to do when climbing solo. When scared, an otherwise climbable pitch becomes impossible. I feel myself slipping, and I am afraid to move up or down. I shift my feet into worse positions and immediately bring them back. The icy drop waits. I lower one hand and hook two fingers into a minute crack. It's insecure, but I pretend that it'll hold. Leaning back, I shakily swing my feet to a lower stance. My confidence begins to return and I climb clumsily down. I reach the snow trembling. Double damn.

My last hope is the snow ramp, so I return to the rock pitch that leads to its base. I carefully clear the snow from the holds, trying to safeguard what little remains of my courage. I gingerly stand up on the tiny ledge, but I have nothing to hold on to. Cautiously I probe with one foot. It sinks deep and then settles. Not knowing if it's safe, I take a step with the other foot. It too sinks deep. Spreading my arms against the wall, I inch to the left, sliding one foot behind the other. I ignore the rocky fissure below, and I concentrate on moving up. I slowly plow a furrow up the ramp. Reaching its end, I am nearly at the top of the cliff.

I attack the last bit straight up, climbing almost vertical. The rock is bad, and the snow is worse, but it's only a short way. After a few yards, my left foot slips. I lunge desperately, pushing with my right foot and grabbing at a higher hold. I miss, and I know that I'm falling. As I slide, my left hand catches on something and I pull up, kicking a foot in and thrusting my body upwards. Another pull and I'm over, gasping for breath as I kneel in the snow. I'm up.

I look back at an easier way that I could have done this last part and I mark the spot for my return. The clouds move in, but I can already see the summit clearly. The top section is unstable and the last few pitches are blocked by a large crevasse. It would be impossible to climb solo. I'm both disappointed and relieved. Nevertheless, I continue climbing.

Above the cirque of cliffs are gentle slopes of mixed snow and rock. Where the rock ends I strap on my crampons, and I follow a sinuous route that avoids the scattered crevasses of the peak's central glacier. The surface is concave—it steadily steepens as I move up—so my climbing accommodates by progressing from normal stepping, to herringbone stepping with my toes pointed out, to upward side-stepping, and finally, to climbing on my crampons' toe points and using my ice axe as a hand pick. The last 2 meters are vertical. Confidently I tiptoe up and haul myself over the lip.

This is where my high camp would have been. At 18,500 feet, it's a good spot—large and nearly level. I'm granted no view; the clouds obscure everything. I take a little walk, as though I'm inspecting the spot prior to building a house. Now comes the long descent, and I'll have to go heedfully; most accidents happen on the way down.

I ease myself over the lip and move slowly. As the pitch gradually slackens, I climb more at ease. Down and down, past the glacier and onto the rocks where I remove my crampons. With extra caution, I down-climb the snow ramp, and when I'm out of the rock groove I breath a sigh of relief. The boulder field is as bad going down as it was coming up, but I'm too tired to curse. I stumble up and down the last low ridges and arrive in Lobuche in the late afternoon. I've come down faster than I had expected, and I'm tired.

I look for Jeff and Dan in the huts, but they have already started back to Namche. Thomas is out, so I settle down by the fire and the Didi gives me a cup of tea and some flat bread *chapati*.

As I eat, a trekker comes in and asks, "Is that your green tent?"

"Yeah... Why?"

"You'd better go take a look. A yak got at it."

I hurry out. My tent is flattened. Triple damn. I survey the damage. Two poles are broken, the vestibule is ripped nearly in half, the top grommet has been pulled out, and the outer fly has a large tear. I pick at the ruins, and I look over at the yak driver, shaking my head with resignation. He comes over and says, "The yak was out of control." He apologizes in his offhand fashion and offers to help, but there's nothing he can do. I jury-rig the tent for the night; tomorrow will be a day of repairs.

April 2

Lobuche

I t's settled. Thomas and I will team up to climb Island Peak. It stands 20,305 feet high, and is situated just south of Lhotse. We will begin the day after tomorrow, first descending to Pheriche and hiking east from there. Other than the fierce winds, the most difficult part is said to be a 200-foot wall of ice at 20,000 feet. "I think we find no tourists up there," says Thomas.

I spend all day repairing the tent. The sun is warm enough that I'm able to work outside. I sew and sew, using the heavy thread and nylon fabric that I carry for emergencies. I fix the poles by inverting the broken sections and splicing them together with tent pegs inside the tubes. The tent sags in the back, but it's the best I can do.

Dinner is a surprise—*kshekpa*, otherwise known as Sherpa stew. It's made from boiled potatoes, mysterious green strands of vegetable, and flour dumplings that sink like lead. I eat with abandon. "He who eats the fastest, gets the most," says a trekker who sits near the pot. The system is a good one for those of us with big spoons.

Alone in my frosty tent, I try to sleep beneath my burden of Sherpa stew. I roll from side to side as I half-dream and half-remember distant events.

"Philipsir, when you go home to Amaarika again you can b-b-bring me b-back a ring, and a watch, *Hunchha?*" said Shyam Krishna, the spectacled owner-operator of Aiselukharka's tiny store. I had always liked his stutter. It made him speak so slowly that he was very easy to understand.

"*Hunchha*—OK," I replied. "But I won't be going to Amaarika again. It's very far and to go there costs much money."

Shyam Krishna was not surprised that I had been to America during the summer monsoon. Even before I had left the village, I'd had to insist that I was *not* going home for the holiday. The other teachers all went home, so why not me? They asked how far America was and how much it cost to go, but the answers were beyond their comprehension. Kathmandu was far, and anything beyond that was plain *faaaar*. America, Japan, Russia, and Europe were just names that described a distant land of wealth and magic.

"What is the way to Amaarika?" asked Aiselukharka's champion card player.

"It's ah—well, you can go east to get there, or you can go west to get there. It's on the other side of the world." I formed a globe with my hands. "One has to go *around* the world to get to Amaarika. See?"

My explanation only gave him the impression that America was a land both mystical and unreachable. My friends and students had some novel views of America, which I never managed to fully dispel.

A boy told me a secret in private. "Philipsir, I have heard the reason that everyone can be so rich in Amaarika."

"Really? What is that?"

"Everyone prints their own money, so you can have all you want."

"No, that's not true. Many poor people live in Amaarika." But the boy was no longer listening. He knew America was rich, and that Nepal was poor; I was just being modest about my home country.

I collected magazine articles that had pictures of America's poor. I showed the clippings to the students and the teachers, and I told them stories of babies dying from rat bites, but my words had little impact. It was like telling a fan of Tarzan that no tigers exist in Africa. People believed exactly what they wanted to, and then arranged the facts accordingly.

I was given proof that America was rich and Nepal was poor. A neighbor asked me, "Philipsir, how many rupees in your money?"

"One dollar is about twelve rupees."

"Twelve of our money equals one of yours? You're twelve times as rich!"

"No, that doesn't mean anything," I protested. "Japan is very rich, isn't it? But their money is just the opposite. It takes almost twenty yen to make just one rupee."

This was a trifling detail. The man replied, "Nepal is the smallest, poorest country in the world, and Amaarika is the biggest, richest..."

I found it strange that the Nepalis, who were generally so noncommittal, would talk in absolutes about the biggest and the poorest. I was often asked, "Is it rainy here, or is it rainy there?" "Where is it warm? Here or there?" "Which is good? Is Nepal good, or is Amaarika good?" How could I answer? They left me with no compromise, no middle course.

I roll over in the tent and let out a belch that smells of fermenting Sherpa stew. My stomach grumbles, and I return to my troubled dreams.

Classes didn't resume until a week after the official end of the monsoon break. The NDS ladies had finished their year of service and they had returned to the university in Kathmandu. That worsened our teacher shortage, so I gained a class—tenth mathematics. The ninth grade had always been disruptive and rude, so I was surprised to find that the tenth grade was attentive and energetic. To help them get used to my strange accent and limited vocabulary, I spent the first couple of days talking about America. They had a lot of questions, but no one asked about my now-healed finger.

After hearing that my oldest brother had died before he was half-grown, Raadhaa, the school's top student, was shocked. "In Amaarika do people die?" he said.

"What are you saying?" I countered. "Of course people die in Amaarika."

"No, I mean—Amaarika is advanced and has doctors, so *children* don't die." I shook my head sadly.

Another student asked, "How many castes are in Amaarika?"

"No, Amaarika has no castes," I said. "Everyone is the same.

"Are both black and white people not living there?"

"Yes, but they are not different castes."

"Not different castes?" The class took a moment to digest this. "Do a black person and a white person marry?"

"Yes, they can, but usually they don't," I answered.

"But they are one caste? ...and white is rich and black is poor..."

"Philipsir," called a boy in the back. "Do the black people live in the south and the white people live in the north?"

"No, not really like that..."

"Yes," someone interrupted. "It's like here. In the north are the white people and in the south are the black people. The Indians are very dark. Also in Europe are white people and in the south, in Aafrika, are black people."

"*Hunchha hunchha*," chimed in another student. "And if we live in Europe we become light."

"Yes, it is true," said the first student. "And if they come here, they become dark. You can already see that Philipsir is becoming dark."

"No," I objected. "It's just the sun that makes me dark."

"Ah! So it's the sun that makes the Indians black. Now I understand. That is very clear."

"Philipsir, Philipsir," beckoned a faint voice. "If you and a Nepali—ah—would it work?"

"What? Say it again?"

"If you marry a Nepali girl could you..."

"Could we have children? Yes, it would work."

As the class considered the possible ramifications of my answer, they voiced a collective "*Ahhhh.*"

When the students felt more at ease with me, they began coming to my room for help with their school work, to get medicine, and mostly just to talk. I usually had something new to show them—my gelatine duplicator for copying exams, a propeller that turned when held over the heat of a lamp, or a wind-up snail that Kay had sent me. And I always had *Newsweek* magazines for them to paw through.

The magazines prompted the children to ask difficult questions about digital watches, oil rigs, and the Egyptian pyramids. One day Netra Prasaad, of the eighth class, spotted a picture of two American children—a boy and a girl—and he asked why they were featured in the pages of *Newsweek* alongside the generals and presidents. When I translated the gist of the article, he looked at me in open-mouthed disbelief. The two children had murdered their father. Their mother did not live with them, and since the father had refused to let them do everything they wanted, the children had hired a local teenager to shoot him. The fee was $60. For a week and a half, the brother and sister enjoyed total freedom while their father's body decomposed in the utility room.

Netra Prasaad spread the story and a stream of students came to see the picture of "the ones who killed their own father." They found it impossible to reconcile in their minds that such a thing could happen. They could accept the magic of jets and television, but they could not acknowledge the loss of humanity that would allow children to commit patricide. It was unthinkable.

The boy's face was pained. He had heard a rumor, an evil persistent rumor. He didn't want to believe it was true—it was a very horrible thing—but he kept hearing talk and now he had to find out. He hoped that his fears were groundless, so he came to me, the one person who would know for sure.

"Philipsir," he said timidly, "in Amaarika do they really eat the flesh of the cow?" His voice carried the same blend of disgust and disbelief as if he was asking about cannibalism.

"Yes," I answered him, and he was appalled. I was glad that the whole village knew that I ate no meat at all. Peace Corps Volunteers were often asked about the consumption of cow meat and only much later would I hear the perfect solution. A friend of mine would answer, "Yes, in America they eat the flesh of the cow, but American cows and Nepali cows are of different castes."

We were thumbing through *Newsweek* when a seventh-class student suddenly asked, "Sir, do you have a helicopter?"

"A helicopter? No, I don't have a helicopter."

"But over there, many people have a helicopter. Does your father have a helicopter?"

"No, my father doesn't have a helicopter. Very few people have a helicopter."

"Oh," he answered, both surprised and disappointed. A few pages further, we came to a picture of a Ford, and the student's friend asked, "Sir, can you make an auto go?"

"You mean drive? Yes, I can drive."

"You're a *Driver?*" they said with astonishment. When I nodded, they gasped as though I had just revealed myself as the latest incarnation of the Lord Krishna. "Driver" was as honored a title as "Doctor."

Their amazement caught me off guard. Moments before they had assumed that I flew about in a helicopter, and now they were awed by the fact that I could drive a car. I needed some time to resolve this. It seemed that people could only relate to things that they had personally experienced. Some of the students had traveled to the road and they had seen buses and trucks. Cars were real to them, while rockets, planes, and helicopters existed only in their minds. So to learn that I was one of the elite *Drivers* was more tangible—and thus more awesome—than to believe that I could fly a helicopter.

After another few pages, the boys asked if I would one day fly a rocket to the moon. I answered, "No," and they looked surprised.

I roll over and back again. The Sherpa stew has moved to a lower stage of my digestive system, and my stomach is at peace. The tent fabric shines green in the morning's first light.

April 3
Lobuche 16,175 feet to Everest Base Camp 17,700 feet

I follow the same route as to Kala Pattar—up the moraines of the Khumbu Glacier to the frozen lake at Gorak Shep. From here, I cross the slick surface of the glacier, following a faint trail of yak droppings. The bizarre shapes of the ice create a crystal maze. With clouds blocking the peaks, I concentrate on the smaller beauty around me.

The blocks of ice are carved by the wind and the sun into abstract shapes, and many of them stand alone. I feel much the same—isolated and so desperately alone. I have been unable to explain this to Dan, Jeff, or Thomas. They seem connected to people and places, but I am detached from my past. America is a distant memory, and Aiselukharka, now three months behind me, is just a collection of photographs. I am cut off. When I consider the possibility of dying in the mountains, I feel nothing at all. I'm already half dead. It's not an urge that makes me climb, but the lack of one that permits me to. Freezing or falling would be a pleasant release from perpetual isolation.

The telltale yak droppings lead me to some dead ends, but I'm in no hurry. I zigzag through the pinnacles of ice and then climb the jagged rocks of the moraine to a vantage point overlooking Everest Base Camp.

The camp dogs bark at me. They scrounge for food among the piles of trash—the refuse of twenty-nine years of Everest expeditions. This season the Spanish and the Basques are making attempts in two mutually hostile expeditions. Their red, blue, and orange tents are scattered among the rocks and I keep my distance. I know they dislike strangers poking around. An outsider might actually be a thief.

I settle myself on a comfortable rock and look around me. The mountains are peaceful—sky and stone and snow, a world in harmony, enclosing a small pocket of chaos. The climbers arrange and re-arrange their tents, ropes, and equipment, causing a stir that has no effect on the mountains around them. A pocket of confusion—just like my thoughts during my first year in Aiselukharka.

I woke to the sounds of the morning. The chickens and roosters cackled while my aged next-door neighbor cleared his throat. He hacked and coughed, then spat phlegm into the courtyard. Someone chopped wood, and up on my roof I heard footsteps and voices. Surendra and Nilam were up there spreading out *kodo* rye on a mat to dry in the sun. Next came the sound of dried corn being thrown on the flagstones for the chickens. Aamaa ground *daal* and Radio Nepal broadcast a Hindu prayer. Since it was Saturday, I had slept till very late. It was nearly seven o'clock.

I looked up at the surrounding cloud of my white mosquito net. Krishna Bhakta said that Aiselukharka was mosquito-free a month after the monsoon, but I for one was still being bitten. I attracted mosquitoes like a magnet.

I got up and opened the wooden shutters. On one window sill sat the guavas that Ek Nath of tenth class had brought me. Everyone else ate them green—if you could mark it with a fingernail, it was ripe enough to eat—but I preferred to wait until they softened a bit. I had missed the summer season of vegetables, so every piece of fruit was precious to me. Winter would soon arrive, and with it would come a resumption of monotonous meals. Through the window, I watched my neighbor reclining on the little roof covering his doorway. He relaxed in the sun and drew smoke through his brass hookah, *blub-blub-blub-blub.*

In Aiselukharka life was peaceful, and no one in the village was aware of the turmoil that swirled in my brain. My thoughts revolved about my private joys and unrevealed depressions, while my emotions whirlpooled around every memory of Kay.

Over two months had passed since I had last seen Kay and only a single letter had arrived from her. I still wrote as diligently as ever and one of my recent letters had contained this passage:

Last night I saw you very distinctly a few times. You were wearing jeans and a T-shirt. Lying on your stomach with your arms folded and crossed to make a pillow, your hair flowed freely over your back, and you were looking at me with clear eyes full of love and caring. I like to think of you that way looking at me with love in your eyes. I like to think that you still feel that, that you still love me, but I really don't know what you're feeling towards me. Perhaps you're not too sure yourself. I remember once asking you what it felt like to fall out of love with someone. You said that you had never been so in love before and so you didn't really know. I know that you're not in love with me now, so I wonder how it happened. I imagine that I'm just slowly and continually fading out of your thoughts and feelings. That seems fairly painless. At least I hope it is.

Letters to Kay were the principal release for my emotions. I wrote about my longings for her and I described the myriad events in Aiselukharka: a festival of men dancing in costume and wearing wooden phallics at their waists, the arrival of a new teacher, the backyard sacrifice of two chickens to the Water Buffalo Deity, my experiments in science class, and my latest illness. Besides recording these happenings in letters to Kay, I kept a small date book. It had space to write just a dozen words for each day, and my jottings for the previous week had read like this:

Saturday: sit around; read; write to Kay; bathe & fetch water; feel miserable

Sunday: hydra hunt in 8th science; start taking flagyl; upset by roll in 6th science—mispronounce numbers; clean water filter

Monday: 9th math exam; grade exams; boil water

Tuesday: rain; good classes; mail comes but no letters; read about new Pope; play recorder; write

Wednesday: 8th class science exam; show spinner on lamp top; picture of house; read D. H. Lawrence

Thursday: new volleyball comes; look at mold; eat P.B. and sugar, eggs & guava; write Ambika & Roger

Friday: Indra Jatra, but no bidaa; look at yeast; picnic on hill; play recorder & sing; talk with K. B. about Durga's temper

Saturday: clean & sort stuff; write Kay; bathe; (Tauni has now been gone 1 week); correct homework; fast walk to Nawalpur; full moon

I had made no entries for the following week. The little boxes were completely blank. Something had filled my brain and had kept me from writing.

Daal-bhaat came. Today's vegetable was pumpkin greens, and I had no choice about eating it all. My friend Tauni had disappeared, and no one knew what had happened to her.

When I finished eating, I put a piece of cloth and some money into my pocket, slipped my feet into my rubber sandals, and went outside, locking the door behind me. Krishna Bhakta insisted that I lock the door. He felt responsible for me and he was afraid of thieves.

A few dozen strides took me across the courtyard, between the houses, and around the corner to Shyam Krishna's *pasal.* The three wooden doors of the shop were open. Shyam Krishna followed no routine in his business

Shyam Krishna's wife at the village 'pasal'

hours. He just opened when he felt like it or when someone came in need of something. *Namastes* were passed around and I squatted on the porch with the other men. The shop was as important for socializing as it was for business, and Shyam Krishna would get to me eventually.

I peered into the half-light of the pasal. Each time I came here I found something new hidden among the dusty goods on the uneven shelves. Shyam Krishna squatted in a small rectangle of floor space and he kept everything within arm's reach. The five-gallon Nebiko biscuit tins in front of him contained mustard oil, kerosene, corn, potatoes, and occasionally peanuts or flour. The shelves at his back held everything needed in a small village: paper, ink, and candies for the schoolchildren; cigarettes, matches, and betel nuts for the men; soap, tikaa powder, and scarlet hair yarn for the women. Half a shelf was piled with Nebiko biscuits, and an old box held a supply of rope incense and leaking flashlight batteries. Stashed in the dark corners were mysterious jars and tins of raw spices and medicinal powders. And there was the newest thing I had seen—metal canisters of ground chewing tobacco.

"*M'saab, tapaailaai ke ch-ch-chaahiyo?* Master Sahib, what are you n-n-needing?" Shyam Krishna used "sahib" to show respect and not to imply any master-slave relationship.

"Please give me four *maanaa* of *chiuraa*," I said, with a gesture to the proper container.

Shyam Krishna measured two quarts of pounded rice onto my piece of cloth and tied it into a bag. This would be my snacking food for two weeks.

"And two packages of matches," I added. "*Kati rupiyaa bhayo, Daaju?* How much is that, Older Brother?"

"*Das p-pachaas*—Ten tw-twenty-five." It was less than a dollar.

I paid Shyam Krishna and we traded pleasantries before I moved to the edge of the porch to watch the men playing cards. They argued whether to shift their mat into the shade or to keep it in the sun. I watched them only with my eyes; my mind was far away.

A letter had finally come from Kay. She had put off writing because she had difficult things to say. She had written about the men—actually it was four men—that she had been with during the past year. Two of these relationships had been before I had seen her during the summer and two of them had been after. I felt like she had lied to me through her silence. When I had been with her I had delicately asked her about other men, and she had said nothing. My mind was in a jumble. I watched the card players, but I spoke to Kay—

"Why is it so hard for you to write these things to me? I know you're interested in other men. Remember Don? How can I be jealous when I exist only in letters to you? You say that you don't want to sleep with any of them again. What is it that you *do* want? Love? But you find only friends and sex partners? You're bemoaning your lack of cake to one who has no bread. You seem to feel guilty... Maybe it would be easier for you if I didn't write so much, or if I wasn't so chaste. Maybe I could arrange something... Fantasies and masturbation aren't enough. I need love too. I love you, honey. I know we'll be together again. I can wait. *Srimati jastai*—just like my wife, is what you are to me. I love you. How much longer can we survive with just an airmail romance? I know the end will come when you find a new lover, but I can't be the one to say the final goodbye. It will hurt, but in time it'll be easier for us. I can't make the move; I'm too alone, and I have no strength. I love you. The uncertainty is slowly killing me. I love you and I always will. That will never change."

The men slapped their cards onto the mat as they played them out. The cards were faded and worn from the rough use. They spoke in Newari and this added to my alienation. Prem Prasaad began to tell a funny story, and I could see from the other men's smiles that it was a story that they had heard many times before. At the end they all laughed together and rocked on their heels. Everyone liked the old jokes best.

A half-dozen children played down by the shrine to Ganesh, the elephant-headed son of Shiva. They rolled wire hoops over the stones and they shrieked and laughed as they chased each other around the temple They were at a good age—old enough to run free of their mothers, but too young to do much of the work.

I stood up with my legs stiff from so long in a squat. I took my chiuraa and matches home, and I searched out Nilam to get my wash basin returned. Between one and two o'clock was the warmest time of the day, so this was when I preferred to bathe myself and to wash my clothes. I sorted my laundry.

My pants were so dirty that they had to be washed, while my jacket could wait another few weeks. I washed clothes only once a month, though I bathed almost every Saturday—depending on the weather.

With one hand balancing the basin of clothes on my head, I walked carefully down the steep path to the *dhaaraa*. This was a stone and cement reservoir shaped like a small house. It collected the flow from a spring and delivered the water through a waist-high pipe. The tank had been built by the village guthi and Krishna Bhakta was very proud of it. *Dhaaraa* literally meant current, but during the driest months of early summer the flow was a mere trickle. The shortage of water was one of Aiselukharka's greatest problems.

But now, during the post-monsoon months, water was abundant and we all took turns at the pipe. During my waiting times, I watched the women bathing and washing. The hookah man's wife and her full-grown daughter washed clothes in two basins—one of brass and one of baked clay. They kneaded their laundry in a one-two rhythm and pounded it on the stones with a wooden paddle. Their wash water turned dark gray. Another woman hoisted her baby son by one arm and dangled him screaming and kicking beneath the flow of chill water. As soon as she was done, an older lady moved over to rinse the soap from her hair and eyes. She was bare from the waist up and her breasts swung freely as she bent her head under the tap. Once a woman had borne her first child she could reveal her breasts both to bathe and to nurse her children. The younger women, however, carefully wrapped a cloth *lungi* around themselves when they washed. The men, too, bathed with their clothes on. Only the small children, who ran around half-naked anyway, could bathe in the nude.

One woman waited long past her turn to fill her jug with water, but she was in no hurry. She was listening to the talk. While the men gossiped at Shyam Krishna's store, the women socialized at the dhaaraa. The talk was mostly in Newari, so I could only pick up bits and pieces: a child was sick, a daughter was learning to speak, someone had a new pot, and the people in Jyaamire village were going hungry. This was a story I had already heard. Jyaamire was an hour's walk up the ridge, and last spring a terrible hail storm had destroyed the wheat crop and had killed three men who had been caught outside. The shortage of food in Jyaamire was just now being felt.

After I finished bathing, I waited to rinse my clothes. One of the young women bathed with her eyes closed and rubbed soap over her legs. The wet lungi clung against her stomach and the brown of her thighs showed through the dripping cloth. Her teeth glistened white and the cool water caused her nipples to stand erect. I took a deep breath and tried to look away. Why did she have to do this to me? I felt something inside of me about to burst, and I held it tight. I spoke to Kay again—

"It's not fair! It's not fair for you to be there when I'm here and we ought to be together. What a tragedy for lovers to be separated. You're in America searching for love and I'm in Nepal living alone. But I don't feel sorry for myself; I could always leave if I wanted to... What can we do? I have a solution! A crazy, beautiful solution. You can come to Nepal! I'm serious. The people here would call you 'Didi' and you could teach beginning English at the school. You wouldn't be bored. Perhaps you could come when you finish at the university in June. That would be only eight months from now. What a beautiful thought! Altogether I have about $500, which you can have. That should be almost enough for you to fly here. You can come when you like, if you like. I would love it, I think. I can picture you here now..."

I finished at the dhaaraa and took my clothes home. They would quickly dry on the branches of the plum tree. Inside, I worked on lesson plans for my Sunday classes. I sat at the table which had been constructed four months after I had first requested it. The bench, which was too wide to fit under the table, had been built during the monsoon. The bench and table, along with the new grayish-green whitewash on my walls, gave my room a very modern appearance. I munched chiuraa while I hurriedly read the tenth-class math book. I wanted to finish so that I would have time enough to write to Kay about my invitation to come to Nepal.

After daal-bhaat, I wrote the letter by lamp light. Even before I had finished, I realized that I was dreaming. Kay wouldn't come to Nepal; she wouldn't even comment on my offer. I remembered that when I had been battling with the decision of staying for the full two years, I had written Kay a very short letter, asking a single question—would she like me to come back early? She had never answered the question, nor had she ever mentioned it.

I blew out the lamp and crawled under the mosquito net. Before I slept, I rolled onto my hand. Around me, the people of Aiselukharka dreamed peacefully, but my own dreams were filled with turbulence.

Here too, the mountains are at peace while the climbers at base camp are in a state of turbulence. Have they had an accident? More likely, it's a fight between the Basques and the Spaniards.

The clouds thicken as I scramble down the moraines and begin across the glacier. After a dozen wrong turns I discover the subtle trail of yak droppings. Some of the paddies are well dried and in a couple of days the Sherpas will collect them for fuel. Fires of yak dung cook much of the food in Lobuche.

I reach Gorak Shep as the snow begins to fall. Hardly able to see, I pick my way slowly down. The wind stiffens and the air turns white with snow. The blizzard closes around me and I'm alone. Suddenly I hear a faint sound. *Klink-klang*. It grows louder, and I'm overtaken by a train of four yaks and two drivers. The yaks' black coats are plastered with heavy snow and the drivers lean forward against the freezing wind. They must be returning from carrying a load of firewood to Everest Base Camp.

I fall in behind them. *Klink-klang* go the yak bells and for once I am happy to be following. I sing a song as we come into Lobuche:

The yaks go marching two by two
Hoorah! Hoorah!
The yaks go marching two by two
Hoorah! Hoorah!
The yaks go marching two by two
The little one stops to tie his shoe
And they all go marching down,
into the ground,
to get out of the rain...

My thoughts are as chaotic as ever.

April 4 & 5

Lobuche to Pheriche to Chukung

Thomas and I descend to Pheriche in only two hours. It's so easy going down! We eat fried potatoes and eggs.

In Pheriche we prepare ourselves to climb Island Peak. Thomas has top quality clothes and boots, but he lacks crampons and an ice axe. He goes to rent these from one of the three shack-hotels while I repair my boots. The leather has split along the back seam and I painstakingly sew it with heavy thread. Thomas returns with his equipment. It's old and shabby, but usable. Now we also have a rope, which I don't carry when climbing solo.

He has rented a full climbing harness that fits around his legs and across his chest. "You have no harness?" Thomas asks me.

"No, but I have some webbing that I'll wrap around my waist."

"Ah. That's dangerous." Thomas reminds me that a climber hanging by a waist sling can stay conscious for only ten to fifteen minutes before passing out.

"But neither of us can afford to fall," I say. "We have no one to help with a rescue."

In the evening we canvass the huts, searching for climbing food. Canned meats and porridge will be Thomas's staples, while I'll rely on the food that I have carried from Namche.

Leaving Pheriche late the next morning, we hike up a passable trail to Chukung at 15,518 feet. I travel considerably faster than Thomas. He compliments me, saying, "You hike like a bear." As he lags behind, I worry that he might need more time to acclimatize.

In Chukung, the Didi gives us sleeping spaces on the floor of her hut. She cooks Sherpa stew, and fries unleavened chapatis for Thomas and me to carry with us tomorrow.

We discuss our strategy. Thomas favors a two-day sprint to the summit and back, but I would prefer a slower pace—using two days to establish a high camp and then resting a day before going to the summit. We will see what happens, everything depending on the weather. My excitement and the stones poking me in the back make sleeping difficult.

April 6
Chukung 15,518 feet

We pack our sleeping bags in the early-morning darkness, and while the others in the hut are still sleeping, Thomas and I start across the broken moraines. The Didi has told us about a small yak path, but we can't find it. The jumbles of rock confuse us and we stumble over the tottering boulders. We take turns guessing at the best route and Thomas's choices are the best. He has a good mountain sense.

One thing bothers me—our loads. I'm carrying more food than Thomas, which I consider to be our emergency supply; of the shared equipment, Thomas carries only the rope, while I have the tent, stove, and 3 pints of fuel. Thomas says that I already hike faster than he does, so if anything I should carry even more. He has a point, but I'm still irritated.

We stop to eat at a frozen stream. Thomas chops a hole in the ice to get water and I warm the chapatis over the stove. The wind threatens to blow out the flame, so I shield it with a pile of rocks. Today is both Easter Sunday and Thomas's birthday. "Happy Birthday! Happy Easter!" I say as I hand him his present—a bar of Indian chocolate wrapped in notebook paper.

"Thank you," he grins and he immediately gobbles it down. *"Ah.* That's good." Thomas sits himself on an icy rock. "At home in the army, I ate so much chocolate as I wanted."

"Of course! Swiss chocolate is very famous."

"Yes, and on one side of my home village is a chocolate factory. That is good. But on the other side is a soap factory. When the wind comes from one way it's chocolate and from the other it's soap. We know what the weather will be by smelling the air."

We continue over the rocks. As we lug our packs over a moraine separating the Lhotse and Imja glaciers, Island Peak comes into view for the first time. It's a double peak and the higher, further summit is barely visible. A ridge connects the two summits and a glacier blankets the center of the mountain. Leading to the glacier are easy slopes of dead yak grass. As we approach, the peak disappears behind its lower ridges. As with most mountains, we'll see little of Island Peak as we climb it; we must keep on route by remembering its features and by consulting the map.

At midday we arrive at the yak pastures of Pareshaya Gyab. This is where climbing groups will generally put their base camp. Thomas and I feel fine and the weather is good, so we continue upwards. The slopes are much steeper than we had thought and Thomas drops far behind. I hike alone, setting my own pace and choosing the route.

The yak grass gives way to rocks and the air thins. Here and there are signs of a trail, but I find no place flat enough to set our camp. Every few dozen paces we stop to catch our breath. Thomas is well below, but I keep him in sight as I plod upward. Past the 18,000 foot mark, I begin to take sitting rests with my pack on—to take it off and put it on again is too much work. Now with each step I take one breath, gasping the air through my open mouth. My pack weighs a thousand pounds. Thomas sits on the ground and rests. We can't go much further today.

The way steepens even more and the slope above narrows to a rocky gully. Praying for a level spot at the gully's mouth, I press on. Thomas waits. The climb of a few hundred feet seems to take all day. At the top is evidence of Sherpas at work—three tent platforms cleared from the rocks. I drop my pack on the ground and I wave my arms to Thomas.

I estimate the altitude at 18,400 feet. When Thomas arrives, we slowly erect the tent. Each exertion is a chore that leaves us panting.

"How do you feel?" I ask.

"All right... Tired."

"So I think we should rest here tomorrow, and then the day after..."

"No," he says. "Tomorrow we go to the top. Maybe we can then come back to Chukung."

"But we have plenty of food and we'll both be stronger if we rest a day."

"The weather is important," he protests. "It may change. It's so good now..."

"Yeah, you're right. Tomorrow to the summit!"

We shake on it. We can't expect the weather to stay good for two more days, so we'll climb tomorrow.

Within the tent's vestibule, we cook a fabulous meal of tinned meat and Tibetan noodles. I work long past dark, melting vast quantities of snow. Dehydration is a serious problem at high altitude, so I insist that we drink as much water as we can hold. We use a plastic bottle to piss into and thus avoid cold trips outside of the tent.

To keep the canteens and my boots from freezing, I bed down with them at the bottom of my sleeping bag. This is my twenty-third night of the trip; three months have passed since I said goodbye to Aiselukharka, and over two and a half years since I left America. I sleep without dreams.

Island Peak High Camp 18,400 feet

"**M**y feet are cold," complains Thomas. "I can't feel my toes."

We crouch in the rock gully just above camp. At 6.15 a.m. the cold is intense. I'm wearing nearly all my clothes: wool knee socks, rag socks, and boots; underwear, long underwear, long pants, nylon overpants, and gaiters; long-underwear tops, T-shirt, long-sleeved shirt, sweater, windbreaker, and down jacket with hood; scarf, knit cap, wool gloves, and nylon overmittens. I wear neither my extra pants nor my cotton jacket; it's not *that* cold.

We move slowly up the gully to a vertical jumble of rocks. The stones are covered in verglas and I can't get my hands and feet in the right places. My mind works in low gear and I take a long time to get over the obstacle. Thomas does a little better, but then he's taller.

We exit the gully to the right and climb toward the ridge. We stop repeatedly to get air and to examine the way up. We loathe taking even a single step in the wrong direction. Sunlight sweeps onto the ridge and warms us. We put on our dark glasses, and where the rock turns to snow, we get out our ice axes and crampons. I slip on my nylon overboots, hoping that they will help keep my feet warm.

We tie ourselves into the rope. Thomas wears his harness, while I use a simple sling wrapped around my waist. The rope unites us in a bond of security, but Thomas discourteously calls it a "string." After a quick snack and a slurp of water, we move up. We take turns in the lead, plowing the way through the snow. We climb without conversation; we're each locked into our private worlds of raising one foot after the next.

As the sun warms me, I remove first my down jacket and then my sweater. To the left we come onto the glacier, crevassed and nasty. We go cautiously now, on the lookout for hidden crevasses. We circle further to the left, around most of the difficulties. The calf-deep snow drags us down. Every ten steps, we stop and gasp for breath. My head is fine and I still feel strong, though I have trouble getting enough air.

Using a snow bridge, we cross a crevasse and come to a large flat area at the top of the glacier. Here we're stopped. The ice wall rises vertically up and blocks the way as far as we can see. It looks a mile high, but we know that it can't be much more than 200 feet. We see no feasible routes. It's impossible.

"What about those Italian climbers you talked to?" I ask Thomas. "What way did they go?"

"They didn't get up the ice wall. 'Too much wind,' they said."

"But weren't they having a celebration? I thought they got to the summit."

"They climbed to over six thousand meters."

"Ah yes." Climbers have certain elevations that become vainly important. For a European the height is 6,000 meters, and for an American it's 20,000 feet. We scan the cliffs looking for a possible route.

"I think the way to go is there," I say pointing to the left. "Across that lower ice, then up under the rock band, and off at an angle climbing the ice to the top of the ridge."

Thomas's face grimaces in disbelief and lack of confidence. "It looks very hard. I think it's not possible. We do better to go around to the right and see what's there. It must be better."

I shake my head. I see no reason why it would be easier that way. I put down my pack and take out my binoculars, handing them first to Thomas so that he can study the route I've suggested.

He looks for a moment and says, "I see a string! It comes down to near the rock."

I look too. It's a white rope, probably left by Sherpa climbing guides for the next time that they have European clients wanting to reach 6,000 meters.

We are now certain of the route, and without discussion I take the lead. We move slowly across the snow and angle onto the ice wall. To reach the base of the rock band requires a risky traverse. I should ask Thomas for a safety belay, but I don't. I step nervously across and reach the slope at the lower edge of the rock band. The ice is broken and is covered with fresh snow. I can't see where to put my feet. I move slowly up and Thomas follows at the lower end of the rope.

Just past the rock, I come to the fixed line. Though it withstands my yanking, I doubt its security. I tie into the rope with my prusik sling as a self-belay, and I hope that it'll hold if either of us falls.

I climb vertically up, using the rope only for moral support. The pitch is extreme. The dark ice is unyielding and the holds are obscured by powdered snow. It's like climbing an invisible ladder that has half of its rungs missing. I'm scared and I imagine that Thomas is too.

I climb on all fours, using the ice axe as a claw to pull myself up, and moving only one hand or foot at a time. Every two or three steps I am forced to halt. I gasp for breath and my lungs work in spasms. All the air seems to be gone. We move tenaciously up, laboring with each upward step. Periodically, I must dig out the fixed line where it's frozen into the ice. I stop to rest, bending forward and leaning my head against the ice. I can see Thomas without turning around. Looking straight down between my legs, I watch him toiling upward. After three more steps, I must rest again. I chop a handhold and call a warning to Thomas as the fragments of ice fall away. To my amazement, my goggles fog up—it's 20,000 feet and I'm sweating. Now I stop after each move to take four or five breaths. Thomas calls for a halt and I slump against the ice to get my breathing under control. We climb, concentrating on each move, pulling up, stopping for a fit of panting, clearing snow from a hold, taking another step, sucking more air, chopping a footstep with the axe, and moving up again.

Kathmandu
street scene

Phil's arrival

Indra Jatra festival in Kathmandu

1. Bathing at the dhaaraa

2. Morning assembly

3. Village scene

4. Aamaa preparing daal bhaat

5. Village kids at Nilam's gupha ceremony

5

1. Philipsir teaching soil layers
2. Students washing science equipment; Jagat Man in center
3. Girls browsing through Newsweek; Nilam far right
4. Students cooking daal bhaat; Ram Prasad Nepal far left
5. Sixth class
6. Teaching about saturated solutions

6

▲ Phil on summit of Pharchamo
▼ Route finding in Solu Khumbu

▶ Solo on summit of
Kangchung West

▼ Pharchamo's summit
ridge

2011
Aiselukharka

Aiselukharka's
Ganesh temple,
dhaaraa, and
power lines;
Krishna Bhakta
in white shirt, vest,
and glasses

In central
Kathmandu people
engulf cars

Krishna Bhakta and Philipsir

Suddenly the snow is smooth and I realize that the top of the ridge is only a few feet away. I rest again halfway. Standing on the crest, I look to the right, toward the summit ridge of Island Peak.

I drive in the axe and wrap the rope around the shaft to belay Thomas up the last part of the wall. He swears in German and asks for slack. He descends a few yards, then continues up haltingly. "I've lost a crampon," he says as he reaches my stance. "It's about twenty meters down." I offer him the prusik sling so that he can go and retrieve it, but he shrugs his shoulders and starts off toward the summit with just one crampon.

The ridge angles gradually up and we climb easily but slowly. The soft snow packs up beneath our feet. Now the ridge steepens and Thomas stops so that we can take the last few steps together. But it's not the summit, just a level area topped by a layered snow lump. A crevasse guards the approach and we give each other a belay to jump it protected. Stepping to the top we spot a second pinnacle of snow that's 6 or 7 feet higher—the true summit. We trudge around the level area searching for a way up this little spire. To climb it would not be difficult; the trouble is that we can't reach it due to the crevasses.

For an hour we fruitlessly try to climb the last six feet. Finally we sit down in the snow. We tell ourselves, "This is the summit," and we take pictures. The air is completely still. At 20,300 feet, this is the highest either of us has climbed, but we don't jubilate. Perhaps we're too tired, or perhaps we're disheartened by the last few unclimbable feet. We sip water and share a chocolate bar, and I feel that something is missing. We start down.

Without glancing back, we descend the ridge. The wind picks up as we down-climb the ice wall. Thomas retrieves his lost crampon and I shiver. When we reach the safety of the glacier, I put my parka back on and we take a good rest. Thomas eats cold sardines and fossilized bread from Namche. I'm appalled. My stomach churns and only accepts a few pieces of dried fruit.

We continue downward, shuffling one foot in front of the other, and thinking solely of getting back to the tent. We climb down benumbed, moving unconscious of our steps. The way down seems longer than the way up. Past the snow, we remove our crampons, and scramble down the rocks. The thicker air revives us and Thomas points to our green tent far below.

We reach camp with an hour of daylight remaining. We crouch among the rocks as we look across the valley. We have climbed our mountain; now it's time to rest.

April 8
Island Peak High Camp 18,400 feet

We are packed and ready to go. I feel like we've left something behind, but I look around and find nothing.

Thump-thump-thump. Our thundering steps jar us as we descend. We literally fly down—past the rocks, through the yak grass, and onto the flats at Pareshaya Gyab.

A small Japanese expedition has arrived to scale Island Peak. Two of the climbers approach us with eager faces. They speak English with rich accents.

"You to *Irrand* Peak? Yes? Yes?"

"Yes, we were to Island Peak."

"*Ah. Ah.* You have success?"

"Yes, we had success."

"Verry good. *Verry* good." The Japanese smile broadly and are truly happy for us.

A success? Of course it was a success. We climbed the mountain. Though I feel we missed the summit. Shouldn't we be celebrating our triumph? We scaled a peak nearly as high as Alaska's Mount McKinley. Sure it was a success, certainly more of a success than my first climb in the Himalayas.

It was Dasai, the same autumn festival that during training I had spent with Jim riding crowded buses to Lumbini. This year I was headed to the Annapurna Sanctuary, a high mountain basin surrounded by 20,000-foot peaks which was five days' walk north of Pokhara. The Dasai holiday lasted only eight days, but I knew from experience that classes would not resume until two full weeks had passed. I bade farewell to Krishna Bhakta, and I assured him that I would be back in a fortnight.

In Kathmandu, I met up with Rob from my group; from the capital we would journey to Pokhara to join Billy, the third member of our party. Rob was penniless. He had an unused pay check, but to cash it would have wasted a day. So we took all the money I had and rushed around the city buying food for our expedition.

"I hope Billy likes peanut butter," I said as we bought three big cans full.

Our bus to Pokhara broke down and we spent a day traveling the last 100 kilometers on the back of a truck. In Pokhara, Billy and Rob rented climbing equipment for themselves and we hired a porter to help with the load as far as the last village. Billy was also short of money, but he borrowed enough to get us through.

The first day we were assailed by countless ground leeches. They crawled like black inchworms and they could smell our blood from yards away. They got down our shirts, up our pants, and into our boots. They could squirm through anything. The bites were surprisingly painless; only by seeing them did we know that the leeches were on us. But once they were attached, they were nearly impossible to remove. They would only drop off when they had drunk their fill. Since they injected a natural anticoagulant, the wounds they made bled profusely for an hour afterwards. At the end of the day we removed our boots and found our socks full of blood.

That first evening, we met a solitary British lady who was on an organized trek. She had a guide, a cook, and two porters. A tent was set up for her, but when night came she refused to leave the house-hotel. She was terrified of the leeches. "I'm not scared of most things," she said, "and I could look a rat in the face, but I simply can't bear leeches."

Billy then told her about sleeping in a tent in a leech forest. Swarms of leeches had tried to squeeze through the tiny holes of the tent's mosquito

186

net. The leeches that were too fat to get in had pushed themselves halfway through the mesh with their bodies swaying like hundreds of small tentacles. Billy told the story very well and the British lady was horrified. She slept in the loft with the rest of us, and in the morning Billy complained that he had hardly slept at all. The lady had kept him awake with her screams. "The room was full of rats," she said. "They were using me for a springboard." Poor woman—she should never have come to Nepal.

In three days, we reached the furthest village. We sent the porter back and added his load to our own. Two more days put us in the Annapurna Sanctuary, and two days after that we established our camp just below the snow line at 15,500 feet. Our goal was to climb 18,500-foot Tent Peak. A Nepali man had boasted, "Our people climb it barefoot." But this we discovered to be an absolute fabrication. The peak required technical climbing ability and high-quality equipment. The three of us made an aborted attempt, but Rob was then out of time and he had to return to school. Billy escorted him down to 14,000 feet, and from there he hiked back alone.

Billy and I tried the peak again. We reached 18,000 feet by mid-morning and tackled the 200-foot cliff of fluted snow that led to the final ridge. We were nearing the crest when Billy called up to me.

"How do you feel about going on alone?"

"What?!" I called back. His question was as absurd as asking the name of my brother's cat. My whole being was focused on reaching the top.

"I'm not feeling very well," he said. "I don't think I could hold you if you fell, but I'll come as far as the ridge if you want."

I was shattered—we seemed so close! Clouds blew across the slope, making it seem very high and steep. I was too frightened to climb it alone, so we went down.

The descent was a nightmare. On the way up, I had been fired with enthusiasm and I had been unaffected by the altitude. But going down, my will was broken and I felt sick. Billy went first. He enlarged the holds and talked me back to camp. The trip was a failure. He had been right to halt the climb when he began to feel weak. I couldn't blame him for that, but I began to suspect that the best way to fulfill my climbing goals was to pursue them alone.

I had already been away from Aiselukharka longer than I had wanted, so we hurried back, reaching Pokhara in just four days. The last day walking in, one of my upper right teeth began to hurt. Nearly a month before, I had chipped that tooth while eating roasted corn. It hadn't hurt, so I had forgotten about it. Now the pain grew with each step. I stopped several times and futilely brushed my teeth. The pain only intensified.

That night a demon spent eight hours swinging a sledgehammer in my mouth. I couldn't sleep at all. I took aspirin and moaned. In the morning I boarded the first bus to Kathmandu. We had gotten the money for my bus ticket by selling our surplus peanut butter.

The bus left at 6 a.m., just as the orange ball of the sun rose over the dusty bus-park. I was lucky to get a third of a seat, but that was the only good part of the trip. That beautiful sunrise was the start of a scorching day. The tooth throbbed and I sweated. I munched codeine like candy, but it didn't help. I leaned forward with my elbows on my knees and my head in my hands. My mouth dribbled saliva onto the floor. I kept thinking that I had reached the limit of pain, only to discover the pangs steadily growing. I hardly noticed the people who shoved against me. My thoughts centered on that single tooth. I wanted to throw myself out of the window and under the wheels of the bus. In nine hours we arrived in Kathmandu.

I stumbled to the Peace Corps office, got the address of a dentist, and received a diagnosis that evening. I had an abscess that required a root canal operation. I was put on a mega-dose of penicillin and eye-crossing painkillers. For the next couple of days I sat in the Peace Corps office feeling like a zombie. Friends who saw me said straight out, "What's wrong? You look terrible."

The doctor decided that the root canal should be done in Bangkok, but I resisted; I had to get back to my village. By chance I met an American dentist who was vacationing in Kathmandu. He agreed to do the root canal if he could get the right equipment. He needed a particular set of tiny files. The dental facility at the mission hospital had the files up to size number thirty-five, but the American dentist thought that he might need a number forty. So, for the lack of a single tiny file, I was sent to Bangkok. This was as ludicrous as traveling around the world for a broken pinky. Ambika sent word to my Headmaster that I would be very late for classes.

The dental facilities in Bangkok were excellent—much better than any that I could have afforded in the States. A week of antibiotics had eliminated the infection, and the root canal, though it required a half-dozen appointments, was painless. I stayed in a cheap hotel—the Peace Corps supplied me with money—and I met Anna, an Australian medical student.

My third night in Bangkok, Anna came to my room to see the black and white pictures I had of the Annapurna Sanctuary. We talked a bit about mountains, but mostly she wanted to hear about Aiselukharka and my life there. She was sincerely concerned about my awkward adaptation to Nepal and my frustrating relationship with Kay. We talked till very late and I eventually realized that she had no intention of returning to her room that night. Nothing like that had ever happened to me before and I hardly knew what to do. I slowly gathered up the pictures that were still lying on the bed...

The next day Anna moved into my room and we had a fine one-week affair. We weren't in love, but we liked each other's company and we enjoyed sleeping together. In many ways meeting Anna was exactly what I had needed. She liked me the way I was, both the American and Nepali parts, and she helped me overcome some of the dependency on Kay which had been making my life so hard. When she left, I felt contented, as though I had just finished a big Christmas dinner.

By the time I returned to Nepal and started back to Aiselukharka, my Dasai break had stretched to six weeks. I slept a night in Lamidada, which put me in Aiselukharka in the mid-afternoon. I had missed a month of classes, so I went directly to the school.

When I was halfway across the playing field the first student saw me. *"Philipsir aaunubhayo!*—Philipsir has come!" he shouted. Other students took up the cry and they came pouring out of the classrooms, climbing through the windows, running down from the ridge top, and racing from around the corner of the temple. The teachers came too, and everyone crowded around me, laughing and jumping, all talking at once.

"Philipsir aaunubhayo!" "Philipsir aaunubhayo!" They had received no message about me coming a month late. "Philipsir, what happened? What happened? You were gone and you didn't come back. We were so very worried. Older Brother Krishna Bhakta heard on the radio that two Amaarikans died on Annapurna.* We knew that couldn't be you, but we were afraid. You've come back!"

"Philipsir, you've come back! Our classes were broken without you to teach us."

"Haamilaai kushi laagyo!—We're so happy!" they called. I was engulfed by their feelings of joy. I turned around and around, looking at everyone, smiling and trying to tell the story of my trip. I wanted to soar. I felt so good to be back. Such a reception!

One of the girls remembered that no one had said *Namaste* and everyone immediately raised their hands to their foreheads while 200 voices called, *"Namaste."* I spun around with my hands in a *Namaste*, returning all their greetings at once.

It was a great excuse for a celebration. The younger students threw their topi hats into the air and the day's remaining classes were cancelled. The story of my journey to Annapurna and Bangkok was passed around and it grew

---

* Vera Watson and Alison Chadwick-Onyszkiewicz of the Women's Annapurna Expedition died high on Annapurna while Billy and I were on the other side in the Annapurna Sanctuary.

considerably with each telling. I was glad to be home; I was becoming truly acclimatized.

Thomas and I hike past Chukung without stopping, and we slowly convince ourselves that we have accomplished a great feat—up Island Peak and back to Pheriche in just four days. We walk into Pheriche feeling like heroes. It deserves a celebration. We buy a can of chopped meat and Thomas supervises its preparation in a skillet of potatoes and greens. It's almost, but not quite, delicious. Thomas sighs contentedly, but I would have preferred a large helping of daal-bhaat.

April 9

Pheriche almost 14,000 feet

We take a rest day to organize our things prior to heading west over the Chikim La pass to Gokyo. I wash my socks with hopes that they'll dry before they freeze. The cracks in my boots need more sewing, but I put it off. I prefer to just sit in the hut.

The lodge is staffed by two boys. They laugh gaily as they cook for us. Their grubby pants smell of smoke.

"Do you ever go to school?" I ask them.

"Yes," they answer. "We sometimes study in Khumjung, north of Namche."

They can both read, and the older brother can do the sums of the travelers' bills. They're very bright, and it's a shame that they can't continue in school. But like most Nepalis, they seem content. What would they do with more schooling? Some schools are such a sham that they might be better off with a minimal education.

The pile of exam papers sat before me. They were the tenth grade's final exam in science and they had to be corrected that day. Tomorrow was the deadline for the results to be submitted to Chautara. The tenth grade's finals had been given while I was away in Bangkok, a month earlier than the other classes, because the school had to prepare the students who would go on to take the standardized national exam. The science papers were the last ones to be graded and I procrastinated.

The math exams had been a chore. The students had obviously copied from the book and from each others' papers. I had been inclined to fail them all, but the fault was partly mine for missing that last month of classes. The exam had been prepared by the district office and it was much too hard, especially since we had finished only 60 per cent of the curriculum. Before Dasai I had been teaching triple-long classes trying to complete the material. Next they would have to take the national SLC exam and they were far from ready.

I had graded the math exams very leniently, giving points for any glimmer of understanding. I had told the other teachers about the extra points that I was giving and they had giggled like children stealing cookies. I was ashamed. Who were we kidding? Even with my helpful grading, the results had been pitiful. Of the thirty-one students who had taken the math exam, only eight had achieved the passing score of 40 per cent.

I sat in the storage room and stared at the ungraded science tests. The room contained two heavy wooden tables and the floor was cluttered with garbage that couldn't be thrown out because we had no place to throw it. Under one table were piles of old exams, rolled into bundles and tied with string. I was the only teacher in Aiselukharka who returned exam papers to the students, and I felt that few of the other teachers actually read them. The tests were just a formality to justify the scores that they assigned on a whim.

I returned exams for a purpose. I wanted the students to see the reasons behind their grades. I wanted them to study their old exams and to learn from their mistakes. Students and parents often implored me to "give" passing grades, and I would reply that their grades depended on how well they did on the exam. They would just look perplexed. Students asked me, *"Kati aayo?*— How much came?"* as though their scores fell from heaven. They saw no relationship between the results of their tests and how much they studied.

Cheating was another matter. It was institutionalized. The teachers regularly allowed the students to cheat by leaving the room during difficult exams. After all, the teachers had passed their school exams by cheating, so why shouldn't these students do the same?

In my own classes, I limited cheating first by structuring the course so that they could pass without cheating. Then, whenever possible, I had the students write their exams outside on the ground and separated by 10 yards or more. Finally, I would subtract points from cheaters or withhold a paper for part of the test time. I hated giving exams and I loathed grading them.

I certainly didn't want to grade the science exams. I had never taught tenth science and I couldn't understand the students' answers. The material and the vocabulary were all new to me. I had spent a full day using my dictionaries and textbooks just to decipher the questions and to figure out the right answers. At first, I had planned to read every answer carefully and to look up each new word, but now I realized that this was impossible. In three hours I had graded just two exams. The papers were mostly illegible and the few that I could read were written in double-talk. The students had tried to bluff me, to make it look like they knew more than they actually did. The papers were too difficult for me, but I wouldn't admit this to the other teachers.

I wished that someone else could do it. During the past year, two Nepali teachers had come to Aiselukharka who had the ability to teach science. One had taught for a month and the other for two. They had both left saying, "I can't live here. I have no family here. There's nothing to do and there's nothing available. I am bored."

This was a problem throughout Nepal. College-educated teachers were unwilling to work in the remote hill regions. They preferred to stay in the cities doing any simple job. In Kathmandu I knew a man with a degree in economics who worked at a tiny restaurant serving pie to tourists. Nepal had few jobs for economists, but he was unwilling to work as a teacher. This was why Aiselukharka needed me. It was too bad that I was proving to be incompetent.

While the papers waited, I thought about what sort of teacher I was. I certainly put a lot of time into my classes and I didn't hit the students—at least not often. The first time that I hit a student had shocked me. During science lab, a boy had been close to breaking a test tube and I had slapped him on the back of the head. The entire class, including the boy, accepted my violence as being completely proper. Originally I had thought that if I ever struck a student it would be a sign that I needed help. But now I rationalized that a well-timed slap could be a form of communication; it showed that I was serious about what I said. I was just expanding my vocabulary.

I pushed aside the papers and I stood up to look at the science equipment littering the other table. It was always filthy. When the wind blew, dirt sifted through the slate roof and covered everything inside. I picked up two gadgets I had made: a light bulb that used a strand of steel wool for a filament and a kaleidoscope made from the pieces of a broken mirror. Our home-made pan balance leaned against the wall and a box overflowed with the interesting rocks that we had collected on our field trips to study plants and insects.

Below me was the eighth grade's room. Even without a teacher, they were studying. Through the gaps between the floorboards, I could hear Netra Prasaad's voice. He was reading from their history text, chanting the words aloud. The other students were listening and I knew that Netra Prasaad would be hunched over the book, rocking with the repeated intonation of his recitation. He was a Braahman.

I glanced at the papers and went to the window. Just outside was the plot of land that the school had repeatedly tried to convert into a vegetable garden. The Headmaster wanted the school to become a vocational high school specializing in agriculture, but none of us teachers were farmers. The crows got most of the newly planted seeds and stray goats broke through the inadequate fencing to eat whatever managed to grow. Despite this, the plot had produced some seto mulaa, and after someone had stolen the biggest ones, the rest were quickly harvested and sold. Past the garden stretched the village terraces, now brown and fallow for the winter.

I heard a sound at the door and I quickly sat down to make it look as though I had been working. A young knock-kneed student came in looking for the volleyball pump. Durga marched right in behind him to give him the pump and to shoo him out.

"*Disturb bhayo**—You're disturbing Philipsir," he scolded.

"No, he didn't disturb me," I countered.

Durga looked at me as I shuffled the papers. "Are many passing?" he asked. His younger brother—actually his nephew—was in the tenth class and was doing poorly.

"Some are passing," I said indifferently.

Durga watched me for a few minutes before going out. He was concerned about the coming SLC exam. This was the school's first tenth class, so it was the first time that we would be sending students to take the School Leaving Certificate. We were discouraged by the knowledge that no students from Sindhupalchowk District had passed the previous year. The test was too hard; it was designed to challenge the students from the quality city schools. Only Raadhaa, our top student, had the slightest chance of earning his SLC. If he passed the exam he might become a teacher, or perhaps he'd work in the civil service, or maybe, just maybe, he would go to the university.

I stared at the papers. Now I *had* to do something. I took an exam. On the first page was written, *"Ek nambarko uttar 225 ho*—The answer to number one is 225." It was the right answer, but the student had shown no work, no formulas. He had surely copied from someone. I wrote a big number five. Five points—full credit. Question number two was an essay. The page was a quarter filled. That was worth two points. I didn't even read it. The next question was also descriptive and the answer was about the same length but included a diagram. That earned him an extra point—three points. I continued that way. Without reading their answers, I gave credit according

* With no Nepali term for *disturb*, the English word has been borrowed. Nepali also lacked common words to say *garbage, bored, yes, no, please,* and *thank you.*

to how much they had written. How could I sink so low? It was a mockery of education, and I was disgusted with myself.

I remembered something that I had tried with the tenth-grade students after I had first taught them for a few weeks. I was assigning a lot of homework which they were dutifully handing in. The quality of their homework showed a high level of understanding, but I wanted to know how many of the students were doing their own work and how many were copying. One day, I drew three boxes on the blackboard and left the room while the students took a head count. In the first box they were to write the number of students who always did their own homework. The second box was for those who sometimes copied and the third box was for those who usually copied. I didn't care *who* copied; I just wanted to know how many. I waited outside for a half-hour. When they let me back in, I saw that my three squares had been greatly enlarged. Inside the boxes were written the roll numbers of all the students who fit into each category. They were unworried that I would know who copied; it was nothing to be ashamed of. The first box was the smallest—three students did their own homework. Fifteen students sometimes (or often) copied, and thirteen usually copied. If this was an indication of their attitude towards school, then it was fitting that I graded their exams without reading them.

I wrote a five next to a solitary number and then a four by a nearly full page of scribbles. Was this education? What had become of my principles? I had traded them for expedience, to save myself embarrassment. No one would know how I had graded the exams. The papers had no connection with learning. They were only a means of getting numbers for the register book. I was just supplying the numbers. Most of the students would pass and that would make them happy. Was that such a horrible thing?

I re-graded the first two papers, giving them twice their original scores. I recorded the grades and turned in the list. Twenty students passed the science exam and I hoped that they would do as well on the SLC. I rolled up the papers and tied them with a string. The exam would never be returned. I put it in the pile, where it would slowly gather dust, along with the others.

If *that* is education then the two boys in Pheriche are well off without it. To sit by the fire and to joke with your brother amid the beauty of the high Himalayas is certainly a good life.

A New Zealand climbing expedition arrives in Pheriche, coming down from Lobuche. They are well outfitted and organized. In the evening, their leader talks with me over tea. He teaches climbing and has been on expeditions all over the world. Next season he will be on a team to climb Ama Dablam. I am impressed. From Pheriche, his party will go over the Tasi Lapcha pass and he hopes to climb Pharchamo on the way.

Unexpectedly he asks me, "Were you up on Lobuche East?"

"Yes," I answer. "Why do you ask?"

"We saw your tracks."

I wonder how he knew that they were my tracks. "Did you climb it?" I ask.

"Well, almost," he shrugs. "Two of us made it to the last 200 meters and there we were stopped by a wretched crevasse. I tried crossing it on a snow bridge but it collapsed from under me. We had climbed up the rock face just behind Lobuche Village and we discovered your tracks at the top. Quite a surprise. We followed your route down."

I go to sleep feeling exonerated that I chose to forgo Lobuche East after only a reconnaissance. I'm more judicious than I had thought.

April 10
Tshola Tsho 15,000 feet

The frozen lake, called Tshola Tsho, is a mile long. Its surface is so smooth and white that it seems unreal among the jagged rocks and sharp peaks. It gives me an eerie feeling, like seeing a ghost. If I climb down to touch its edge, would it vanish?

Thomas and I have hiked a half-day west of Pheriche. We scramble cross-country over the rocks and twice we lose track of each other. We're more tired than we ought to be.

Toward evening, we drag our feet into the summer settlement of Dzongla. Only one of the three huts is unlocked; we see no people and no yaks. I get water from beneath the ice of a stagnant pool and Thomas starts a fire with scraps of wood and pieces of dried yak dung. A candle gives me light to chronicle our climb of Island Peak. Lastly, I write a stream of complaints against Thomas. I get upset by little things he does. He now makes a terrible noise as he scrapes the soot off the bottom of his pan with his Swiss army knife. Doesn't he realize that it'll get just as black the next time he cooks in it?

I feel better after eating, but I still wish for some time alone. I won't brood over it though. Living in Nepal has taught me to recognize the triviality of our daily worries. Things in life are so uncertain, so unexpected.

My hands were cold and I shoved them into my pockets. Winter mornings in Kathmandu, remarkably foggy and cold, always made me melancholy. It was a week before Christmas and I was waiting at the bus-park for Matt, one of

199

the remaining math/science volunteers. We were going to Chitwan National Park and I couldn't understand why he was late. It was nearly 5 a.m.

Aiselukharka seemed far away. The final exams for grades one through nine had gone as well—or as badly—as could have been expected. I managed to complete the textbooks in all my classes, except tenth math, and I felt satisfied with my work. In eighth class we spent a bonus week doing a unit on health and disease. To finish the first year of classes was an important milestone.

I had now been in Kathmandu for four days and I was abreast of the latest news. One more from our group had quit. He had never liked Nepal and he had been wanting to leave for a year. He spoke the best Nepali in the group and it was too bad that he had left. Another teacher from N/71, Tom, with the arm-length blond hair, was getting a free trip home for Christmas. A volunteer from another group had freaked out and Tom was escorting him to Washington for therapy.

The bus-park was a simple dirt lot and the brightly painted buses were lined up in rows. *"Pokhara-Pokhara-Pokhara-Pokharaaaaa!"* A man called the bus destinations so fast that they were unrecognizable to the untrained ear. Porters scurried about in ragged clothes carrying baggage to the roofs of the buses and attendants pounded on the buses to guide them as they backed in and out. *Thump-thump. Thump-thump. Thump-thump. THUMP!* Two thumps meant go, and one loud thump meant stop. I watched a pair of tourists looking for their bus. The girl's long sandy hair hung over her pack and I sighed. My melancholy increased.

The far edge of the lot was lined with ramshackle tea stalls. They looked as if a strong gust of wind could knock them over. I waited in the cold and drank tea.

The bus came and so did Matt. We spent half the day riding the bus out of the Kathmandu Valley and down to the Terai. Another bus took us from Hetaura to Tadi Bazaar, and as evening fell, we hiked the last few miles to Chitwan National Park.

We found a small lodge outside the park entrance and got a room that had walls of woven bamboo encircling a floor of loose dirt. The night was fantastic. A heavy mist hung over the jungle, and the nearly full moon made supernatural silhouettes of the banana trees. We heard snorting noises and the Nepalis said that it was a *gaida*, a rhinoceros.

In the morning Matt and I registered at the park headquarters and paid entrance fees of sixty-five rupees each. The park rangers warned us about the rhinos; deaths were common. They explained that rhinos were extremely fast, but that they couldn't turn quickly. This meant that a gaida in open country could be outmaneuvered by running in zigzags. The safest escape, though, was to climb a tree.

Matt and I started toward the nearest of the park's two observation platforms, called *machaans*. We had to ford a sluggish stream, and as we approached we saw a group of long-antlered deer. They leaped through the water and it sprayed into the air. After they were across, a bird dropped from the sky, hit the water, and soared up with a fish clutched in its talons. We waded through the stream and continued to the machaan. At the far side of the clearing around it, we came to the edge of the elephant grass where I saw more deer. I was afraid to follow them into the grass. It grew to 15 feet high and it was no place to meet a rhino on foot.

We hiked back through the jungle. It was too thick to see more than 10 yards ahead, but not so thick that it prevented us from walking. Twisting vines interlaced one bizarre tree with the next, and swift exotic birds disappeared into the leaves almost before we could spot them. Suddenly we heard a deep snort, just to our left, followed immediately by the crashing sound of something *big* running deeper into the forest. The rhino must have been very close, but we didn't see it. Matt and I felt extremely vulnerable standing half-concealed within the bushes.

The next day we took safer transport through the jungle—an elephant. We arranged the trip with a private elephant camp and arrived an hour before sunrise. We climbed a ladder to get atop the elephant; the howdah that we sat on was just a big sack of straw tied to her back. The driver steered with his feet behind the elephant's ears, guiding her out of the compound and into the elephant grass. The tall grass swished against her sides like waves, giving the impression of riding in a boat at sea.

The driver chose the direction by intuition and the elephant sniffed the air. Her long strides took us into the jungle and she crashed straight through, breaking down trees and flattening the undergrowth. Matt and I looked about eagerly, but we figured that the noise was scaring the animals away.

Suddenly we heard a snort and saw the rump of a rhinoceros disappear into the brush. We tracked it to a clearing. Two gaida had stopped to examine us. They were huge, with thick skin that was sectioned like armor. Their small ears turned toward us, and they watched our every move. The one stayed between us and the other, but they didn't mind the elephant coming close. We followed the pair for a half-hour and Matt took a dozen pictures.

Circling around, we crossed the main river and entered the forest. We scared off a herd of deer and glimpsed the tail of an Indian python as it slid down a hole. The elephant abruptly turned, and we found ourselves looking down at a half-eaten deer carcass—the sign of a tiger! It was a fresh kill from the night before, and the driver dismounted to cover it with branches. He would come back later and secretly take the meat home. "*Bhaag pheri aaunchha?*—Will the tiger return?" we asked expectantly, but the driver said, "No. The tiger, he never returns."

As we traveled back to the camp, Matt spotted a *jaraayo*, a type of large elk, but I missed it. The ride lasted about three hours and I was enthralled. I would have gladly ridden all day.

Matt and I walked back to the park office and halfway there we saw three Nepali girls in a tree. They had sighted a mother rhino and its young grazing across the river. We watched them through my binoculars. Incredible.

Two hundred yards before the office, we heard a noise in the brush and two Nepali farmers said, "*Gaida*." Feeling very bold, we went in to see. Matt circled to the right and I went to the left. The sounds moved away as we approached. I slipped off my pack and slowly stepped through the heavy green undergrowth. The rhino was to my right, standing still and staring toward Matt. Rhino ears are very directional and since he was concentrating on Matt, he didn't hear me. The rhino charged forward a few steps to drive Matt away and I came very close to him on the left side. I wasn't scared at all. Suddenly the rhino saw me, turned to one side, and retreated further into the forest. Perhaps he sensed my confidence and was intimidated. Thinking it best to get to a safer spot, I tried to climb a tree.

My tree was a poor choice. It was only 8 inches in diameter and its bark was slick. It forked 5 feet above the ground, and I had a lot of trouble getting up. Matt cautiously came over and joined me. We watched the rhino and the rhino watched us. With time passing, and after nothing had happened, I got down from the tree to attempt getting closer. I still felt no fear.

"How about getting a picture of me and the rhino?" I joked to Matt.

I slowly put my binoculars beneath a heart-leafed plant and I pulled on my headband. I didn't want the hair to fall in my eyes at a crucial moment. Carefully placing each foot, I crept through the tangled vines toward the rhino. He weighed over 2 tons and he had already shown his temper toward Matt. I approached silently and I watched his eyes more than I watched my feet. As I came closer, nothing but air separated us.

Further ahead and to my right grew a solitary tree. It had that same slick bark and it didn't fork till 15 feet up. Being just 6 inches across, it would be impossible to climb. But I wasn't thinking of escape; I was still moving forward and the rhino stood motionless. I reached the edge of some low grass and I froze in mid-step with my right arm partially extended. The rhino and I could almost hear one another breathing. He was less than 20 yards away and I could see the tufts of hair growing from his ears. Neither of us knew what to do; we just stared into each other's eyes.

We exploded simultaneously into action—we had realized who was truly in control. I had only one option—I had to run straight *at* the charging rhino. I leapt forward, toward the oncoming rhino and toward that useless tree. The rhino's 2 tons came at me full speed and the pounding of his legs literally shook the ground. His horn flew at me impossibly fast. I didn't think at all—there was no time. I lurched up and grabbed desperately at the tree as high as I could reach. Holding on with both hands, I swung around with my back to the rhino, but it was already too late. He hit me from behind, knocking me forward and up. I clung to the tree. The rhino's side scraped against the tree, and he continued forward with my legs dragging across his back. In 10 yards he came to a stop and turned around for a second charge. I pulled myself higher, and the tree leaned sickly to one side. He charged again and his feet thundered. Just before reaching the tree, he veered to the side and crashed into the brush. The sound of his rampage echoed in my ears until he was long gone.

I climbed to the fork and examined myself. I saw no blood and I felt no broken bones. What had happened? My torso had been high enough to avoid the rhino getting his horn into me. He had only managed to ram me. My right buttock throbbed, but I was otherwise unharmed. Matt was babbling. He had thought that I would be killed and that he would be next. As I hung in the tree, I began to laugh hysterically. I was amazed to be alive.

We waited twenty minutes before climbing down from our trees. I picked up my binoculars and limped back to the trail. Somehow I missed my pack on the way, and I had to go back into the jungle to retrieve it. I didn't want to return. The place scared me. I was still seeing that strange rhinoceros face—his ears pointed toward me and his eyes watched me.

Matt detailed our escapade to a park warden who replied, "Yes. To survive a gaida attack is a sign that one is in grace with God." He explained that a rhino usually attacks its victim three times. "First it gores with its horn, then it returns to bite, and finally it licks with its tongue. Its tongue can take the skin off a man." A month later I would hear that a German traveler had been killed by a rhinoceros in Chitwan. I was numbed by my close escape and my hands shook for the rest of the day.

That night, Matt and I, along with two British travelers, went to the far machaan to spend the night. The machaan overlooked a watering hole, and since this was the dry season, we expected it to be much used. Matt and the others took positions down close to the water, but I stayed up in the machaan. The sun set with an orange glow and the water reflected the colors. We all noticed a slight movement in the grass. A large rhinoceros stepped slowly into the water. It lowered its head to drink and the world seemed to stand still.

After the rhino had slipped away, Matt and the Brits came back to the machaan. They talked loudly about the heredity of intelligence. I wanted to quietly enjoy the growing darkness, but their chatter broke the mood. I took my blanket and went down into the night. I had something that I needed to do. Wild places had always been havens of refuge for me, places to relax and to feel secure. But that morning's rhino attack had made the jungle a place of dread. I was afraid to walk among the thick growing trees, so I wanted to face my fear and to overcome it by meeting the jungle at its worst—alone at night.

I walked through the dark and found a clearing big enough to sleep in. I meditated and then rolled up in my blanket. I heard sounds all around me—rhinoceros, or wild boar, or tiger? It was cold and I shivered though the night, looking out into the dark. Animals moved in the brush, but nothing came closer than 20 feet. The dew was heavy and by early morning it dripped from every leaf and twig. I was cold and stiff, but calmed. The forest was still safe.

I joined Matt at the machaan and we followed the jeep trail back to the lodge. Two hundred yards from the machaan we found a line of tracks in the fine dirt. The prints were clear and unmistakable—tiger. A park surveyor happened by and he confirmed that they were tiger tracks. That night a tiger had roamed within smelling distance of me and had left me alone. Perhaps the warden had been right about me being in grace with God.

Two days later we returned to Kathmandu. The city was as dirty as ever, but somehow Christmas made it seem romantic. Windows were strung with colored lights and the big hotels displayed Christmas trees in their lobbies. The strings of lights were actually in celebration of King Birendra's birthday on December 28, and the Christmas trees were only to attract tourists, but we didn't care. I had long talks with Klaus, Pesout, and the others in our group. Some of us had not seen one another since we'd sworn in a year before. We walked through the cold nights and our breath billowed in white clouds. Everyone was invited to Christmas parties at the ambassador's residence or at the Peace Corps director's home. We exchanged very few gifts and no one mentioned what Christmas was like at home.

On King Birendra's birthday, the Thursday after Christmas, Sudharshan handed me a fat envelope—a thirty-two page letter from Kay! She had described everything that had been happening with her, and she had written an account of a short romance that had ended badly. I read the last two pages till I had them memorized—

> . . . because of getting hurt I've been wanting to be closer to you. I have really been longing for the relationship we had all along. I want the closeness we had, and to be able to understand and share as well. Nobody seems to think quite like you do; that very natural, practical insight that you have about things. It's so good to read in your letters that you still hope we'll fall back in love. That's something that's deeply reassuring. But, Phil, I don't have the strength to try not to find the love I want from you in other people. I'll go on looking till you come back (just as I've done since you left). I am sure it will be in vain; I hope it will be in vain.
>
> I'm in such a screwy state right now! I don't want to have any heavy relationships when you come back. I wouldn't feel

good about that (unless they give the kind of love that you do—there are very few that do). Damn. I know my words will be very ambiguous. Phil, do you get their meaning? I feel so selfish and childish. I just want you to come back right now. I want us to be in love again and as close as before and us together (wherever).

I'm sorry if I've hurt you by not being able to comfort you and through my silence. I feel foolish at the fickleness of my feelings, but I can't deny them.

Sweet Phil, Take care of yourself,

I love you much, Kay

Happy Christmas—
I'll be thinking of the ones we were able to share.

I felt her love very strongly. In a year I would finish the Peace Corps and we would be together again. I was more lonely than I had been in months.

Two days later, I was back at the bus-park waiting in the cold of the early morning. I still felt melancholy, but I also had hope. Small tears welled up in my eyes. Classes would soon begin and I needed to get back to Aiselukharka.

April 11
Dzongla 15,889 feet

Thomas hikes well ahead of me. Lacking a trail, we follow a compass bearing based on the map. The surrounding peaks are awesome, but I ignore their beauty. I grumble to myself about Thomas going so fast. He wants to reach Gokyo in one long day, but what's his hurry? I'm still carrying four days of food which I would rather eat than carry back to Namche. I stop to drink and to piss. I decide to hike at my own pace, and I find that I soon pass Thomas. The canyon broadens, making it easier to walk on the frozen stream than to scramble over the rocks. This is also gentler on my boots, which continue to crack and split.

I have seen on the map a 20,000-foot peak situated on the other side of the pass. I have the necessary food and equipment with me, so why not climb it? I could meet Thomas in Gokyo in a few days, or perhaps later, down in Namche. The idea excites me and I hike faster.

The best route to the pass appears to be along the top of a moraine and I'm happy to find a few cairns marking the way. Reaching the base of a cliff, I traverse to the right and come to the glacier. From here, a gradual snow trudge leads to the pass, so I wait for Thomas. I can't see him at all and I worry that he has had an accident. Finally I spot him through the binoculars. He is propped motionless against a rock. Is he hurt? I'm relieved when he stands up. He sluggishly puts on his pack. I know that he doesn't like carrying it. At Thomas's home in the Swiss Alps people seldom carry heavy loads, but in the Himalayas everything is carried on the human back.

The porter lifted the load and we continued the climb. He had hiked very slowly all day from Lamidada and I wondered what the problem was. The load was not so big: a dozen books, three tins of peanut butter, two reams of paper, a gallon of kerosene, and a rolled-up cotton mattress. (I had finally grown tired of sleeping on a lumped-up cloth pad.) Altogether, the load weighed about 55 pounds, which was far less than the 110 pounds or more that porters sometimes carried. So the weight wasn't the difficulty. Nor was the trail too steep. One of my students had shown us a gradually sloping trail that just happened to pass the student's home. Neither was the load too awkward. The mattress made a nice cushion against his sweating back and the naamlo, head-strap, was a good wide one. I concluded that he was just slow.

When we reached Aiselukharka, I used the naamlo to carry the load up to my room. It's a good system. You lean forward with the weight distributed between your back and the strap across your forehead. What I disliked about using a naamlo was that I couldn't turn my head. The neighbors had come around to say *Namaste*, and the sight of me bearing a load with a naamlo made everyone grin. They weren't shocked, though. They had already seen me

doing such undignified tasks as chopping wood, hauling stones, and milking the family water buffalo. I was finding it harder and harder to surprise them.

I paid the porter his twenty-five rupees and added an extra five because the trip had taken longer than I had expected. It was already too late for him to return to Lamidada that night, and I expected that he would ask around for a place to sleep. But instead, he just sat on our raised porch looking woebegone. For a Nepali to be alone among strangers was a great misfortune. He acted very surprised when I took him to my own room and gave him a plate of chiuraa. "Won't you eat too?" he asked me, and I joined him. He was a sad-looking man of twenty-five, and throughout the day I had asked him about his family. He had a brother and a sister of eight and nine, but their father was quite old—the porter had crooked his index finger to show me how old and bent his father was—so he did most of the work himself. His family owned a piece of land that was too small to feed them, so he earned money doing whatever jobs he could find: portering, or working on other people's land, or laboring with the road crews. He had a hard life and he was used to being treated as an inferior.

I called him *Tapaai*, in the honorific form, the same as I spoke to all adults, and this embarrassed him. After he had seen all the people who welcomed me back and who called me *Sir*, he decided that I was someone important. We were both hungry and I made sure that Aamaa cooked enough for the porter too. The daal-bhaat was excellent and the porter gave me a big grin when I asked if he had eaten enough. I arranged a place for him to sleep and I soon realized that he would be too cold with the single blanket I had given him. I went out and roused Mahendra to bring a thick comforter. The porter tried to refuse, but he had no choice. He rolled up in the soft warmth and he watched me for half an hour before he slept. I wondered what he dreamt about.

I felt good being back in Aiselukharka after my Christmas break, and I was soon into the routine of classes. I taught two periods of science and two of math, and the students complained that I had so few classes. They all wanted me as their teacher. They said that they *understood* when I taught them.

The district education office relocated a few of our teachers. One was transferred and promoted to be the Headmaster of a primary school near his home village, and Durga was sent to Kathmandu for teacher's training. They had been sharing a room with Kedar, the geography/history/government teacher, and Kedar now came to me with tales of how bad it was to live completely alone. He needed me to be his full-time friend. Other than Krishna Bhakta, my best friends were not the farmers and the landholders, but rather the outside workers: the teachers, the transient porters, the Carpenter, the Priest, and the Tailor. Perhaps being non-Newari brought us closer together. Kedar wasn't alone for long; he too was transferred to a new school.

Three new teachers arrived, and after only a year, I became one of the senior teachers. I did much more talking and gossiping than I had the first year. I had learned something important. The villagers would not invite me to their homes—I was considered welcome at all times and it was up to me to just walk in. I still felt occasional spurts in my language ability, and I had much more free time. Two of my classes were repeats from the previous year and that saved me hours of lesson-planning. I could have fully settled into my life in Aiselukharka if not for one thing. My longings for Kay had been rekindled by her recent letter. My world felt incomplete without her, and I continued to write her long amorous letters.

At night I had vivid dreams—some frightening, some silly, and some just strange. In one I was approached by a rat who offered me a partially eaten peanut. When I ate it, I immediately shrank to rat size. The rat led me through a hole in the wall and into a confusing world of tunnels and passageways. The dream didn't frighten me; it was just fun. Another dream concerned a woman who had Kay's face and body, but who was an absolute stranger. As in the previous year, I was immersed in a life of loneliness.

I was sometimes depressed, but little things unexpectedly brightened my spirits. One night I was alternately writing to Kay and warming my hands over the lamp when a boy whom I hardly knew came to my room. He handed me a bag of roasted soybeans. "A special present from my father," he said. I had recently seen the boy's father and his older brother in Lamidada when I had spent the night there before returning to Aiselukharka. They had been trying for a bus to Kathmandu. As they waited, a full bus drove by without stopping. An hour later another bus went by, and then a third one passed that didn't even slow down. They tried to jump aboard each moving bus, but they had no luck. They just came back to me, laughed it off, and had another cup of tea. The three hours of inconvenience would have enraged many Americans, but the boy and his father were completely calm and even a trifle amused. *"Ke garne?"* they smiled. The fourth bus took them to Kathmandu, and as I sat in my room, chomping on their soybeans, I felt myself absorbing a portion of their composure and tolerance.

My friendships deepened with the Carpenter, the Priest, and the Tailor. The Carpenter was a pleasant little man who wore the Nepali *suruwaal* trousers. The traditional pants were voluminous in the seat but close-fitting from the knees to the ankles. The Carpenter always talked with great determination and confidence, but he could hardly stay on his feet when he heard a joke. His craftsmanship was crude though functional. He took pride in owning all of his own tools, and even when he was away from his work, he kept a chisel in his hand or a nail behind his ear to display his profession. Presently he and his apprentice were making window frames for the student hostel that was being built. One day I was surprised to learn that he had never been paid for the bench and the table that he had made for me.

The Priest lived in the large brick house that stood in the main temple's courtyard. Many priests lived in the area and any Braahman could charge fees for doing pujaas, but the *Priest* was responsible for the temple. His family had overseen the temple for three generations and he was proud of this. He liked to give me tea on holy days and he would tell me old stories and recount the history of the temple. In several ways he and the Carpenter were opposites.

The Priest spoke with great hesitation and uncertainty in his voice. Though he smiled most of the day, he would shut his mouth whenever he heard a joke. He would look puzzled, unable to grasp what was so funny. But that just made any joke even funnier, and the Priest would become even more puzzled.

My talks with the Tailor seldom consisted of more than "*Namaste*," but for some reason he was my favorite. I never knew his name; the villagers called him just *Damaai*—the Tailor. We were all addressed by our stations in life rather than by our names: Aamaa, Shop Keeper, Younger Sister, and Teacher. Damaais were of the lowest occupational caste and the Tailor associated with the Newars only when it involved his work. He wasn't local. He had just popped into the village one day and had moved his wife and daughters into an abandoned house. They had few possessions: some blankets, a few cooking pots, and their precious hand-crank sewing machine. The Tailor was very dark, extremely thin, and incredibly tall. He was a good deal taller than I was, and that made him a true Goliath by Nepali standards. Our great heights in a Lilliputian world were our private joke and he smiled from ear to ear whenever we met.

The Tailor never stood straight up; he walked with his knees bent. This gave him a strange gait and I wondered if something was wrong with his legs. I passed his house going to and from school each day and I often lingered to watch him work. He sat on a mat, with his body hunched over the sewing machine and his long legs awkwardly folded. He took measurements by sight and he used no patterns. He sewed and cut at the same time, never taking the cloth from the machine until the article was finished. He could make anything and he never wasted cloth. But no matter how skilled he was, he was just a Damaai, and he earned only a few rupees per frock or shirt. I saw him twice a day and he always stopped his work and raised his long hands to his forehead. A magnificent smile would spread across his face, and we would say "*Namaste*" in unison. These were moments of true friendship.

I talked with only a few of the many porters who passed through

Aiselukharka, but besides the man who had carried my mattress from Lamidada, I met one who had a very distinctive charm. In February, the school was performing a pujaa in honor of Sarasvati, the goddess of wisdom and learning. As we began preparing for the afternoon feast, a middle-aged woman walked in bearing a large pack-basket filled with seto mulaa. She was a Tamang, from one of the Buddhist tribes akin to Sherpas. Her feet were bare, but her wrists and ankles were encased in heavy brass rings. She wore a long cloth wrapped around her as a skirt, and her hair was braided with red yarn and tied across the top of her head. She refused to put down her load of mulaa until she had seen the teacher who had paid for it the day before. We asked her, "Which teacher was it? What was his name?"

"I don't know," she said, "but he wasn't any of you."

We laughed and told her to give us the mulaa.

"No," she insisted. "You didn't buy it, so you shan't have it." She had to give it to the right one.

Another teacher came, but it wasn't him either. We respected her for protecting goods that had been sold to someone else, but we needed to start the mulaa cooking. *Ke garne?* More teachers arrived, but none of them was the right one. As we tried to figure out who the teacher was, the Tamang lady smiled serenely with the basket resting against her back and the leather naamlo pulling across her forehead. Porters were rarely in the limelight, but when they were, they made the most of it. I thought she looked extremely lovely. Prakash, the third grade teacher, walked in and she shook her head. "That's not him."

"It's not me what?" asked Prakash.

"It wasn't you who bought the mulaa," we explained.

"What do you mean?" he said as he turned to the lady. "Don't you remember? I paid you for the mulaa yesterday."

He *was* the right teacher, but she hadn't recognized him. We all burst into laughter. The Carpenter nearly fell to the ground in mirth and the Priest looked around in search of the joke. The Thamang lady put down her basket

214

and laughed as loudly as any of us. She was delighted to be the focus of a gag. And perhaps she was also happy to be relieved of her load.

Thomas drops his pack next to mine. Already I've been sitting here for two hours, but now Thomas needs a rest. We look across the canyon at Island Peak, which stands slightly above the intermediate summits.

With worries about the softness of the snow, we start across the glacier. A slight track is marked by an off-white color. This is where the group with the yaks must have crossed. The path is flush with the surface of the glacier, but it's firm and walkable. A step to the side plunges us into hip-deep snow. Moving over the nearly invisible track gives us the sensation of walking on water. The top continually recedes, and Thomas lags behind.

At 17,782 feet, the crest of the Chikim La, the glacier abruptly ends. The route down is a steep drop of scree and rock. I wish to wait for Thomas, but the wind chills me and I begin the descent alone. The rocks are all loose and as I scrape my way down, a triangular chunk of leather breaks off my right boot.

At a slight leveling, I stop to take out my map and binoculars. Just north of here are the two peaks of Kangchung Himal, 20,023 feet and 19,977 feet. The afternoon wind drives clouds between the two summits, making them appear both frightening and irresistible. My whole attention is drawn to the higher peak. The glacier leading up to the col will be the hard part. I ponder which will be best—a route up the middle or along the right flank? Both seem dangerous... but who cares?

Thomas joins me and I tell him my decision to climb Kangchung. We agree to meet in Gokyo in three days or in Namche in five days. We have only one map, so we discuss his route down to the next village and he wishes me good luck.

By evening, my solitary tent rests on a patch of frozen ground a mile or so south of Kangchung Himal.

Nyimaganoa Camp
17,300 feet

I lie contentedly in my sleeping bag as the morning sun warms the tent. I can't understand why I was irritated with Thomas. The high peaks surround me like fingers and I doze in the palm of the Himalayas. In my mind's eye, I fly up and over the mountains: ice-covered freedom. *Nyimaganoa,* it says on the map, but I have no idea what it means.

I move my camp a half-mile, to the foot of the glacier. It's a rough business, plowing through thigh-deep snow, lunging forward, trying to hop from one island of rock to the next without sinking. A 100-yard stretch takes nearly an hour. My hopes of getting a better look at the peak are thwarted by the clouds. My route is still uncertain.

The tent, looking like a giant green beetle, now sits on a frozen mud flat just above a lake of ice. Lethargy keeps me from doing the important repairs on my boots. I'll be wearing overboots, so it doesn't really matter.

I melt snow for water and I eat leisurely. At dusk the clouds open, giving a glimpse of the glacier above—tottering ice blocks and threatening crevasses. It's no place for a solo climber.

The last rays of light strike the clouds over the Chikim La. Clouds of orange, red, and blue mix to form purple and deepen into night. After a last look, I zip the tent closed and sleep.

April 13

Kangchung Himal Camp
17,700 feet

Bebeep, bebeep... My watch alarm sounds from the side-wall pocket. At 3.30 a.m., it's cold and dark. Wind shakes the tent, but it's not strong enough to worry about. I light the stove in the vestibule and it goes to work warming the tent and melting the snow that I collected last night. As the temperature rises, so does my activity: stuffing odds and ends into my pack, eating granola with warm milk, melting more snow to carry on the ascent, pulling on my thick socks, and finally lacing up my boots. All this takes one and a quarter hours and I'm soon moving up the glacier...

I plunge my ice axe into the slope and lean forward for a short rest. I'm already halfway to the col. I've opted for the route up the right side and it's been a good choice. So far I've met only step-over crevasses. My plan is to traverse to the center of the glacier just below the section of ice blocks.

I continue up and step over another crevasse. I dismiss the ever-present danger of falling into a crevasse that's concealed by snow. The climbing is pleasant. The surface of the glacier is firm and my crampons bite securely with each step. I encounter only small patches of hard ice. A few small clouds hang over the Chikim La and the wind has stopped.

Suddenly I see a movement and I jerk my head up. An ice block the size of two railroad cars slowly topples over. It picks up speed and the sound comes a moment later—a deep groan and crunch, like a train crash in slow motion. The falling ice creates its own wind and a cloud of snow billows up.

I'm directly below the avalanche, but where should I go? I have the crazy notion that I can dodge whatever comes my way—like dodging a tidal wave? The falling ice consumes everything in its path.

As I realize the hopelessness of my situation, the entire avalanche begins to sink, plunging into a chasm just above my proposed traverse. Ice missiles the size of footballs whizz by, but only the smallest pieces hit me. The glacier shakes and grumbles as the ice drops into its bowels. I'm awed and intimidated.

With nowhere to go but up, I continue climbing. Just below the scene of the avalanche is a ramp leading to the left, toward the center of the glacier. It gives me some tense moments. I move swiftly along a line of ice blocks and I stop to rest when I'm above the ice fall.

From the top of the col, I look down on the Gyubanare Glacier and across to Tibet 4 miles distant. The east summit of Kangchung looms 1,500 feet above. The face is steep and featureless, so I contour around the col towards the north ridge. The pointed summit looks broken at the very top and I'm unenthusiastic about making another nearly complete climb, like the ascent of Island Peak.

The north ridge is steeper than I had expected, and I'm soon stopped by a crevasse. I traverse to the right, climbing far across the face before I can skirt around it. Instead of returning to the ridge, I proceed straight up, using the inside points of my crampons and the pick of my ice axe. The angle is severe, and I feel very exposed.

Another crevasse divides the face. It's bottomless and its sides taper in a deep, cold blue. Because of the steep slope, the crevasse's near edge forms an acute angle and its far edge is almost directly above. I could balance on the near edge, step over the crevasse, and continue on the face above. But if I slip, the game is over. I decide to traverse around this one too. I hold the lip of the crevasse like a guard rail, and keeping my right hand on the axe, I confidently begin. After two steps, I FALL!! My body pendulums across the ice and my feet swing through the air. Suddenly I'm hanging by my arms, one hand holding the lip of ice and the other hand clutching the axe. I kick in my front points and pull myself up. I regain my footing, but not my confidence. I had slipped. *Slipped?* I stand motionless for five minutes, pondering the steep ice and my near fall to oblivion. Reluctantly I start down. Slowly. Descending the slope is awkward, and I'm acutely aware of the exposure.

Back on the col, I eat a chocolate bar while I assess the prospects. The west peak looks easier. Its summit is 46 feet lower than the east peak, putting it just under 20,000 feet, but it's certainly a challenge. I'll be pressed for time, and I warn myself to start down by 1.30 or risk losing my way in the dark.

I recross the col and start up the steepening and narrowing ridge of the west peak. My progress is good and I encounter no crevasses. After an hour of steep climbing, the ridge narrows to an arête of ice too thin to stand on. I straddle it with a leg on each side, like a child trying to slide up a banister. There must be a better way.

Passing this, the ridge broadens and then ends in a magnificent rock cliff. Removing my crampons and overboots, I scramble down and around. As I climb along the bottom of the cliff, I spot a route of descent that would circumvent a return to the glacier. I'll have to find just the right rock chute; the others all terminate in cliffs.

Back on the ridge proper, I look up at the apparent summit, but remembering the view from the col, I know that it's just a leveling of the ridge. The deep snow makes for hard climbing, but this is offset by the sight of Everest rising far above the other peaks. The Chinese northwest face is completely exposed.

Reaching the false summit at 1.15, I eat another chocolate bar and take the day's first squat-down rest. With wool gloves and nylon over-mitts off, I photograph Everest and then change the film before resuming the climb. The ridge is less steep than further down, but the softer snow is exhausting. My time limit expires and I have no thoughts of turning back.

Keeping clear of a cornice, I slog higher and see the end. It's not the summit, just the end. The route is blocked by a crevasse and an overhanging wall of ice. The crevasse ends to the left and is replaced by a drop of vertical ice—broken and dangerous. The crevasse continues to the right, though the slope on the far side is climbable. I could jump it, but the lip is undercut and unstable. I look back and forth between the possibilities, each becoming more frightful with every glance.

Impulsively I start to the left, committing myself before my growing fear forces me down. I traverse directly out and around, cursing myself for not taking a rest before beginning; I'm already worn out. The ice is bad and I try not to look down. With each step, pieces of ice break loose and hurl themselves down the face. I reach the point from which I hope to climb up and regain the crest of the ridge. With laborious swings of the axe, I chop out a shelf that gives me a space to stand with both feet while I catch my breath. The ridge top is only a short ways, but from here up the ice is all hard and fragmented.

Standing on the pseudo-security of my little ledge, I hack out the first eight steps and then begin up. As I move higher and become more tired, the steps I cut become smaller and more precarious. The chipped-out pieces of ice fall away noiselessly. I forgo chopping holds on the final 6 feet, and decide to use the last of my strength to pull myself onto the crest. My lungs pump for oxygen as I stand in my topmost steps. I jab the pick of the axe into the ice on the top, then, praying that it'll hold, I pull up. My hands clutch the axe and my feet tiptoe higher, till I can swing my right leg over the crest and onto the snow of the far side. Except there is no far side; my leg finds nothing!

I have climbed the side of a wafer of ice and I kneel on the edge, which is just wide enough for my two knees. My hands still cling to the axe, but my body slides down the arête as it crumbles beneath my weight. It will hold only minutes longer and I know it's the end. They'll find my tent and nothing more. *Ke garne?*

Damn it, Phil, climb! I try to pull myself up the arête, but nothing happens. I'm physically done in and I'm terrified of breaking away more ice. *Pull, damn it. Pull!!* This time I manage to shift my knees a bit. A section of ice falls to the right. Again I pull, bringing my knees up to my hands. This amount of progress lessens my fear, though I still crouch like a child. I gingerly kick in my front points, one foot at a time, then I pull out the axe and drive it in further along. I creep and pull, bringing myself up to the axe, and in this way—like an inchworm—I move along the arête.

Further up, the ice widens and becomes more stable. I stand, and continue upward towards the summit.

Again in heavy snow, I step to the top of a rise and look around. The mountain has another lump some distance further, but this one seems higher. I'm on the summit, so I do what's expected of me. Setting the camera with the self-timer, I sit in the snow and the shutter clicks.

Elsewhere in the world, a 19,977-foot peak would be an important mountain, but here it's insignificant. This is possibly Kangchung West's first ascent, and certainly its first solo ascent. I feel no elation, only numbness and exhaustion. I look at my watch, but I don't see the time. I only know that it's late—too late to get back in the light. I don't even know *how* I'll get down. It doesn't really matter. I wonder why I didn't fall back there. One of those peaks to the north must be Cho Oyu, but Everest is truncated by the clouds.

I stay ten minutes and start down, toward the east face. I don't think or ponder over this decision; I just go. The face is very steep, but the snow is soft. I climb facing out by kicking backwards with my heels to make steps. I'll descend the face to the col and then return to camp. *In the dark? Down a crevassed glacier?* Maybe I'll dig in for the night.

Not expecting to make it, I lower myself one step at a time, down and down. The slope worsens, giving a scary view toward the Gyubanare Glacier. I'm stopped by a rocky band of cliffs and I'm forced to traverse to my right, toward my ascent route. The entire face is vertically corrugated into mammoth waves, so every 10 yards I must claw my way through and around a crest of ice. I take no time to be careful. What difference does it make? It's just a matter of falling rather than freezing. I promise myself that I'll never climb solo again.

My full attention is focused on stepping and balancing, and I'm startled to find tracks in the snow. It's the false summit where I ate a chocolate bar a lifetime ago.

A reassuring line of tracks points the way home. I follow, cautiously now, hoping to find that rock chute that I spotted on the way up. I pause only once—taking off my snow goggles to better see those faint, encouraging ice-axe holes and crampon marks. Despite this, I lose my way in the growing clouds and darkness. I try to stay in the light areas that mean snow and away from the dark ones that mean rock as I head down the south buttress in the general direction of camp.

I saunter dreamily down the middle of a tributary glacier that I suspect to be close to the bottom. I'm abruptly awakened when a large section of ice drops a meter beneath me. Unhurt, I climb to the moraine and away from the danger. Looking over the moraine's crest, I see the small frozen lake where my tent stands. I skirt the shore and reach camp under a starless sky.

April 14

Kangchung Himal Camp
17,700 feet

I wake to find the tent coated with a layer of fresh snow. Eating and packing consume three hours. At this altitude little chores become real work.

On Kangchung's long southern ridge is a notch that should give me a direct route to Gokyo. I fight through the soft snow to the notch at 18,000 feet and I am relieved to see that the way down the other side is steep and rocky, but climbable. I eat lunch and look up at Kangchung. I remember my promise to never climb solo again. I'll be crossing the Tasi Lapcha Pass with Thomas and a porter, so the promise will be kept. As I look at Kangchung in perspective, I feel uneasy, unsatisfied. But unsatisfied about what? I went to my limits and beyond, doing everything but get myself killed. I should accept this feeling of unfulfillment. It's surely what makes us seek higher mountains to climb.

The downward route is 2,000 feet of rocks and boulders, scrambling and sliding. My boots continue to disintegrate. At the bottom I must cross the kilometer-wide Ngozumpa Glacier. Its surface is sun-sculpted into hills and valleys and is covered with loose rock. I swear that I can hear the music of Radio Nepal being played in Gokyo. For two frustrating hours, I backtrack up and down searching for a way through the maze. The lateral moraine at the far side is a steep wall of sliding gravel and I'm done in when I reach the top. The craggy huts of Gokyo look very inviting.

I'm anxious to tell Thomas about Kangchung West. *"Ma mero saathi khojdaichhu*—I'm looking for my friend,"* I tell a Sherpa woman. She looks at me inquisitively and I explain, "He came the day before yesterday. Very tall, with curly hair."

"Ah!" she grins with her crooked teeth. "Frenchman, isn't he? Yes, over there!" She points to a row of orange tents.

"No, no. He's a Swissman and he came alone."

An older woman emerges from the hut's dark doorway. Her teeth have the same irregular pattern—they are probably mother and daughter. She's been listening. "Yes, your friend," she says with conviction, "he came yesterday. Speaks Nepali…"

"No, he doesn't speak Nepali. He…" I cut myself short, realizing that she has no idea who my friend is. I check the other huts for places to sleep and signs of Thomas. I eventually learn that Thomas left for Namche this morning. He must be tired of Sherpa food.

The only vacant place to sleep is atop a yard-long box of potatoes. "I'm too tall," I say with a shake of my head and the Sherpas laugh. I erect the tent begrudgingly; I had been hoping to sleep indoors.

As the night deepens and the cold strengthens, I sit wedged between two Germans in the smoky hut. We warm our dank stocking-clad feet by the fire. Another European walks in and says to the younger of the two crooked-teethed women, "*Ai, Didi, ek glas chang dinus na*—Hey, Didi, please give me a glass of *chang*, OK?"

I strain my eyes to see who this is speaking Nepali. He's no Peace Corps Volunteer that I've seen before. Then I recognize his horn-rimmed glasses and long square jaw. "Richard, is that you?" I call to him. He's an American anthropologist who's studying the Rai ethnic groups for his doctorate thesis. Richard squeezes himself into the corner and nurses his cup of chang—a Himalayan beer brewed from a mash of fermented rice. It's a white viscous drink that always looks ready to solidify. I don't drink it, but all the Sherpas in the hut slurp steaming cups full.

"Richard, what are you doing here?" I ask. "I thought you were living far south of here."

"Yes, I was," he says between draughts of chang, "but I'm also researching trade routes. I came with a group of Rai porters who bring goods to the Saturday market in Namche. Once I was that far, I thought to come to Gokyo and see Everest. But *aai*, it's certainly cold!"

We talk of his work, and I tell him the full story of my trip till now. Richard isn't a climber, but he acts interested and I'm grateful for his attention. As I get up to face the cold outside, I suddenly remember something. "You said you've seen Klaus? How are the rabbits? Did you see the rabbits?"

"Yes. They look big and fat. Klaus takes them out every day to munch on the grass behind his house. He's like a proud papa."

April 15
Gokyo 15,720 feet

In the tent's half-light, I carefully push the needle through the leather. I've already broken two needles and I can't afford to lose a third. The work is tedious and I repair only the boots' most impressive holes. They looked good when I bought them secondhand in Kathmandu, but the leather must have been rotten. Fortunately the cracks breach only the outer layers of leather.

Evening finds me holding a cup of Sherpa tea and sitting by the fire. Richard sips chang and we discuss politics. "I wonder if it'll make any difference who wins the referendum," I say. "It's only an advisory thing. The King can still do whatever he wants."

"Yes, but if the Panchaayat System wins and still no changes are made, there will be big problems in the east. The people have been riled up since last year..."

The problems had actually been building for over two decades. The domination of the King, no matter how benevolent it happened to be, was still totalitarian. If a group of people are discontented, they will always hold the government accountable. It began in 1951 when a bloodless revolution overthrew the century-long rule of the repressive Rana family. The King reclaimed governmental power, opened Nepal's borders for the first time, established schools, and introduced limited democracy. The country was flooded with Western ideas and an educated class was born. This group of intellectuals soon developed a hunger for opportunities and commodities that Nepal could not provide. Their dissatisfaction steadily increased.

In the villages, though, the people were concerned about simpler things: the crops, their children, and the weather. Up in Aiselukharka I was far from any political tensions, and I too dwelled on other matters. I had suddenly become superfluous.

Three new NDS teachers had just come to do a year's service in Aiselukharka. Their postings were supposedly chosen at random, but the new teachers were all Newari women from Kathmandu, the same as their predecessors. That was well enough; the problem was that they were all three qualified to teach math and science. And since a second science teacher had come at the end of the previous year, I was now one of five math/science teachers. The school didn't have enough classes for us all. The Headmaster asked if I would like to teach fewer classes, but I refused. I would have been bored without a full teaching schedule. What the hell was my purpose there? Prior to this, I had felt almost self-righteous when I had considered the good that I was doing for the school, but now it made no difference if I was there or not—there were *three* other teachers ready to do my job. I became depressed, so to boost my spirits, I made plans for extra projects that I would do in the village.

Meanwhile, down in the capital, the dissatisfaction of the educated class burst forth. The spark was a seemingly unrelated event. On April 4 and 1,000 miles away, Zulfikar Ali Bhutto, the former president of Pakistan, was executed for complicity in a political murder. The world was outraged. Bhutto had been a highly respected Third World leader, and the university students in Kathmandu staged a demonstration of protest. Their goals seemed unclear, but during the course of their demonstrations, they realized that they had considerable power if they formed a united front. The college students went on strike across the country and their leaders wrote a list of demands. Among other things, they pressed for a reduction of tuition fees, the elimination of college entrance exams, and a lowering of the minimum passing grade from 40 per cent to 33 per cent.

Some of the students became violent and threatened to ravage shops if the city merchants didn't join the strike. Many discontented Nepalis, such as unsuccessful businessmen and my friend the economist who worked in a pie shop, joined the disturbances. It grew into a movement and they next made political demands. They wanted a true democracy with a multi-party political system. The present one-party Panchaayat System had to go, and the monarchy itself was under attack.

Up in Aiselukharka, we didn't understand the grievances behind the disturbances in the city. Most of the villagers *liked* the Panchaayat System. It was a type of tiered democracy. *Panchaayat* means literally a council of five, but a Panchaayat could have any number of members—five was just an extremely auspicious number. At the local level came the Village Panchaayat, a council elected by the adults of the community. In our case, the Village Panchaayat was elected from Nawalpur and Aiselukharka combined. The head of the Village Panchaayat was the Pradhaan Panch and the Panchaayat members elected representatives to the District Panchaayat. Then the District Panchaayat elected representatives to the Zonal Panchaayat, and so on up to the National Panchaayat. The people had no direct voice in choosing the members of the National Panchaayat, which was perhaps a good thing. The average villager knew little of national and international affairs. A country-wide election would have to emphasize national issues like Indian trade restrictions and the use of foreign aid. For most farmers, such matters were irrelevant. An election for them was a simple matter of voting for the most respected and popular men in the village. This was a good criterion at the village level, but even these local elections were plagued with difficulties. The previous year, I had read the following article in my weekly *Nepal Press Digest*:

ELECTIONS

According to an RSS report: "Nearly 75 per cent of the votes cast in village and town-level elections in the Mahakali and Janakpur zones have been found to be

invalid. In one village Panchaayat of Darchula district,
a candidate who had secured 34 votes was declared
defeated because only eight votes were found to be valid,
whereas his rival, in whose favor only eleven votes had
been cast, was declared elected, only one vote having
been found to be invalid. There was confusion also about
election symbols. Voters in the Tarai areas could not
identify a spade. A plow was mistaken for an umbrella,
an eye for the sun, and a maize-pod for a butterfly. In
Sarlahi district, some voters who wanted to affix marks on
the symbol of 'eye' did so on their own eye."

The Election Commission expressed surprise at the report and maintained that it was itself not in a position to indicate what percentage of votes had been found to be invalid. A press note published by the Commission in this connection added, "The same system of secret ballot has been followed in the current election as in the past... Symbols have been used because most of the voters are illiterate... the Election Commission has affixed posters at different places indicating the correct method of marking ballot-papers."*

I felt that Nepal was unprepared for a true democracy, but many people in the cities disagreed. In Aiselukharka we heard tales of riots and widespread strikes. Radio Nepal broadcast reports of skirmishes and unrest, but the BBC announced that hundreds had been killed in clashes and that innumerable people had been arrested. I thought the truth lay somewhere between these two extremes. *Newsweek* devoted a full page to the disturbances, but the Nepali government banned that issue. We heard a rumor that Durga, who was attending teacher's training in Kathmandu, had been arrested. Krishna Bhakta, the Pradhaan Panch, the teachers, and a few others in the village closely followed the political maneuvering, but the majority of the villagers were unconcerned with it all. Kathmandu was a foreign country to them. When they referred to a journey to Kathmandu, they said, "*Nepal jaane*—I'm going to Nepal." Nepal meant Kathmandu; Aiselukharka was their home, not Nepal.

---

* From the *Nepal Press Digest*, Vol. 22, No. 13, Kathmandu, March 27, 1, as translated from the Gorkhapatra, March 19 & 21, 1978.

Throughout the spring, the problems intensified and even the villagers became concerned when the protests focused on the King. The present King, thirty-four-year-old Birendra Bir Bikram Shah Dev, was venerated as the incarnation of Vishnu. Both the constitution and the general public deemed him to *be* the government of Nepal. I heard schoolchildren chant, "The name of our government is Birendra." Color photographs of the King and Queen hung in all public buildings and in many private homes. At the start of every school program, the framed portraits of His and Her Royal Majesties were brought out to be honored with a pujaa and draped with flower garlands.

I felt that the monarchy was a good government for Nepal. The country could not afford the inefficiency of a fluctuating democracy. Fortunately, the present King happened to be a good one. He had been educated at the University of Tokyo and at Harvard, and since the death of his father, King Mahendra, in 1972, he had steered the country down a middle course that had convinced the world's powers to give Nepal considerable foreign aid. High on the list of donors were India, the U.S.A., China, the Soviet Union, the United Kingdom, and Japan. Over half of the national development budget was supplied from external sources and the King wisely used the funds to develop education, transportation, and health services rather than to expand the army or to complete showy projects. In regard to being a God, King Birendra was asked the following in a written interview:

Q. How do you feel about being looked upon as a God?
A. It is not a question of how I feel about it. These are local
   customs and traditions. This relates to our religious background.
   I have the responsibility (under the Vedic scriptures) to protect
   the people against injustice. The concept of God is there among
   the people.*

---

* From *An Introduction to Nepal* by Rishikesh Shaha, 1975, Ratna Pustak Bhandar, Publisher.

King Birendra also stated that "the King embodies the collective identity of the people." Lately, however, that identity had been changing. The college NDS system had teachers working throughout the country and they were efficient conduits for spreading the unrest. All the college campuses and many of the high schools were on strike. A number of Peace Corps teachers left their villages and assembled in Kathmandu. The King eventually appointed a new Prime Minister, requested the resignation of the Minister of Education, and accepted many of the students' educational demands. Only the loss of the Minister of Education would have an impact on Aiselukharka. Our classes continued as usual.

A representative from the dissenters came to the school to persuade us to strike. The Headmaster kept him away from the students, and when he was allowed to talk to the teachers, his words were heard with interest but without response. He left defeated; we felt that our purpose was to teach, not to strike for political change.

Even though many of the students in Kathmandu were mollified by the King's educational reforms, they next focused their resources on a single issue of wide appeal—political freedom. The partyless Panchaayat System prohibited the formation of political action groups. Dissent was permitted, but not by organized bodies. When the students and intellectuals had originally gone on strike and had bullied the shopkeepers into following suit, scores of outlawed political parties had sprung up. Now the full force of the movement centered on the right to form political organizations. King Birendra responded with a call for a national referendum to decide between continuing with the Partyless Panchaayat System or switching to a new system that would include political parties. The protest movement transferred its energies away from general disruption and began to campaign for the defeat of the Panchaayat System.

Things slowly returned to normal, and the King decided to minimize further unrest by disbanding the NDS. The college students who had incited the disturbances in the far-flung villages were called back to the towns, and the strikes in the rural high schools ended. The loss of our lady science teachers put me back in a needed position, but the school was once more short of teachers. I would have little time for special projects after all.

The country soon split into pro-Panchaayat and anti-Panchaayat factions, and for many people it became a matter of those who were pro-King and those who were anti-King. When asked which side they would vote for, many responded, "I will vote for the King, of course!" They missed the point of the referendum. My friends in Aiselukharka were in favor of political parties, but I avoided talking with them about it. Peace Corps policy was to steer clear of political disputes.

Some of the villagers were extremely vocal about their beliefs, while most everyone was just relieved that the cities were calm again. They all hoped to be on the winning side when normality resumed. Few would have guessed that logistic problems would delay the referendum for a full year.

Richard and I sit in the smoky hut and mull over the future of Nepali politics.

"I wonder which side will win," I say as I rub the dirty skin off my hands.

"It's difficult to guess," says Richard. "Kathmandu is full of banners and the roads are painted with political graffiti. The mood is very tense."

"I hope that the anti-Panchaayat wins. They were the ones causing all the trouble. If they lose, they'll make problems much worse than last year."

"Well, there's nothing we can do," he replies. "*Ke garne?* We'll know in a few weeks."*

---

* The referendum was duly held on May 2 1980, and the results were announced two weeks later. The Partyless Panchaayat System won in all districts with an overall vote of 54.8 per cent. The anti-Panchaayat movement quickly protested the results, but they had little following. In a major concession, King Birendra proclaimed that the Prime Ministership would become an elected position. The attitude of the anti-Panchaayat faction seemed to be that full democracy would eventually come, but that it would require a few more years of work.

April 16
Gokyo Kang 17,600 feet

The rocky knoll juts 2,000 feet above Gokyo. The view of Everest, as advertised, is fantastic. I share the windy crest with a group of French tourists—red knee socks and movie cameras. The morning light shines on Kangchung West and I study its summit with binoculars. The right lump of snow, the one that I climbed, looks a shade lower than the left lump. A German says that he can't see a difference, and I wait for Richard to arrive with his verdict.

He comes up huffing. "The one on the left looks slightly higher to me," he says. I scratch my head sadly, but Richard can't understand my disappointment. "Tell yourself that the other is higher, if that's what you want," he suggests.

"No. I want to *know* that I climbed the higher."

"How much might the difference be?"

"Maybe a couple of meters."

Richard shakes his head mockingly. He has a point—the depth of the snow varies by more than 2 meters.

"It's a matter of aesthetics," I explain. "Of vanity," I confess.

We return to Gokyo and pack for the two-day trip to Namche. Throughout the afternoon, we stride easily downhill and we cover an amazing distance. It's so easy to walk on a trail! We come around a corner and I stop short. It's green! A tiny patch of meadow bristles with new shoots of grass. After three weeks totally engulfed in rock and ice, anything green looks like a vision. Each blade grows with a full life of its own. Spring has climbed the slopes during my time up high.

Below the 14,000-foot level, we encounter scraggly dwarf trees. We stop for a rest and I look fondly at the stunted pines. Their roots grip the rocks and their branches are twisted with the prevailing winds. I wonder about the growth of my own trees.

"*Malaai taar chaahinchha*—I need some wire," I told the topi-capped man at the construction warehouse. We went through his stock and picked out the type I needed—medium-weight steel wire, an eighth of an inch thick, strong but workable. "*Raamro.* Good. I want a thousand feet."

"A *thousand* feet!?" The warehouse clerk pulled his tongue back into his mouth and then measured out the wire by counting the loops in the coil. He calculated the price according to its weight, and the bill for both the wire and a pair of heavy pliers came to just over 200 rupees—the full amount of my Peace Corps special project allowance. The Peace Corps was designed to provide expertise, *not* materials. We were allotted 200 rupees, about $16, to do a project and anything over that amount came from our own pockets.

I had come to Kathmandu to get my gamma globulin shot, cash a check, have a cavity filled, and buy the wire. I shipped it to Chautara by jeep and then had it portered to Aiselukharka along with a supply of farming tools for the school's expanding agriculture program.

The arrival of a 3-foot-wide coil of wire caused a stir. I had talked over the idea with many of the villagers, but only now did they realize that I was serious. My plan was to plant trees and to protect them against hungry goats and cows with fences of wired-together bamboo. The site of the future trees was important and I took each of my classes there for a talk.

We stood on the slope above the dhaaraa. The hillside formed a bowl-shaped basin, and the dhaaraa's only source was this tiny watershed. The slope was dotted with a dozen century-old shade trees, but I could count the spots where a dozen more had once stood. They had been cut for lumber

234

to build the new classrooms and the student hostel. Even the stumps had been chipped away for firewood. A few goats and sheep grazed beneath the remaining trees while a woman filled her water jug at the dhaaraa.

I looked at the eager faces of the seventh-grade students as they gathered around to hear why I had brought them there. "Who remembers how this was three years ago?" I asked. They looked at one another and said nothing. "Were there more trees here?"

"Yes, yes," said one of the local boys. "So many trees were here that it was dark in the daytime. Now they are gone."

"And did the dhaaraa have more water?"

"Oh, yes, Sir. We had much water all year, but now very little comes."

"Why is that?" I asked. "Trees drink water, don't they? After the trees are gone, shouldn't more water come? Isn't that so? But now the trees are gone and there comes less water. Why is that?"

One boy, who carried a coin stuck in his ear, suggested, "It rains longer where many trees grow." But his classmates shushed him with the wisdom that "it's only the dripping leaves that makes it rain longer."

The class made no other guesses, so I kneeled on the ground and dug my fingers into the dirt. I explained the basics of ground-water retention and I described how tree roots and forest cover are important for water absorption. I told it all simply, but only a few of the students could really grasp it. The rest of the class preferred my second explanation: "If we have no trees, the sun shines very hard and then what happens?"

"*Sukchha!* It dries up!" the class shouted.

"*Hunchha,*" I agreed. "If it dries up, no water comes for the dhaaraa. So we need to plant new trees. But what happens if we plant them just like that, without doing anything?"

"The animals eat the trees," said a boy.

"Yes, yes," said another, "the goats and the cows."

"And water buffalo and sheep."

"And chickens."

"Hunchha? And chickens? They eat seeds, but not small trees." We discussed the necessity of protecting the trees with fences. The students all agreed to help, though none of us realized how much work it would be.

A forestry expert came from Chautara and showed us a way to prepare the planting sites a month in advance. First, we dug a narrow, 2-foot-deep hole. Then we scraped up all the dead leaves and twigs from a 3-foot radius and crunched them into the hole as mulch. This would give the trees a soft, fertilized bed in which to grow. This would also make a good science lesson. The expert began to pace out the area to mark planting sites at 6-foot intervals, and he was saddened when I told him that we couldn't fence so many trees.

One day after school, a couple of dozen students and I chose sixty spots for the trees. We borrowed hand shovels from my neighbors and we set to work digging the holes. Only the students who were highly motivated and who lived near Aiselukharka came to help. The digging was much work because of the hard ground, old roots, and numerous rocks. I groveled in the dirt along with the students, and I scurried about measuring the depths of the holes and joking in the few words of Newari and Thamang that I had learned. We needed a second day to finish the holes and afterwards we ate packaged Nebiko biscuits from Shyam Krishna's store.

Next came the matter of the bamboo. Krishna Bhakta and I discussed how high the fencing would need to be and how far apart the pickets could be placed. Fifteen posts, in a circle 18 inches in diameter, and hip-high would do it. In math class we calculated how much bamboo and wire would be needed. The students were surprised to find that their math had some practical use.

Getting the bamboo was like pulling teeth. Due to the lack of water, Aiselukharka had no bamboo of its own and we had to beg for it from the surrounding villages. Either Krishna Bhakta or the Pradhaan Panch came with me on these 6 a.m. forages—we had to talk with the farmers before they went to work in the fields. Each precious cluster of bamboo grew on private

236

land and the owners begrudged parting with it. Krishna Bhakta was adept at persuasion. He never mentioned that we were planting the trees for the dhaaraa. He realized that Aiselukharka's water problem was unimportant to men living in Nawalpur, Gupha, or the further villages. He talked instead about the schoolchildren needing to learn to plant trees.

The farmer stood with his arms crossed and Krishna Bhakta offered him a cigarette, saying, "The bamboo can be your personal donation to our Philipsir. He's just like us, not a *thulo maanchhe*—big man—like the stuck-up officials in Chautara." The farmer looked at my rubber sandals and agreed. Next we discussed which bamboo stalk or stalks to cut. Krishna Bhakta proffered more cigarettes and cajoled the man into letting us have a good tall one. Two of my students brandished their kukuris and down it crashed.

One man couldn't give us any bamboo because his brother had died three days before. He and everything he owned were jutho for a total of ten days, so we would have to come back in a week. He also told me that bamboo could only be felled on certain days of the week. If cut on an improper day, it would warp and rot too quickly.

Throughout May, we spent our mornings searching out bamboo, and our afternoons carrying it back to the house where the students cut it into lengths and split it. The green bamboo trees, some of them 8 inches across and 40 feet long, were extremely heavy. A half-dozen unenthused students were needed to carry each one along the steep winding trails. The task was even more difficult when I couldn't find the exact spot where we had cut the bamboo that morning. I easily went the wrong way through the maze of small paths and terraces, and the students would laugh; they knew every rock and bend by heart. The only time I could do my school work was at night by my lamp. I was busy every moment and it was one of the happiest times I spent in Nepal.

The bamboo mounted, but the number we needed was staggering. Each of the sixty circular fences would require fifteen pickets, making a total of

900 bamboo pieces. And I planned on having a minimum of one thousand to account for breakage. Our backyard became filled with bamboo sticks laid out to harden in the sun.

Talk circulated in the village about the trees bringing extra water to the dhaaraa. The Carpenter lent us a small saw for sectioning the bamboo and the Priest offered to do a pujaa to ensure that the trees would grow tall.

Mahendra and Surendra helped me cut the wire into 41/2 foot lengths, which we twisted into rings. Two rings each would form the fences' shape and the bamboo would be held fast with 3-inch pieces of wire. I soon discovered that I had underestimated the amount of wire needed; we would only have enough for fifty trees.

Twisting the rings together was difficult and only the older students who had strong hands could do it. Even though we had two pairs of pliers, I realized that wiring the fences around the young trees would be a long hard job. The trees couldn't be planted until the rains began, and then putting the fences around them would take two weeks, making it well into July before we could finish. But that would be several weeks after the close of school and I needed to be in Kathmandu before then. Krishna Bhakta found the solution.

"Put up the fences now," he said, "but leave a gap for planting the trees later."

Great! We could wire up the fences, leaving out two of the pickets. And when the monsoon began, we could plant the trees through the fence openings. In two afternoons, we pounded all the bamboo pickets into place and lashed the fences together with thin strips of cane. The hillside was now quite impressive. Viewed from a distance, the fifty bamboo fences, rising above the green leaves, looked like a field of white tombstones.

To fasten the strips of bamboo to the wire rings was even harder than I had feared. The job had to be done well so that the fencing would last a minimum of three years. I expected that the trees would need that length of time to grow above the heads of the cows. None of the students were strong enough to cut the short pieces of wire and then twist them around the bamboo strips. And for me to crimp 3,000 ends of wire myself would have taken an eternity. The fairest way would have been to divide the work among all the men of the village, but this was impractical. My method of fastening the bamboo was complicated, and none of the men, except the Carpenter, had used a pair of pliers before. Each worker would have needed a couple of days to get the hang of it.

The easiest solution was to take just two men, let them learn to do the wiring well, and then pay them for their work. This, however, was against my principles. I remembered the Peace Corps slogan, "Helping people to help themselves."* I didn't want it to become a matter of *paying* people to help themselves. I wanted the villagers to be responsible for the project. I wanted them to come away feeling that development depended on their own efforts. But I also wanted the project to be successful. Finally, I hired two men to do the wiring at seven rupees a day. I, too, wired fences, both before and after school, and my bill came to fifty-six rupees. The unfortunate part was that the people of Aiselukharka began referring to it all as "Philipsir's trees." The project had become mine instead of their own. At least the students were learning a lot from it.

The government ran a nursery near Jyaamire, the village where hail had destroyed the wheat, and the Headmaster wrote a requisition to get the trees. I was now ready to fetch them, but all the students, including Mahendra and Surendra, disappeared. I thought that the trip would be fun and I was surprised that the students were so reluctant to go. The reason turned out to be that they all refused to wear pack-baskets. I eventually collared two gullible students and I outfitted them with make-shift Western-style backpacks. The trees were only 6–10 inches high, so along with my big Kelty pack, we were able to carry seventy-six of them in one trip. As we hiked back

---

* The slogan was later changed to "The hardest job you'll ever love," seemingly characteristic of the American emphasis on one's self—a shift from the 1960s altruism to the 1980s egoism.

to Aiselukharka, the two students took off their packs whenever we passed a house. They then carried the packs in their hands, for they were *students* and they didn't want to resemble lowly porters.

The planting beds had been prepared, and the fences were done, and we had the trees. All that remained was to plant the trees and to wire up each remaining pair of bamboo pickets. Throughout the project, I had often been frustrated, feeling that work was done only when I was personally there. But the fact that it was done at all convinced me that I had made points for enterprise and self-help. The *bholi-parsi* and *ke garne* attitudes had been beaten for once.

Yet now, with everything ready, the trees couldn't be planted. The ground was too dry and we had to wait for the pre-monsoon rains. After all our work with the bamboo and the wire, it was ironic to be delayed by the uncontrollable weather. The monsoon was late and the impatient American was helpless. Even Philipsir had to wait and say, *"Ke garne?"*

The trees thicken as Richard and I descend. He leads the way to Dole Village, where he stayed on his way up. I'm content to walk behind and to look at the tiny yellow and blue flowers. The house in Dole is even darker than most. After a full day of hiking, I'm not the least bit tired. This low altitude is delicious.

April 17

Dole Village 13,400 feet

The Didi cooks daal-bhaat, which I hope will be good. Three weeks have passed since I last ate rice. I wait in the sunshine and gaze dreamily at the new greenness. Tiny flowers push upwards and a yak looks pleased as she munches the fresh grass. I close my eyes and lean back with the sun shining on my face.

The sun still shone in Aiselukharka. The monsoon had not yet begun, and until it did, the trees remained unplanted. But in another sense, the late monsoon was a blessing—the new school hostel was lacking a roof.

Work had first begun on the hostel just before I initially arrived in Aiselukharka. The money for its construction came from a government development grant and the labor was done completely by hand. The workers quarried stones from the hillside below the school and mortared them together with a mixture of mud and dung. The building stood two storeys high and had eight large rooms on each floor. If completed, it would have space for one hundred students.

All the hostel now lacked was a roof, and our school construction fund was far short of the amount we needed to build one. If left uncovered, the hostel's mud and stone walls would be easily destroyed by the summer monsoon.

Originally the shortage of funds had not been a worry; the school had friends in high places. The Minister of Education had personally pledged to provide the hostel with a first-class roof of tin (actually corrugated galvanized iron). He had a vested interest in the district: he had bought land there, claimed residency, and been duly elected to the National Panchaayat. He was one of the richest men in Nepal and he had been a great boon to the district, that is, until the recent political upheavals had forced his resignation. Thus ended his pledge of money to roof the hostel.

Krishna Bhakta and I talked over the problem one night in my room. *"Ke garne?"* he said with a note of defeat. "It's June and the rains will soon begin. We still have no roof for the student's hostel and if it sits through the rains it will be broken. We don't have enough money for a roof. What to do?"

"Kati rupiyaa chaahiyo?—How many rupees are needed?" I asked.

"We have ten thousand rupees," he said sadly, "so we need twenty thousand more."

"What about a bank loan?"

"No. The Headmaster tried that."

"Does it have to be a tin roof? Wouldn't a slate roof be cheaper? There's enough slate in the mountainside just two hours away."

"Yes, but it's much work to dig out slate and that too eats money. Also the slate is very heavy and we would need many more wooden beams. It would cost as much as a tin roof."

We had few alternatives and I knew better than to suggest building a thatched roof. Newars made their roofs solely of tile or slate. A tin roof would be a mark of status, but a thatched roof would have been the Nepali cultural equivalent of eating with one's shoes on.

The villagers of Aiselukharka were very proud of the school and the mood was one of helplessness. We could do little to get a roof even though we all understood the importance of the hostel. With only four high schools in the district, some students undertook a daily round-trip walk of four hours in order to study in Aiselukharka. Those who lived further away than that tried to get a place to stay in the village or just didn't come to school. A

242

hostel would allow many more students to attend high school and would save others hours of walking. The Headmaster expected the students to use this saved time for studying, and he assumed that more girls would be sent to school once we had a place for them to stay.

Having a hostel also carried an economic advantage. With more students coming to school, more tuition would be collected. Nepali schools were financially dependent on both student fees and government funds. Schools had been known to close due to a lack of regularly paying students. A high student-teacher ratio was necessary to avoid bankruptcy. How ironic that the hostel, which would bring in revenue, was actually putting the school in debt.

When the student unrest had ousted the Minister of Education, I had begun writing letters in search of a foreign aid organization that could help. At first I had thought that we could get $1,000 through the Peace Corps Partnership Program, but I was told that this was only for projects in which all the labor was voluntary. The people in Aiselukharka had done very little unpaid work on the hostel; after all, it wasn't *their* children who lived far from school.

Then I learned that UNICEF could supply tin for school roofs. While the monsoon was being sluggish in its arrival, I made an emergency trip to the UNICEF office in Kathmandu. I spoke with the man in charge of development projects. He was well-dressed and very British:

"Yes, yes, we furnish rural schools with corrugated roofing material of galvanized steel. We now have some coming from Calcutta. It will arrive in a month or two. You need to submit these applications with the dimensions of the building. You can arrange the portering from the roadhead? Good. It's for the *high school* you say? For the hostel? I see. You understand, of course, that our number one priority is building *primary* schools. Basic literacy is the most important thing, you know. But *we* don't determine the roofing sites. No. That's decided by the local government officials, your

District Education Officer. What district was it? Ah yes, Sindhupalchowk. Your district has an allocation of three roofs per year. That's all correct. We'll be hearing from you? Good."

What he said about the priority going to primary schools upset me. Sindhupalchowk had an abundance of primary-school buildings, and a shortage of primary-school teachers. Where did he think those teachers would come from if the district lacked high schools? Nevertheless, the news of getting the tin through UNICEF was good and I rushed the applications back to Aiselukharka.

Three months might pass before we could get the roofing, and in the meantime the school's construction committee decided to buy large rolls of plastic with the remaining money. The plastic was carried from Kathmandu and a dozen men used bamboo crosspieces to tack it over the roof supports. It would protect the hostel through the monsoon, and then a real roof could be built in the fall.

The clouds soon gathered and the rains began just two days after the plastic roof was completed. This was always a joyous time. The monsoon brought new life to the crops and the forest. Men and women sang as they went to work in the fields.

We planted the trees on an auspicious Wednesday. We danced in

the mud and everyone agreed that the hillside of bamboo-fenced trees was a beautiful sight. We were all happy, but I felt embarrassed to be given the credit.

"A plaque sh-sh-should be erected to Philipsir's tr-trees," suggested Shyam Krishna.

"You'll have a great name in Aiselukharka," said the Priest.

"You must return here when they are very big," said Guru.

Only to this last statement did I agree.

I wired the final two bamboo pickets to each fence, and I left the trees in Krishna Bhakta's care for the summer. I would take a short trek to Gosaikund and I would then spend the two months of the monsoon recess speaking English with my Peace Corps friends. I also hoped to get a letter soon from Kay. Two months had passed since her last letter and I felt certain that something was wrong.

The monsoon soaked me as I hiked out of Aiselukharka. The tree project was finished and the leaves of each young tree glistened with drops of rain.

The day's sunshine turns to grayness, putting Richard and me in a light rain as we reach Namche. We get beds at the lodge that he recommends, *The International Footrest*, and I go to meet Thomas. The Didi hands me a scrap of paper:

Philip,
I could not wait. I go today to Lukla.
Thomas

"*U gaisakyo*—He's gone," she says. "He left yesterday morning."

I'm baffled. What's his hurry? I'm here on just the right day. Perhaps he's worried about his soon-to-expire visa. If he gets a flight from Lukla, he could be in Kathmandu tomorrow. How strange! So that leaves me with only a porter on the Tasi Lapcha Pass, and then alone on Pharchamo. Perhaps it's best.

Namche Bazaar is shops and food and people, a place to rest and recuperate before going up again. Namche is the lowest I will go.

April 18, 19, 20, & 21
Namche Bazaar 11,286 feet

I don't feel like doing anything, but much has to be readied for crossing the Tasi Lapcha. I need to buy food and package it, re-repair my boots, wash my clothes and myself, and engage a porter. I inquire about a porter, but the responses are all negative. The Tasi Lapcha pass, and especially its far side, has a very bad reputation. The Sherpas are unenthusiastic. Someone will turn up, but the ultimate would be to do it alone. Other people are just trouble—unpredictable and unreliable. I take short walks, around and around, or lie in my sleeping bag. And each day, I eat as much as I can hold, trying to replenish my reserves for the last climb.

I gobbled granola as I peered into the fog and clouds. Three days from Aiselukharka had brought me through Helambu to a 12,000-foot ridge on the way to Gosaikund. I still wanted to see those sacred lakes that I had missed last year. Throughout the morning, I had hiked and climbed without a break; the swarms of leeches and mosquitoes had kept me from stopping. And I had been lost much of the time. Myriad yak paths diminished into nothingness and monsoon clouds lay heavy on the mountains, making it impossible to see. I chomped on the granola's mixed nuts and rock-hard dried fruit and dreamed of a soon-to-come letter from Kay.

Suddenly I felt something grate in my mouth. It made a sickly sound like gnashing gears. I spat out chunks of tooth and bloody granola, and I probed with my tongue. The hole felt enormous! It was the tooth in which I'd had the root canal done. The dentist had said that it would be brittle and would perhaps break off one day, but I had certainly expected it to last longer than eight months.

The trip to Gosaikund was now out. The tooth's root was still embedded in my jaw and a broken piece was connected to the gum. I had to get to Kathmandu as soon as possible. Taking the wrong trail, I spent a frustrating day hiking in a circle, but I then righted myself and reached the road two days later.

The first thing I did in Kathmandu—even before seeing the doctor about my tooth—was to pick up my mail. Sudharshan handed me three news bulletins, a copy of *Newsweek*, and a hefty manila envelope. The envelope was no doubt from Kay, but I hesitated before looking at the return address. In her last letter she had written about a guy she'd met in Sacramento. She had explained that it wasn't anything serious, but she had also mentioned the possibility of moving in with him. Wasn't that a contradiction? My eyes shifted to the left-hand corner of the envelope. Kay's new address was in Sacramento, California.

I stood motionless in the hallway, holding my mail. My boots were caked with mud from the hills above Helambu and my head felt fuzzy, like it was filled with monsoon clouds. I shuffled around the corner and went up the stairs to the third-floor balcony. I closed the door behind me and sat on the floor to open the packet from Kay:

Dear Phil,

As always I have much to say; I saw the King Tut exhibit in San Francisco, classes are finished, and I will be firefighting this summer. But what usually keeps me from writing is that something has come up that's a little more difficult to write about (unfortunately it's true) and that is that I have moved to Sacramento with Kevin. I'm sorry that I've had such a hard time writing but even now I'm not sure what to put down (I know you have a million questions).

I love you, but it's really hard to think about my future with anyone at this point. It just doesn't cross my mind and I don't want you to get carried away in your dreaming. I am really shying away from letting expectations be built on dreams that I can't be sure of fulfilling. I hope that will be enough said for the time being . . .

When I think of Kevin the feelings come so strong. I have come to think that I never loved you as much as you loved me, nor was I quite in love with you. For it seemed that as I fell in love with Kevin I was feeling and acting the way I remember you acting: overwhelmed, full of compliments and concern... When you write about the future (meaning future dreams together), I just feel empty. I don't see the future . . .

She had closed the letter with "Love, Kay." The packet contained pieces of denim for repairing my jeans, information on universities that I was thinking about attending when I returned, and miniature photocopies of all the color slides that I had sent back for processing. Part of the letter mentioned that she had somehow lost the silver and turquoise ring that I had given her five years before. This seemed shockingly symbolic. I felt that I had just died.

Kay didn't see the future, while I saw nothing but the future. I had been living for the future, waiting until we could be together again. The present was agony. The occasional letters from Kay only made me hunger to be with her. They tortured me with memories of kisses and caresses. A merciful ending of the relationship would be the best thing for me, but despite such great wisdom, I sat on the balcony and cried. The monsoon had truly begun.

I got appointments with the doctor and the dentist. Their decision was unanimous—I had to go back to Bangkok. The tooth needed a gold post and a porcelain crown, which Kathmandu couldn't supply. The dentist began preliminary work on the gum around the tooth, and two weeks would pass before I could leave for Thailand.

In the meantime, I walked the city streets, trying to escape my gloom. Sometimes I carried my umbrella or my raincoat against the bursts of monsoon rain, but other times I preferred to be wet and cold. I explored the ancient temples and I listened to the holy men at prayer. The Hindus chanted in a nasal monotone, and the Buddhists muttered to the rumbling of drums. The days passed in despair and throughout the nights I lay awake reviewing every past conversation with Kay.

I could accept that she had met someone new; I had expected that. And I could understand that she needed to live with the one she loved; I needed that too. But I couldn't conceive of her believing that she had never been in love with me. It was the worst thing that she could have said to me. Had we lived a lie for five years? Perhaps she had been fooling me—and herself—all along. Or perhaps she just needed to make a clean break from me.

As my mood darkened, I attempted to talk with Klaus and Pesout. They could only suggest that I take a trip. Klaus and I made plans to hike around Annapurna together when I returned from Bangkok. But Pesout wouldn't be able to come; he was convalescing from a case of hepatitis. Another friend advised me that love was irrational and that looking for explanations was futile. *Ke garne?*

With each day I felt myself slipping into a black abyss. All my hopes of the future had been built on dreams of Kay and now she was gone. Summer was the time that most of the volunteers got together for a holiday, but their gaiety only isolated me. All I wanted was to escape...

The bay curved away from me in a wide horseshoe. The sand was fine and smooth, and the waves fell against the beach in their eternal rhythm. Behind me were coconut palms, rubber plantations, and jungle—the Isle of Phuket, off the coast of southern Thailand. I had made my escape.

Five days before, I had flown to Bangkok and the dentist had begun work on my tooth. A gold post was set into the root and a porcelain cap was being cast. The cap wouldn't be ready for a week, so I had journeyed south.

I sat in the sun, and though the surf was calming, I pondered too much on past events. I felt abandoned. My implicit faith and trust in people had been shattered. In addition to Kay's rejection, other broken promises occupied my mind: in the spring I had assisted a woman from Vassar with her study of science education in Nepal. For two weeks I had interpreted for her in village interviews. When she left Nepal she was to return to me copies of the surveys, but she never did, and she kept much of the money that I had given her to send me supplies in Aiselukharka. Before leaving for Bangkok I had learned that much of what she had said about herself was a lie. Another breach of faith: when I had left Aiselukharka for Gosaikund, I had given Krishna Bhakta a pack of things that he guaranteed to take to Kathmandu in a few days' time. They were items that I couldn't carry to Gosaikund, but that I needed for the summer. I had waited and waited, but the pack was brought to Kathmandu only the day before I was leaving. Some guarantee! These unrelated events gathered importance in my mind and I began to recall countless other times that people had let me down.

But Phuket did its best to relax me. The jungle was luxurious and the water sparkled a deep blue. The sky occasionally released a dose of monsoon rain, but this only freshened the air and kept the tourists away. I lived on fresh fish and tropical fruit—bananas and pineapple and papaya. On my second day I spotted two small monkeys riding contentedly on the back of a man's bicycle. He cycled down a dirt road and I followed him with curiosity—around a bend and into a gated yard.

The monkeys were trained to pick the coconuts! With ropes tied around their waists, they clambered up a palm tree. Following *keech-keech* commands from their trainer, they grasped one of the big in-the-husk coconuts and twisted it around and around until the stem broke and it fell to the ground. Another man swung a machete, removing the husk. Then he cut a hole for us

250

to slurp the milk through. Another swing laid open the nut and we scooped out the sweet coconut meat using a palm-sized sliver of husk as a spoon. They were fresh green coconuts, not the old dried-up ones that are common in American supermarkets. I talked with the workers in my hundred-word Thai vocabulary and we ate coconuts until we were bloated and feeling sick.

Phuket was a near-idyllic place, but it was here that I lost all trust in my fellow men. I was on the beach writing, while to my right a French woman and her daughter were pointing toward the streaks of sunlight on the hills across the bay. *"Voilà. Elle se noie,"* they said to each other. Their words meant nothing to me. I was writing to Kay, explaining that I accepted her relationship with Kevin, and that I was already beginning to think of her as a friend instead of as a lover. I told her that I was having a good time. I lied so well that I almost had myself convinced.

After the French women had remarked about the sunlight for ten minutes I stood up. Something was in the water, far down the beach and out past the breakers.

Other people were watching. I jogged down the beach to get a better view and when I got closer I heard a woman screaming. Without thinking, I raced into the water, jumping over the small waves and then pushing through the deeper water. I started to swim and was engulfed by the breakers. The current was fierce due to the monsoon and I had been warned of the undertow—two people had drowned the previous week.

With a struggle, I crossed the breakers. I watched her head, but she went under with each wave and I was afraid that she would sink before I could reach her. She was hysterical, screaming in terror each time her head broke the surface. Another swell came and she went down, swallowing a mouthful of water. When she surfaced again I hollered, "You'll be all right now." Then I saw that she was Thai and I knew that my words were pointless. I felt the tremendous current that pulled us both out. A wave covered us just as I reached her.

I caught her around the waist, and she immediately stopped thrashing. I held her with my right arm across her chest and under her armpit. She was a big woman and I kept her up with my hip under her back. I swam with my free arm and kicked. As I leveled her out, the current was less, but the shore was unreachable. I was sure, though, that I could keep her up until more help arrived.

Except no one was coming. I fought against the current and as each wave washed over us, I pushed her up, and thus myself down, trying to keep her head above the surface. I had trouble getting enough air. Wasn't anyone else coming? I swam and swam, my right arm gripping the limp woman, and my left arm, feeling like lead, churning the water below the surface. We made slow progress with the breakers coming steadily closer. I didn't know how much longer I could keep it up. Then suddenly we were swallowed by the waves, pulled under, and tumbled head over heels. As we were tossed about, I held on to her with both arms, like a wrestler. I wasn't going to lose her now. I caught a gulp of air, and down we went again. I kept kicking with my legs, trying to move us toward shore and trying to reach the surface to breath. We got pulled under twice more. When we came up the third time, we were past the breakers and I could see the beach. Two Thai men began wading out to help.

They reached us just before the water was shallow enough to stand. We pulled her in by her arms and the current against our legs threatened to take us down. Reaching shallow water, they tried to stand her up, but that was impossible. Others came and we half-dragged and half-carried her to the sand. She coughed up sea water and she cried. She would be OK. People congratulated the Thai men who had helped and I stood idle, feeling absolutely spent, like an expelled flashbulb. I had never been so tired. I walked back to my spot on the beach and I lay in the sand with my whole body trembling.

At first I didn't think much about the rescue. I had merely been the first to reach the woman. But then I remembered the people on the beach who had watched her drowning. No one had tried to help until well after I

252

had begun pulling her in. Another minute or two and she would have been lost. How could a hundred people have watched that woman and heard her screams and yet done nothing? I asked that question countless times, but I got no answer. Were they afraid? Didn't they care? Or was it just not real to them? The whole affair was shocking and disappointing. What if she had died in front of an audience? I was disgusted with the world.

During my last few days in Phuket, a number of the local people came and gave me the thumbs-up sign. In Nepal that would have been an obscene gesture, but in Thailand it meant *Number One!* They called me "Champion," and said, "You very strong. You come woman." Their compliments only irritated me.

I had to get back for my last dental appointment, so I returned to Bangkok by the local (seventeen-hour) bus. On the way to the dentist I was nearly robbed of my passport and all my money. Walking close behind me, someone put six slashes in my backpack with a razor, but amazingly they got nothing. I retrieved my traveler's checks hanging by a couple of threads. I didn't even see who it was. Just a bit of Thai hospitality!

I flew back to Kathmandu. The flight was delayed and I didn't get in until after dark. I had to find Klaus. I still planned to hike around Annapurna, and Klaus had promised to be my partner. I transported my equipment to Klaus's hotel and gave him a big hug when I saw him. I was ecstatic; we would have a month hiking together.

Klaus looked downcast. "I'm sick," he said. "I can't go. I'm too weak."

I didn't say a word. Even Klaus had let me down.

The next day I took the bus to Pokhara, alone as usual, and the following morning I hiked north in torrential rain. The route passed through the world's deepest river valley, choked with lush vegetation and filled with thick monsoon clouds. In five and a half days of trails that were quagmires of mud and cow dung, I arrived at Marpha, on the back side of the main Himalayan range. Marpha was in the rain shadow, and received almost no rain.

I dallied a week in Marpha and then advanced north to Jomosom and up the Thorang Pass. I spent a night on the top of the pass at 17,700 feet without a tent. The morning was clear, giving marvelous views, but I didn't care. All I wanted was someone to talk to. Two years in Nepal, being dreadfully alone, then comes my vacation and I go off solo trekking. It was pitiful. This was no vacation. I decided to get back to my friends in Kathmandu as fast as I could. I reached the road in record time—covering 120 miles in just four days—and walking the last 20 miles barefoot through flooded rice paddies.

I had a week in Kathmandu before I needed to be back in Aiselukharka, but I would have been happier with just a day. My friends were a great disappointment to me. Since coming to Nepal I had been continually open to listen to everyone's problems and worries. And now that I was back in town after a summer away I found friends who wanted to talk with me. All their problems dragged me down, but worse than that, I felt that these same people had little interest in hearing my own troubles. We all required a lot of support to handle the difficulties of living in Nepal, but just then I seemed to be getting no aid from anyone. I was as alone as ever, and I was anxious to leave Kathmandu.

After four days in Namche, I've got everything done—washed, repaired, bought, and packed. I'm ready to flee. Richard left yesterday for the south. Thinking it over, I decide to cross the Tasi Lapcha without a porter and without a guide. I feel confident that I'll find the way, but I'm unsure about carrying such a big load. I'll see tomorrow. I just want to get out of here.

April 22

Namche

"When I've got it up, you read the scale," I say to the American. I'm eager to know the weight of my pack before setting out. It's stuffed with climbing equipment, clothes and extra clothes, tent, sleeping bag, foam pad, stove, two quarts of fuel, one quart of water, and food for two weeks. It feels like a load of bricks. The spring scale, borrowed from a trekking shop, hooks on to the upper crossbar of the packframe. Standing atop a wooden sleeping platform, I lift it up.

"Wait until it stops shaking," I grunt to the American. He watches the scale: "Forty-one."

"Forty-one?" I let the pack drop as I convert the weight from kilos to pounds. "That's ninety pounds... Shit."

"Are you certain you can carry it?" he asks.

"Yeah... sure." That's what I say, but what I should be asking myself is: "Phil, seriously, are you *crazy?* You're going to carry a ninety-pound pack—*ninety pounds!*—alone into the high Himalaya? *Really?*"

I have it on now. The weight presses down through my spine and legs, and plants my boots firmly against the ground.

The American wishes me, "Good luck," as I maneuver the pack and myself through the door. After returning the scale with a *Namaste* of thanks, I zigzag between the houses and hike up the switchbacks to the monastery north of town. The way is lined with *mani* walls, their chiseled slabs of stone proclaiming in Tibetan: *Om mani padme hum*—The jewel is in the lotus.* It's the prayer that devout Buddhists continuously chant over their beads, spin on their prayer wheels, and print on their prayer flags.

Slowly placing each heavy step, I reach the crest of the hill and look back on Namche. I won't be seeing it again. I can finally move up.

I hiked slowly through the trees toward the fork in the trail. I took the trail to the right, which was longer but less likely to have been washed out by the monsoon. The red mud was slippery and I had to watch my step.

The fields were still flooded and the second crop of rice was coming up. A man passed me carrying a wooden plow across his shoulder. After the disappointing summer, I was on my way back to Aiselukharka and I would not leave the village again until I had finished my two years of teaching. That would put me among the 55 percent of my group who had stayed the full time. I thought of the others—the ones who had terminated early. As each of them had quit, I had felt sad to lose a friend, but I had also been vaguely glad. When someone gave up it was proof that those of us who remained were accomplishing an uncommonly difficult task. I didn't know if the other volunteers felt this way; I was too ashamed to bring it up.

But was there any big difference between those who left and those who stayed? The key seemed to be our singular personalities. I, for one, had never really been a part of things in the States. I had always felt set apart by the way I looked or by the way I thought. So coming to Nepal and being a novelty was not a shock. In America I was abnormal, but

---

* A more descriptive translation from *Buddha*, by William McQuitty:

    Om—possessing wisdom;

    ma—Buddha;

    ni—whose tranquil nature removes evil;

    pad—and spreads the qualities of goodness;

    me—his power brings people to possess these qualities;

    hum—by his strength he overcomes evil.

in Nepal I felt at home to have my strangeness accepted as a part of my foreign character.

I was further aided by my aversions to American television and a greed-based culture, and by my affinities for clean air and a people-oriented society. The ability to adapt was equally important. I had to accept whatever came my way, and the combined experience had lasting effects on me.

The physical changes were more noticeable to others than to myself. Before I had come to Nepal, people had often guessed my age to be a couple of years younger than it actually was, but now they guessed that I was a year or two older than reality. I had aged five years in a period of two. I imagined that emotional stress and an inadequate diet accounted for this. What I more readily noticed was that my vision had deteriorated. In Kathmandu, I was having to cross the road in order to read window signs, and the doctor had recommended that I get glasses.

The inner changes were a predictable response to the life I was leading. My self-confidence had certainly increased. I felt that I could go anywhere and do anything. After coping with so many extreme situations in Nepal, I felt that I could handle anything that might come my way. My basic beliefs hadn't altered, though they had clearly intensified. Living in an alien world had required me to be very forceful if my ideas were to be heard. Finally, I had become highly conscious of world problems. The nebulous Third World had become very real to me, and international conflicts took precedence over baseball scores. I had become less an American and more a citizen of the world.

Living the external lifestyle of a Nepali had also made me more Nepali on the inside. As I climbed higher on the ridge leading to Aiselukharka, I felt that I was truly coming home. Krishna Bhakta would be there and the daal-bhaat would be hot. I began to consider staying for a third year in Nepal. American Phil was left further behind as I approached closer to Aiselukharka.

Hampered by frequent rests, I come slowly into Thame, the Sherpa hamlet where Tenzing Norgay was born. The pack's weight is extreme to the point of absurdity, but getting through today convinces me that I'll be able to carry it three more days to the pass.

I ask a woman in a potato field for a place to stay and she takes me to her home for the night. The house is large by Sherpa standards, having both a ground floor for the animals and an upper storey for people. We reach the second floor by climbing a rickety ladder. I take off my pack, sit down, and look around. The absence of the most common status symbol—a shelf of shiny brass cooking pots—bespeaks the family's low income. But this is overshadowed by the array of religious articles, which includes a colossal floor-to-ceiling prayer wheel and two shrines complete with water bowls.

I lean back while the potatoes bubble over the fire. On the other side of the hearth, an old woman sits muttering chants over her beads. Occasionally she gets up and circles the room, attending to the sacred objects. A garland-bedecked picture of the Dalai Lama receives an extra share of her devotion.

In addition to the boiled potatoes, we eat oppressive potato pancakes. They taste bitter, but when smeared with globs of yak fat, they ease down my throat. I fall asleep to the old woman's droning chant—*Om mani padme hum*. The sound of time.

April 23

Thame 12,500 feet

I dawdle over my preparations to move on. Only 5 miles separate me from Thengpo, the next and last village. When I'm ready to go, the younger woman figures my bill on her fingers. Using only her right hand, she lightly touches her thumb to successive segments of each finger as she counts. First finger—one, two, three; second finger—four, five, six; and so on. The morning's fare of potatoes is added in and the bill comes to more than I had expected.

The pack feels unaccountably lighter than it did yesterday, though I must still put an effort into each step. Only 6,500 feet left to climb! I recall first-hand accounts of the Tasi Lapcha: a one-time Peace Corps Volunteer told of his trek over the pass, "We couldn't have possibly found the way without a guide. It was physically the most demanding thing I've ever done." A Sherpa climber sincerely tried to talk me out of it: "I've done Nanda Devi.* You know Nanda Devi? Tasi Lapcha is worse than Nanda Devi. More hard. More dangerous." A Sherpa guide, upon hearing that I would go solo, proclaimed unequivocally, "*Sakdaina*—Can't be done." And his American clients agreed, saying, "If I had known it was going to be so bad, I wouldn't have come. I wouldn't have come." "You're *alone?* No, I don't think it's a good idea. Are you really *determined* to go?" "You have a rope? You have to have a rope in at least three places. But even then I wouldn't want to down-climb all that rock." According to the reports, most of the difficulties are on the west side

---

* Nanda Devi is a 25,645-foot peak in Uttar Pradesh, India.

of the pass, the side that I'll be descending. So any problems with the pass will come after Pharchamo. The specter of the dead Japanese mountaineers looms foremost in my mind.

The trail angles up, sometimes steeply, following the Thame Khola, which is a tumbling cascade of white water. Across the canyon rise the imposing rock and ice walls of Teng Kangboche, and overhead, the blue-black sky remains absolutely silent. The sense of peace is overwhelming. These are the mountains that I have wished to feel at one with, but the presence of villages, trails, and other climbers has held me back short of that goal.

In Aiselukharka, too, I had felt unable to fully merge with the village life. The biggest cause of this had been my longing for people who were unreachable. But now the relationship with Kay had evaporated, and in a process that had begun with my arrival in Nepal, my friends in America were neglecting to answer my letters. More often than not, my weekly mail packet contained nothing but a *Newsweek* magazine and some Peace Corps memorandums. My ties to America had become minimal and I felt myself freed of a tremendous burden. I could focus all my energies on the village.

After the disastrous summer, I arrived home in Aiselukharka eager for news of the hostel and the trees. I was disappointed to find progress on the roof at a standstill. Both the DEO and the men at UNICEF seemed to be hedging. The plastic sheets on the hostel had minimized the monsoon damage, but without a proper roof the structure would eventually collapse.

The trees, however, were doing well. Surendra walked with me around the hillside and told me case histories of each one: "This tree was eaten by goats, but grew back from its roots." "That one died and we replaced it with one of the extra trees that you-sir gave us." "Those two are big, but these others are small and maybe they'll die." I was pleased that the trees were being looked after.

The best news was the outcome of the SLC examination. Raadhaa had passed! And not just barely, he had been placed in the second highest of the three divisions. And what's more, two of our other students had passed in the third division. Jubilation prevailed in the teachers' office. From Chautara High School, a supposedly better school than ours, only one student had succeeded in passing. Of all our students, only two had failed the mathematics section of the test, and for this, the Headmaster gave me full credit. I was amazed that they had done so well in math, for I knew that some of my students could barely add. Perhaps I had helped with my vigilance during exams, forcing them to develop ever more cunning ways to cheat. I was glad that they had passed, whatever the means. The three SLC graduates applied for government jobs, but they only got work as teachers.

The weeks slipped by and the days began to shorten, but no miracles helped us with the desperately needed roof. One breezy afternoon, Krishna Bhakta and I took a walk along the slope above the hostel. We looked down at the structure that had received so much time and energy. The hillside below us was ravaged from the excavation of stones and was dotted with five elephant-size holes. These pits were where the mud had been mixed. The Carpenter's handcrafted window frames were already gray from weathering, and the roof of plastic was shredded. The tatters fluttered and snapped in the wind. One of the thick stone walls was already cracking. The unfinished building would not hold up another year.

Krishna Bhakta stood with his empty hands hanging at his sides. "What about the thousand dollars from Amaarika?"

"No, we can't get that money," I said.

I had already explained a half-dozen times about the requirement of voluntary work to get Peace Corps Partnership funds, but I was still asked about this American money. The teachers looked upon $1,000 as a trivial token of friendship from infinitely wealthy America. They didn't realize that the money would have to be raised by children selling candy, or holding a carnival, or washing cars.

Krishna Bhakta ignored my answer. He spoke quietly, "The Headmaster and the Pradhaan Panch and I have been to Kathmandu and Chautara twice. They will not give us the tin for the roof. The DEO says that he knows nothing about it, that it is only the UNICEF that arranges it."

"But what do the men at UNICEF say?" I asked.

"They say that the DEO has the responsibility. He must first approve the papers and then submit them to UNICEF…"

They had an airtight runaround. What could the problem be? I doubted that it was the matter of priority going to primary schools. I suspected that the DEO just needed a monetary incentive to solve the problem—a bribe.

Krishna Bhakta still spoke, "…We went again to see the old Minister of Education. He has forgotten about promising us the money for the roof. He says we should not have built such a large hostel if we didn't have money enough to finish it. *Ke garne?*"

His last words carried a tone of absolute finality, and I realized that nothing more would be done. He had already reconciled himself to the loss of the hostel. It was a terrible waste. Was there nothing more that could be done? *Ke garne?* This attitude was a great strength when facing the tragedies of life, but it was also a great weakness when trying to accomplish development. And after two years in Nepal, it wasn't just the Nepali attitude; it was my attitude as well. Life went on.

Ke garne? were the final words concerning the hostel, but I remained busy with other projects. The district called on me to help with a pair of week-long teacher-training sessions. That was my chance to pass on to my Nepali counterparts whatever expertise I had acquired. My single aim of these sessions was to persuade the science teachers to do simple experiments and demonstrations in class rather than just to lecture at the students. In addition, I was working on a project for other Peace Corps Volunteers—

a list of basic phrases and vocabulary words in eleven of Nepal's secondary languages: Newari, Thamang, Sherpa, Rai, Hindi, and so on. I was seldom idle.

My life in Aiselukharka had been slowly changing. All my concerns had become village matters and I seldom thought about America. The end of the relationship with Kay had severed my last links with the States. I wrote very few letters. What was the point? Even Roger, who had gotten married in July, had stopped writing to me. I felt no connection with anyone outside of Aiselukharka, and the pages of my datebook went unused for the first time. My double life ceased. Nothing more held me back and I fully immersed myself in my role as Philipsir, the Nepali school teacher.

As I approach the houses of Thengpo, a man calls, "You want some tea?" I ignore him. No, I don't want tea. I want nothing at all. I discard my plan to sleep tonight in Thengpo and I hike on. Beyond the village, the trail dwindles to nothing. After all, a trail has no purpose from here on; there are no villages, no people, nothing.

I move unencumbered. I hike and climb according to the shape of the mountainside, ascending where it's easy and traversing where it's not. The higher I go, the easier it feels. No trails tie me to thoughts of others, and I feel myself becoming a part of the mountains. Time is determined by how light it is, and temperature is measured by what clothes I must wear. As darkness settles, I pitch the tent on the last and highest patch of yak grass. Despite my sense of freedom, I am practical enough to be aware of the weight that I carry; for dinner I eat some of my heaviest foods. The pinpoint stars appear, and the high glaciers groan through the night.

April 24

Patch of Yak Grass 15,700 feet

The sun wakes me. The mountains shimmer in the morning light and I relax in the growing warmth. The rising air stirs a gentle wind as the high walls boom with the sound of cracking ice.

My morning tasks are left waiting while I rejoice in the here and now. When shall I begin the climb? *Bholi-parsi.* Any time now. The mountains are timeless.

Pharchamo stands 2 miles away. Its long north ridge rises in unbroken whiteness from the Tasi Lapcha. It's the only route. I toy with the thought of reaching the pass today. But if not today, then tomorrow, or sometime.

"Wednesday or Thursday?" I sat up and opened the wooden shutters to the chill morning. "What day is it?" I wasn't really sure. Since I had stopped recording events in my datebook, I was frequently confused about the days. This was paradoxical, considering that I had become adept at telling the time from the sun. I could even determine the month by noting where the sun rose and set against the panorama of Aiselukharka's surrounding hills. But was it Wednesday or Thursday? I would have to ask someone, or less embarrassingly, I could consult the school roll book.

I carried my pitcher of water out to the backyard and was greeted by the charging bulk of our family water buffalo. The rope around his neck jerked him to a halt just before he could run me down. This happened every morning and it was certainly my own fault. When he was a young calf, I had made the mistake of frolicking with him, playfully butting and pushing. And now, grown to half a ton, he still wanted to play. I scratched his nose while he rolled his eyes in ecstasy and strained mightily against the rope. I had learned why one shouldn't play with baby water buffaloes.

A dark bird with yellow eye patches and an orange beak landed on the water buffalo's back. It hopped about on stiff legs, picking bugs out of the coarse hair. Possibly dissatisfied with the meal, the bird croaked a very un-birdlike tune. It was a common mynah, and though they were beautiful birds, their habits were too gregarious for my liking. I preferred the sparrows that came to my room each morning. They would timidly flutter in and out of the window, snatching up the grains of rice that I had sloppily dropped on the floor.

On my way to school, the Tailor stopped his work in mid-stitch and gave me a jubilant *Namaste*. Up on the school athletic field came a flurry of the same. No more students said *Namaste* to me than when I had first come to the village, but I now sensed a difference in how they said it. Instead of an automatic gesture of respect, their *Namastes* had become intimate, a reminder of shared affection. The scores of initially unfamiliar faces were now my friends and family: Narayan Prasaad was so clever at sports and games, but always got caught when cheating on an exam. Ganga Ram carried a seldom-working pocket watch that he'd inherited from his father's father who'd been to India. Sharmila Devi, with her long tangled hair, chagrined the boys by beating them at wrestling. And Mohan Lal, of tenth class, had gotten married last spring and had recently become the focus of innumerable jokes when his superbly pregnant wife came looking for him at school.

Klang-klang-klang... Guru rang the brass-plate bell and everyone lined up for the national anthem. As always, I had the first period free to prepare lessons and to make ready for the day's demonstrations. Today I had little to do, so I stood on the second-floor walkway, looking out at the expanse of hills and sky. "What are you looking at?" was an often asked question, to which "Everything, nothing," was my usual reply.

As I stood gazing at everything and nothing, a man came across the field whom I had never seen before. He wasn't from Aiselukharka, but since he caused no excitement, he was apparently known to most everyone. What made him unusual was his legs. They were deformed—elongated and bent around. He couldn't walk, but instead he crawled on all fours with his knees sticking above his back. He had the appearance of a walking grasshopper, but he carried himself with respect. Keeping his head up so that he could look around, he moved across the field and down the trail towards the village.

I could well imagine how this man's life must be. He would live at home (where else?) with his family, doing whatever work he could. He would not be expected to hide himself away, and he would not be subjected to mockery. He wouldn't even be stared at. All the people with whom he would come into close contact would be life-long neighbors. How could they fail to accept a man they had known since birth? He would probably marry; even the most unfortunate could find a spouse. All in all, his life—so unlike the shut-away lives of handicapped Americans—would be beautifully common.

Klang-klang. The bell sounded second period. In eighth science we talked about the ways that sicknesses are passed from one person to another. After that came ninth math and the pointless study of square roots. Tenth math was equally irrelevant, but was manifestly important in light of the upcoming SLC exam. I demonstrated methods of factoring quadrinomials. My last class of the day was seventh science, in which we were studying sound.

"*Swarko kaaran ke ho?* What is the cause of sound?" I asked the class as we stood outside the temple.

It was a review from the previous day and the students laughed as they gave the funny-sounding answer. "*Jhananana*—Vibrations," they grinned.

"Is that right? Or is it *jhana-nana-nana-nana*?"

We all laughed and I took out the bamboo strip that I had used the day before to show how vibrations made sounds. I held one end tight against a stone step and twanged the free end. They could see—as well as hear—

266

the vibrations that caused sound. Next we moved to the big 200-year-old bell that hung by the temple. Taking turns, we pressed the palms of our hands flat against the bell and struck it with the heavy iron clapper. Besides seeing the vibrations, they could feel them.

"You can see the vibrations, and feel the vibrations, and what else?"

A thoughtful expression spread from face to face. I was happy to see them thinking rather than giving up or just guessing.

"Can you smell the vibrations?" I hinted. "Or taste them?"

"No," blurted the top two students, each trying to outdo the other. "You can *hear* it also." This rivalry between Ram Prasaad and Megha Nath was often keen, but never unfriendly. For Megha Nath, though, it was unfortunate that Ram Prasaad was always a bit quicker.

Before going back inside to record the lesson on the blackboard, we did a final experiment. I instructed the students to hold their hands against their throats as they said, "*Jhananana.*" Most of them could feel the vibrations with their fingers and it was eye-opening for them to discover that their bodies worked along the same lines as bells and bamboo strips.

These science classes were my single greatest joy. With the students' help, I daily re-experienced the wonder of simple discoveries, and ever more frequently I could see the students learning without guidance from their teachers. This was the most important thing, for in a few years they would be finished with school and finished with teachers, but hopefully not finished with learning.

At the end of the day's classes, the students went off on their long walks home, and I sauntered down the path to Krishna Bhakta's house. Halfway there I stopped in to see a man who had been sick the past week. His wife had come to me for medicine, and I wondered how he was doing. "It's me coming," I announced as I stepped inside. It wasn't the custom to knock; one was expected to just walk in. We had no strangers in the village.

The room was small and the floor was in need of a fresh mudding. The wife, hearing my entrance, greeted me with a smiling *Namaste*. She didn't rise from where she sat shelling corn. Her glass bangles jingled as she worked, and as my eyes grew accustomed to the dark, I saw that her wrap-around skirt was tattered at the edges. This was probably not due to its age, but was more likely a result of the violent beatings that I had seen her give her clothes when she washed them.

"How is he?" I asked.

"He's sick," she said matter-of-factly and got up to show me his place in the next room. He was sleeping on a wooden cot, facing the wall and covered with a thin blanket.

"Does his head hurt?"

"Not so much. And he's eating more now. But he coughs, and has aches in his fingers. His nose drips..." She went on with the description that I had heard before. It sounded like the flu. I could do nothing more than repeat my advice about drinking water and resting, but the woman was still greatly pleased with my visit.

"Perhaps you're having tea?" she suggested when we returned to the main room.

"No, I'm not having tea," I said, putting my hands together in a *Namaste* that meant "no thank you."

"Will you stay to meet my First Son?" she asked with pride. "He comes back from Chautara today."

"When will he be coming?"

"*Ahile*—Now."

"*Hunchha*," I said, with a sideways tilt of my head. I sat back on my heels to wait. She gave me a small pile of roasted peanuts to eat, and when they were gone I gazed at the wall above the fireplace. The stones were covered with layers of fine ash and soot, and the flecks formed delicate patterns of infinite variety. Tiny particles of gray, white, and black were arranged like the most exquisite lace. It was sublimely beautiful.

My thoughts turned to my life in Aiselukharka. I had needed two years to become fully adapted, but now I had only three months left. It seemed a shame

268

to leave so soon. Was I prepared to stay another year? Last week I had wanted to leave. This week I wanted to stay. I was far from reaching a decision.

After I had waited quite some time, the First Son had yet to appear and I noticed that the sky was darkening—I had been sitting by the fireplace for two hours.

"I'm going now. *Namaste*," I said as I left.

I returned home in the twilight and picked up my 20-liter jug to go and fetch water. Evening was the best time at the dhaaraa, for rarely was anyone else there. I was therefore surprised to meet Ram Prasaad and Netra Prasaad coming up the trail. They put down their full water containers when they saw me.

"Philipsir! You've come here alone, at night? Aren't you afraid?" they said.

"What for afraid?"

"Afraid of *boksi!*"

Boksi were witches that roamed at night and could inhabit a person's body. I had heard several stories about people who had gone mad—they had been "eaten by a boksi."

"No, I'm not afraid," I said. "A boksi won't eat me. I don't taste good."

"*Hunchha?*" they questioned, not knowing if I was being serious.

"Yes, and I also dance and sing with a boksi who comes to my house at night. Sometimes the boksi eats my socks, but never me."

"Hah!" they laughed. "That's not boksi. Those are rats that eat your socks." They lifted their water jugs and hurried up the trail, taking care to stay together. Despite my own courage, boksi evoked very real fear.

Evening daal-bhaat came with a vegetable dish of potatoes and beans. When I finished the meal, I left no extra rice on the floor; I tried to discourage the rodent-teethed boksi that came at night to chew on my socks, soap, and toothpaste.

I had lessons to plan for my coming classes, but I could do it in the morning. I assembled the pieces of my recorder and arranged my music under the lamp. Music making had become my daily meditation. My fingers passed over the holes, my foot kept time, and my breathing flowed to the pattern dictated by the melody. The music itself traveled from the written notes, to my eyes, out through my fingers and mouth, to the recorder, and back in by way of the ears, around and around. It was a total presence, in harmony and unity, with no divisions between me, the music, and the recorder. It gave me a sense of timelessness and for my family it was a signal that I had nothing very urgent to do.

As I had hoped, Krishna Bhakta soon came to the door. I put away the music and we talked. We discussed the weather and the latest village gossip. It was too late for the radio news, but it didn't really matter; any events of great concern were things that we would see for ourselves.

I told Krishna Bhakta about the rats running off with my toothbrush and he told a funny anecdote:

"In the old days we didn't have brushes for cleaning teeth. We chewed on a stick, like from the plant that grows along the trail here. But another plant grows with that one. If a man took a stick from the wrong plant his throat would swell up like this. Like a melon."

"Was that dangerous?"

"Oh yes," said Krishna Bhakta. "Very dangerous, because a man looked like such a fool! After a few days he would be normal, but we would always remember. I saw Old Man Jaganath with a melon neck twice."

We laughed over his story, while the jackals on the hilltop began to yip at the rising moon.

When neither of us had anything to say, we sat contentedly and listened to the night. Nothing was that urgent to talk about. Our evening chats were more for sharing our friendship than for communication.

Krishna Bhakta left for his bed in the main house, and I settled down to sleep. As I blew out the lamp, I realized that I had forgotten to find out what day it was.

Time stands still as I climb slowly higher. Step follows step in a ceaseless rhythm and any progress I make is lost in the enormity of the mountains. To hike without apparent movement is strangely reassuring—a world at rest.

My strength ebbs away as I labor up the endless slopes of scree and talus. Somewhere around 18,000 feet, the rock gives way to ice and my breathing becomes a continuous chain of gasps. I put down the pack and pull on my down jacket. I reach into the pocket and discover a chocolate bar, which I immediately devour.

The weather deteriorates, and despite the work I'm doing, I shiver. The slick ice is treacherous and the ungainly pack forces me to crawl. I should get out my ice axe and crampons, but there's no place to stop. My route is simple—I put my feet in any secure spot that leads upward.

With each step, something large and dark grows up ahead. It's the southern cliff of Tangi Ragi Tau—the top of the pass. I lean forward with my hands on my knees and suck in the air. A few steps and another rest. Step by step, I make my way to the base of the cliff.

The wall overhangs slightly, providing a snow-free tent platform at its base. I gratefully set my pack on the ground and begin erecting the tent against the wind. My exhaustion amazes me. Snow swirls about and I have no idea of the time. Crawling into the tent, I'm faced with the task of melting snow and preparing dinner. When my belly is full, I sleep—deep and dreamless.

April 25
Tasi Lapcha Pass
around 19,000 feet

The height of the pass is uncertain—something between 18,900 and 19,100 feet, according to the various maps. My camp, though, is not directly on the pass, but higher up, off to one side. It's a cold spot and is totally blocked from the sun. The tent shudders in the wind as I rotate between reading, sleeping, and eating.

The white cone of Pharchamo's summit beckons me, but there's no possibility of climbing today. I'm sick. My head is tight and I have diarrhea. I start a course of tetracycline and I tell myself that I feel strong and healthy. Three days to climb here from Namche was too fast. No wonder I'm ill. I've lost some acclimatization during the long interval at lower altitude. Regardless of this, I'm determined to climb tomorrow.

The day passes in a half-doze, and I think back on the events that have brought me to this place: dissatisfaction with America propelling me to Nepal, loss of contact with Kay making me dependent on Aiselukharka, and my departure from there leaving me with only the high mountains as a refuge. A Peace Corps friend said, "Leaving your village is like a small death." If so, the Himalayan hills must be shelter to many a ghost.

Night comes, bringing a deep intense cold, chilling me to the core. The sensation of spreading internal ice is surreal, perhaps like the feeling of death.

Klack. Klack. Klack. It began just before dawn. Someone stood on the roof of the house opposite and tossed firewood to the flagstones below. It formed a great pile, and I thought a moment before I realized its purpose. It was for the cremation of Krishna Devi Himalaya. Her death had been expected for weeks, but she had continually surprised everyone by opening her eyes each morning and calling her children by name. At ninety-three, Krishna Devi Himalaya was everyone's mother, grandmother, or great-grandmother. As the stack of wood mounted, I joined the mourners out on the courtyard. Their faces were expressionless, stunned, not believing what had happened. No one knew a time when she had not been there. It was unthinkable that she was now dead.

The mood was in drastic contrast to the activities of the previous week. The Dasai festival had been a time of great jubilation: all the family members uniting, everyone beaming as they tried on their new clothes, the children playing on the high rope swing by the school, and the chickens and goats being sacrificed at the colorful pujaa ceremonies. After all this came the elaborate feasts. I had stayed home in Aiselukharka for the festivities, forgoing the usual practice of surrounding myself with Westerners during school vacations.

The Dasai merrymaking was now long past. The men stood about looking at the ground and not knowing what to do. The women, however, knew exactly what to do. They assembled in the second-storey rooms where they wept and wailed. Their cries started low, but they grew in pitch and intensity as more women arrived. The screams of grief blanketed us all in a thick cloud of despair.

I noticed that no one was wearing shoes of any kind, so I rid myself of my rubber sandals. Most of us were idle while the four men who would act as attendants did the work. They first bathed and then dressed themselves in loincloths of new white muslin. Next they tied the firewood into bundles using grass ropes, and lashed together a bier of green bamboo poles. All the while, the women and girls moaned and howled.

Two men were gazing languidly into the house's open porch and I moved over to join them. There lay Krishna Devi Himalaya, bare from the waist up, her breasts shriveled and dried with age. Her eye sockets were smeared with mascara and a folded paper was tied across her forehead. This was her *chihna*, her horoscope—a record of her name, moment of birth, and home village—information that would guide her in the spirit world. A small brass cup was placed over her mouth, and her body was then wrapped in white cloth. Not knowing if it was proper to watch the preparations, I stepped aside.

Her three gray-haired sons now emerged from the house. They too wore white loincloths, and the priest adorned them with additional strips of material. The elder two sons received bands tied around their biceps, and the youngest had one wrapped about his head like a baby's bonnet. It was the youngest son, Kaanchho, who had the obligation of performing the funeral rites, though it had been the eldest son's duty when their father died.

Presently the body was carried out on the bier and the women's shrieks reached a fevered pitch. The sons, too, broke into sobs and wails. They all three collapsed in grief and the other men rushed to support them. *Aamaa! Aaamaaaa! Aaamaaaaiiiyeee!*

Kaancho's wife came outside to discard a clay pot and a straw mat, and the priest did a small pujaa over the body before the procession departed. A man and a boy led the way with torches, followed by a man sprinkling the trail from a bowl of rice and corn. Then came the four attendants carrying the bier on their shoulders, the inconsolable sons being helped to walk, and finally all the other men and boys arranging themselves in descending order of kin. As we rounded the house, the women pushed their tear-streamed faces out from the windows and shrieked ever louder. Only men would attend the cremation.

We moved slowly down the trail with the women's screams gradually dying in our ears. Cremations were most normally conducted on a river bank, but since Aiselukharka had no river, we shuffled to the village cremation *ghat* which was situated by the gully far below the dhaaraa. The bier was placed on the flagstones to one side of the pyre. The shroud over Krishna Devi's head was then opened and the brass cup removed. The men lined up and carried cupped handfuls of water from a flooded field to pour over Krishna Devi's lips. This was a ritual feeding in repayment for all the nourishment that she had given her offspring.

I stood nearby, looking at her features: the grim lips, the wispy hair, and the protruding nose. It was the same aquiline nose that was so characteristic of her sons and her sons' sons. Her ancient skin was stretched tight over her bones, but she didn't look ninety-three years old, much less dead. I had the feeling that she was about to open her eyes and whisper, "Kaanchho."

The cup and shroud were replaced, and after another pujaa, the bier was carried around the funeral pyre three times and set atop the neatly stacked wood. The attendants removed the shroud completely and covered her with a heap of straw to conceal her nakedness. The straw hid the upper two-thirds of her body and left her feet exposed. The three brothers each knelt in turn and touched the tops of their heads to their Mother's cold toes—the highest possible gesture of respect. After the priest performed a final pujaa, the pyre was lit with a bundle of fragrant-smelling wands.

Everyone, except the four attendants and a few of the most curious, moved up the slope and sat around the stone mourners' hut.

The straw burned first and covered Krishna Devi's upper body with a layer of black ash. As the fire grew, the burning flesh began to sizzle, and the smoke became acrid. The flames crept between her knees, first blackening the skin, then splitting it open, and revealing the white tissue beneath. The heat affected the tendons, causing her feet to rotate, ever so slowly, first to the right and then to the left, as though she was writhing in ultimate agony.

The attendants stood in a circle. They complained among themselves that their shoulders ached and they accused each other of not carrying the bier smoothly enough. The other men and boys lingered in the shelter, with the most distant relations being the first ones to leave for their morning meals. I squatted close to the pyre, watching in grisly fascination as the flames consumed the body.

The tendons must have shrunk in the heat, for the left knee gradually raised itself. The thigh melted away, and the leg burnt through just above the knee. When the lower leg fell to one side, the thigh bone pointed to the sky. Now I understood why most of the relatives preferred to watch the cremation from afar.

My curiosity was more than satisfied and I wished to leave, but my legs would not obey. I sat and stared, unblinking, in hypnotic horror. The attendants used one of the bamboo poles to fold the armless body at the waist. Krishna Devi's face was still whole, but as I watched, the characteristic hooked nose began to bubble and burn. The body was turned again, revealing a large hole in the back of the skull. With another rotation, brains leaked out of that ghastly hole, dripped onto the blaze, and sizzled loudly.

My mouth was dry, but my hands were steady. My eyes watched the burning flesh, but the reality of it was beyond my comprehension. I felt nothing at all.

More wood was stacked onto the body, and I was calmed by the realization that it was over. I would not be witness to more horror, and I knew that all the manipulations of the body had been important. It had to be completely reduced to ash or else risk the possibility that Krishna Devi would be bound to the earth as a ghost. The fire still blazed. Eventually the smoke lost its caustic smell and the pyre became nothing more than a stack of burning wood. Gratefully, I stood up and returned home.

Krishna Devi's body was gone, but the mourning over her loss continued. For a period of ten days all related persons were jutho, ritually unclean, and had to follow certain austerities. We all refrained from washing our hair, and no one consumed any salt, oil, or lentils. The fact that I still ate with the family established that I too was one of Krishna Devi's relations.

During this jutho period came the four-day Tihaar festival. On the third night it was customary to line the windows with candles, but this year not a light was seen. Even the families that were not in mourning kept their houses respectfully dark.

At the end of the ten days, the women carried water from the dhaaraa to wash their hair in the open courtyard. While this was done, the men and boys assembled in one of the fields and shaved their heads, leaving only the sacred *tupi* top-knots. Surendra mentioned that perhaps I too would shave my head, but since I wasn't Hindu, I didn't have it done.

For the trio of sons, and especially for Kaanchho, the mourning rituals were elaborate. During the first ten days Kaanchho lived alone on the porch, wearing a white loincloth and eating one small meal a day. Many pujaas and purifications had to be performed. Most of these required a Braahman priest and some were expensive. Only after the initial ten days had passed could Kaanchho engage in his normal work or socializing.

For the following year the sons would restrict themselves to clothing that was completely white. At the end of the year the most visible signs of mourning would be completed, but the family would still hold annual *shraaddha* ceremonies in the name of the dead. The rites in Krishna Devi's honor would continue for as long as her memory survived, and a shrine might one day be built to honor her. These things would be nice, but her greatest tribute was already established and was self-perpetuating—her lifeblood flowing in the children of Aiselukharka.

April 26

Tasi Lapcha Pass 19,000 feet

I drive in the axe with both hands and lean over it for a rest—legs apart, arms straight, and head down. The frigid air stings my lungs, but this is good; cold and clear conditions are perfect for an ascent. With those nearly complete climbs of Island Peak and Kangchung Himal in mind, I'm ready to reach the absolute top of a mountain.

Raising my head, I review Pharchamo's features: the left skyline is guarded by an ice cliff; next comes an escarpment of mixed snow, ice, and névé; the central slopes are not too steep, but are crevassed higher up; and on the far right is a seemingly climbable expanse of snow. Atop it all is the summit with its unknown difficulties. A twin-lumped leveling hides the highest point.

Pulling out the axe, I scan the white-on-white snow, and I continue climbing. I move one slow foot at a time; with so far to go, I must ration my strength. I stick to the center, knowing that I'll eventually be forced to the right, but not wanting to make the traverse until it's absolutely necessary. The pass drops behind me and I see one reason for the uncertainty of its height. The lowest point of the pass can't be crossed because of an enormous fissure. Should the height of a pass be measured at its lowest point or at the elevation one must climb to cross it?

The grade steepens as it becomes interspersed with stretches of ice. It's frightfully cold and I'm glad that I've chosen to wear all my clothes. Even the four layers around my legs let a chill through, but gradually the temperature rises with the sun. The point comes where I should traverse to the right, but marks that resemble footprints keep me moving up the center. The marks are mere crystallized spots in the snow, but their even spacing, right and left, convince me that a climbing party has passed this way—perhaps the ill-fated Japanese expedition.

I zigzag upwards. I prefer to climb the snow and névé, but more and more I'm forced onto the blue ice. I chop a pitch of steps to reach a dark object in the snow. It's an old-style ice piton. Japanese rarely use out-of-date equipment, so maybe it was left by the expedition of New Zealanders. A spell of chopping dislodges the piton and I add it to my scanty equipment. It might be useful. Also, I wish to leave the peaks unscarred by the passage of mountaineers. It's the ethic of *clean climbing*, to climb the mountains without violating them, leaving no traces behind.

I'm not encouraged by the knowledge that better equipped and more experienced climbers have been here and have needed technical equipment. I'm climbing without even a rope.

I'm stopped by a crevasse. Detouring around it, I encounter a second one. It's narrow and I can step over. An hour passes as I work through the maze. Finally I meet a crevasse that has no route around. On the other side is a smooth white slope leading towards the summit. I pace along the edge looking for a way across. My best bet is to jump it at its narrowest point. How wide is it? Maybe 4 or 5 feet, though it looks like 20. *Come on, Phil. You can do it!* My body is set to go, but I hold myself back. The far lip is higher than this one and might break under my weight. And jumping is very uncertain in heavy clothing at high altitude. It requires the security of a rope. My legs want to jump. The summit beckons, and so does the icy blue depth of the crevasse. I step back, and retreat.

The sense of defeat rises in my stomach as I traverse to the right. Another route might go, but I doubt it. Pulling back from the crucial jump was the end. I move away from the crevasses and head obliquely up. I take the usual, frequent rests demanded by the 20,000-foot altitude, and though my progress seems good, the summit is no closer. The route takes me around the flank, which is unclimbable higher up because of ice cliffs and overhangs. I must get back to the center.

I search wearily for a way up, but every possibility is blocked by a crevasse, a sheer drop, or an ice wall. It's hopeless. The sun begins to dip. Even if I had a safe route, it's already too late to get to the summit and back. I think of the Japanese who climbed the peak, only to fall on the descent. Dejectedly, I start down, but then I halt after a hundred steps. I remember the dictum of Shiro, a Japanese climber who participated in the first winter ascent of Mount McKinley: "When there is only one way to survive in the mountains, you must check every possibility to the very end..." The words pester me and I start up again; I have failed to explore a particular snow ramp that bypasses two crevasses.

Retracing those hundred steps is hard work. I move further up and out along the snow ramp. The powdered snow is heavy and weighs my feet down. Across the ramp, a delicate traverse skirts an ice cliff. I follow it out, but beyond that there is no way to climb higher—a dead end.

Again I start down, knowing that I tried everything, and still failed. *Ke garne?* I descend snow slopes which take me far to one side of all the crevasses. This route is easier than the one I took coming up, but it's worthless since it gives no access to the top. As I plod down, I console myself—Pharchamo has no safe route for a solo climber... But hasn't it? What about the other side? The left side, the mixed slopes of ice and névé? It's steep, but it has no crevasses. Suddenly it seems very possible. I total up my remaining food. It should be enough. Tomorrow I'll rest and then make another attempt.

I come down to the pass, circle the fissure, and tackle the short climb to camp. Only now do I feel how truly tired I am. Before crawling into the tent, I turn to look up at Pharchamo. The summit is not quite visible, but the darkening sky is still cloudless. It would have been a perfect day to reach the top.

April 27

Tasi Lapcha Pass

Once again, a day of rest. Idle days at high altitude are all the same. My mind works slowly as the inactive hours pass in a partial stupor. Simple tasks like collecting snow and cooking meals require a major effort and much time.

The position of my camp beneath the overhang has disadvantages. First: the sun never shines on the tent. Usually a tent in the sun can reach seemingly tropical temperatures, but alas, not here. Even at midday it's like living in an ice-box. Second: chunks of ice continually fall from the cliff's edge a few hundred feet above. Some of the pieces are the size of large water jugs. They whistle as they drop, crashing to the ground within a few yards of the tent. The danger of being hit is perhaps small, but I nevertheless brace myself each time I hear the high-pitched shriek of a falling missile.

The day's big event is going out to photograph Pharchamo. It stands like a mammoth pyramid. Snow and snow and ice. I can clearly see the dead-end routes of yesterday's failure, while on the left skyline is an impassable cliff of ice. This leaves the near left as my only hope. Using the binoculars, I spot a finger of snow that could grant me a route through the ice. It looks too steep, but the view is foreshortened—I'll find out tomorrow. I take the picture: a white cone, a deep blue sky, and a few wisps of cloud.

With evening comes a wind that rattles the tent. It's not overly cold, which is a near-certain sign of bad weather. I sleep as soon as it's dark, and in my dreams are visions of a white pyramidal mountain, a small mountain, with eyes.

I looked again. The mountain with eyes was Krishna Bhakta wrapped in his thick white blanket. It was late November. We were both cold, and I had been daydreaming. I would soon be leaving Aiselukharka, and one of the final things I wished to do in Nepal was to make a mountaineering journey in the direction of Everest. Thin air and snow mountains...

We pulled our blankets tight around ourselves and rocked on our heels. "*Ah ma ma ma... Katiko jaardo chha*—How cold it is," we mumbled in commiseration.

We stared hypnotically at the smoking lamp, imagining that through our eyes we could somehow absorb a wisp of the flame's heat. A rat scurried along one of the roof beams, and three houses away we heard the cry of Shyam Krishna's baby. To sit there in the cold, shivering with Krishna Bhakta, felt like the most natural thing in the world, but in just a few days I would be leaving. Two years of the ease and unity of life in Aiselukharka had seeped into me, and now the world outside Nepal had become unreal. I couldn't fully understand why I had decided to leave. During the periods that I felt good, the difficulties and frustrations seemed very distant. What convenient memories we all have! The rat ran back along the beam and I wished I was staying longer.

Krishna Bhakta looked over at me. He was apparently reading my thoughts. "Is it not possible for you to stay?"

Recently, many people had been asking me to stay in Aiselukharka. They remembered that I had originally said that I would only be there for one year but that I had eventually stayed for two. So why not a third year? They suggested that I remain in Aiselukharka permanently—"Get married and buy some land." Miraa Devi, the girl who lived across the street, was mentioned as a possible bride, but the Headmaster recommended his wife's younger sister. To stay a third year in the village was an inviting possibility, and the thought of a Nepali bride was both frightening and alluring. It seemed like a very reasonable thing to do, and my old friend Dwight, the formerly vegetarian English teacher, was presently arranging his Nepali wedding.

I returned Krishna Bhakta's gaze and answered his question. "Yes, it's possible for me to stay, but I can't. I miss my brothers and my parents." This was the only reason for leaving for which there was no rebuttal.

Krishna Bhakta accepted my answer, but he knew that it wasn't really true. He had seldom heard me talk about my family. "When you walk from here, what will you do?" he asked.

"First I have some days' work in Kathmandu, then I will be going to India..." I described the short trip that I would make before returning to Nepal with the intent of trekking to Everest and climbing the high mountains. I explained about flying to Lamidada, hiking to Namche Bazaar, and crossing the Tasi Lapcha pass.

"Yes," said Krishna Bhakta, "but when you get back, to Amaarika, will you live at home or will you work?"

"What? My family is broken, isn't it? I have no real home."

"But your Father's home..."

"He has no land. He lives in a rented room. And the town where I live is very far from there."

Krishna Bhakta extended a hand from beneath the blanket and rubbed his head. It was hard for him to comprehend this notion of a broken family. And how could a supposedly rich man like me have a father who owned no land? "What will you do?" he asked.

"I will have to rent a room." I shrugged. It was a depressing idea. Living alone in the midst of America's vastness would be a drastic step down from the sense of community that I had in Aiselukharka. I wasn't even certain where I would live. No place seemed overly inviting. Most of all, I wanted to be close to my friends, but who were they? My relationship with Kay had ended, some of my closest friends were now married, and others had moved. I had dropped out of their lives, and I had learned from my short trip home that no one cared about Nepal. I expected that my homecoming would be a lonely occasion.

But before I even went home, I would need time to put myself back together, to assimilate and fit into place the events of the past two years...

Krishna Bhakta brought me out of my reverie with another question. "And when you get back, the government will give you work?"

"No, I must find my own work, though the Peace Corps gives me some money for living."

"But isn't the Peace Corps a government service? Don't they have to care for you?"

"It's not like that. I must find my own job." This, too, was depressing. I could imagine myself handing out resumes: "Anybody want a retired Peace Corps Volunteer?" Why compete against dozens of applicants for a job that I might not like? There in Aiselukharka I had work that was satisfying and for which I was truly needed. In two years I had matured from a juvenile who could hardly speak the language to a capable adult whose opinions were respected. My work had extended from the classroom to include everything that affected the village. Work in health care, water development, and reforestation could keep me occupied for a lifetime. But I was giving this up for an unknown job in a world of concrete and gasoline. It made no sense.

Krishna Bhakta shifted his glance back to the lamp. He shook his head slightly and whispered, "*Naramaailo, naramaailo*—Unpleasant, so unpleasant."

Perhaps he was commenting on the unhappiness of my coming departure, or possibly he was imagining the loneliness I would feel on my return to America. Krishna Bhakta was the only one in Aiselukharka who understood that America was not just fruit trees and sunshine. He was also one of the few men in the village who had been faced with a decision of great consequence. This, too, allowed him to feel empathy with my position. His story was unusual.

Krishna Bhakta's branch of the family had not always lived in Aiselukharka. They originated from Bhaktapur in the Kathmandu Valley. As a boy, Krishna Bhakta spent a good deal of time in both places, Bhaktapur and

284

Aiselukharka, though it was in Bhaktapur that his family always assembled for Dasai. As a young man, he witnessed the important events in Nepal's recent history: the fall of the Rana oligarchy, the reinstatement of the King, and the first arrival of Westerners. By maturity, Krishna Bhakta was firmly established in Bhaktapur. He operated a small but successful shop and his young wife was proving to be a good mother. His only problem was that he didn't like Bhaktapur. Running a business gave him headaches and the commotion of life in a large town, though very exciting, was too unnerving. The family retained land in Aiselukharka and a life in the hills was what Krishna Bhakta preferred. But he was also responsible for the welfare of his growing family, and he was expected to fulfill the mercantile role of a prosperous Newari. It was certainly a difficult decision, but Krishna Bhakta uprooted his family and moved his home to the hills. He had not celebrated Dasai in Bhaktapur since then, nor had he experienced any more headaches.

I was facing a similar decision. In Aiselukharka was the type of place I wanted to live, the type of work, the friends, the mountains, but, but...

Again Krishna Bhakta seemed to be reading my mind. He freed both arms from the blanket, crossed them, and looked at me directly but softly. "You really have to go back, don't you?" he said as he stopped rocking. "We will never forget you. You are just like one of us. But one must be with his own caste, with his own kind. Isn't that so?"

"*Hunchha,*" I replied.

Krishna Bhakta was right, but what was my own kind? That was the crux of my difficulties—the conflict between the Nepali Philipsir, whom I had become, and the American Phil, who had been lost along the way. I felt that there could be no compromise.

April 28
Tasi Lapcha

Bebeep. *Bebeep.* The watch alarm does not startle me. I've been waiting for it to sound. First: start the stove and melt the day's drinking water. Second: pull on successive layers of clothing in preparation for the climb. It's dark and I work by feel—the routine is automatic. Wind buffets the tent and dislodges a shower of ice from the overhang. The weather is not good for climbing.

By first light I am fed and packed. With my legs out of the tent, I begin fitting the crampons onto my boots, but I am stopped when my bare fingers stick to the frosted metal. I don my gloves to finish the job but I remove them again to pull the crampon straps extra tight. Getting to my feet, I kick and stomp to test the crampons' security.

I zip the tent closed and slip the pack over my shoulders. The wind's fury hits me as I step onto the smooth snow of the pass. The wind truly shrieks as it whips across the wide basin. The gusts force me to crouch low with my back to them, while the mightiest blasts threaten to knock me over. At first I follow my tracks which are still visible from two days ago, but then I leave them and angle to the left. The wind slackens as I get around the corner and away from the pass. Down in the valleys, the clouds are already forming.

The lower slopes are easy. The condition of the snow is good and my crampons bite firmly with each step. The angle steadily increases and I stop often, both to catch my breath and to examine the route. It curves up in a great arc, culminating in a narrow finger of snow that threads between two faces of ice. It looks severe at its uppermost, but above the ice the slope eases off and leads to a long *S*-grade to the summit. There are no crevasses in sight.

Two hours pass as I work steadily up, driving in the axe's point with each step and stopping ever more frequently for air. Over my shoulder and far to the northeast stands the Everest massif, the black triangle of the world's top seemingly no higher than its neighbors. With an effort, I could pick out my entire route of the past six weeks: up the Dudh Kosi to Namche, further north to Lobuche and Everest, back around to Island Peak, then over the Chikim La to Kangchung, down to Namche via Gokyo, and finally up to the Tasi Lapcha. It seems long and meaningless. My eyes stay fixed on Everest as the clouds move up from the east and hide the other peaks from view.

I resume climbing, now kicking in my toes with each step, now chopping holds with the axe. At first the surface is yielding, but climbing higher and steeper, it turns to crystalline névé and then to ice. I discover that my climbable path of snow is only a veneer of whiteness over the otherwise solid wall of ice. I hack out steps and my arms ache from the strain. I chop with one hand at a time, keeping the wrist strap tight. With the other hand I cling to the hand holds. I rest looking straight down between my feet. This is the steepest ice climbing I have ever attempted. The mountain drops below me in a smooth wall and far far down it curves off in the direction of the pass. Dreamily, I tell myself that a fall would just send me on a long fast slide. Realistically, I know a slip would send my body hurtling uncontrollably down the face, careening head over heels, ultimately coming to rest at the bottom—bashed, broken, bloodied, and dead.

I reach high with the axe, and with slightly erratic swings, I chop another hold. Turning the axe around, I drive in the pick and grip to its questionable security as I take a careful step upwards. I shift my left hand to the next hold and pant for breath with my face pressed against the ice. A long delicate ladder of steps stretches beneath me. It's dangerous—both precarious and stupid. My arm pulls the axe free, raises it above my head, and begins chopping another step.

As my body climbs higher, gradually tiring, the steps become noticeably smaller and increasingly far apart. A voice in my head pleads for prudence—*Stop. Go back.* Another step is cut and I move up. Putting my head back, I see there, up there, the top of the wall. It's coming within reach. *Go down!* My arms and legs, with no orders from the brain, climb on, hoisting me higher and higher. The face is climbable, but the danger is extreme. Suddenly, as though seeing it for the first time, I discern my risky position—the vertical face, the tiny insecure steps, my growing fatigue, and the possibility of a storm. I realize that I can indeed climb the wall, but by the time I reach the summit and return, I will be too tired to down-climb it. A slip would be... unthinkable. *Turn around! Go back!*

The ice axe arcs, and arcs again. A step is cut and a mindless foot moves up. *Go back!* Each move brings me closer to the top, but going on is foolhardy, even suicidal. I must descend, but my body climbs upward. I plead with myself. *Go down! Please, you must descend!* I gasp for air with my head resting against the unyielding ice. An arm swings up, chopping, and a cramponed boot steps higher, slowly, unsurely.

Stop! STOP!! My left hand trembles as I grasp a hold. *You must go down. Now!* I assert control. I pull out my left boot and stretch it downward, probing for a lower step. There it is. I shift my weight gingerly and bring down the right foot. I extract the axe and send it home lower down. Two more halting steps of retreat and I'm doing all right.

The descent is more difficult, more dangerous, and much more frightening than the ascent. I can't see the steps that are down past my feet, so I must explore for them with the toes of my clumsy boots. This sets me off balance and destroys my self-confidence. I move my mittened hands and cramponed feet with extreme caution. Forced to look down with each step, I am constantly reminded of the space below my feet.

One uneasy delicate step at a time, I make my way down.

Finally below the ice, and onto the steep snow, I chop a perch and squat down to rest. I look aloft, not believing what I climbed, or nearly climbed. My body is numb with exhaustion. I could never have come down that wall after a full day's climbing. Another attempt that failed. Shit.

Continuing the descent with my feet sideways to the slope, I begin to think. The route failed, but from near the top was a view further to the left. I can still see it—around the corner, beyond the cliff, was no ice at all, just an expanse of snow.

Hoping for a long simple route around the difficulties, I halt my descent immediately below the steep climbing. Here I leave my tracks and make an extended traverse towards the far base of the ice cliff. It's a matter of putting one foot ahead of the other, periodically pausing to regain oxygen balance, and moving up again—so easy compared to the vertical wall. As I approach the imposing cliff of ice, its perspective changes, becoming more of a buttress than a precipice. Skirting the base of the obstacle, I look up with gratitude at the miraculous stretch of windswept snow that will take me to the summit.

I climb without hesitation. The way is clear—I take the most direct route while favoring the least incline. The clouds below the Tasi Lapcha churn upward and the climb becomes a race against the weather. As I ascend, my upright rests become more frequent and the chain of ice-axe holes steadily lengthens. I'm now past the buttress, looking down on the ice that I nearly climbed.

The grade steepens, and I move carefully, though I cut no steps. The slope forms a crest and I pull myself over the lip and onto the wide S-shaped bend that leads to the top. I'm on the summit dome at last. I dig three deep grooves into the snow to mark the spot for my return. The slope bulges outward and I see how the Japanese could have easily lost their way.

The wind strengthens and my crampons leave almost no mark on the hard packed snow. Up and up. With head down, I lean against the axe, puffing at the air. Persisting. I move upward and my body climbs automatically, instinctively.

The shape of the ridge reminds me of my forested hill behind Aiselukharka. I pass between two low lumps, the highest point visible from my camp on the Tasi Lapcha. The ridge levels and narrows, and the approach to a house-size spur of snow is blocked by a bottomless crevasse. A snow bridge down on the left spans the gap. It looks dubious, but no matter... It holds me and I'm across.

I tackle the spur head-on, the only way. It's all powdered snow, like sugar, and it's nearly vertical. I flail with arms and legs working in unison. I seem to do more digging than climbing as I lunge upwards. Each spasm gains me 6–8 inches and leaves me panting for breath with my arms sunk deep into the snow. Another thrust, and another. I gulp for air with my mouth wide open, my lungs about to burst. Waiting for my breathing to come under control, I push up. I reach the crest, gasping again, and I crawl on my hands and knees. Standing up, I find myself straddling a razor-edged ridge, an arête. A few steps ahead are objects in the snow: scraps of rope and a metal stake—belay equipment left by expedition climbers. The ridge slopes downward, but it's not the summit. The second crest stands distinctly higher. The top is only 30 yards away, but it looks terribly far. I tiptoe along the windward side of the arête, keeping clear of the cornice.

And I'm here—the summit! 20,580 feet. I look down on all sides. It's a strange sensation. I feel exposed and naked. The fierce wind is unnerving. The clouds bubble up from the valleys and blot out the view.

I have two flags: a red tattered bandanna from California and a white Buddhist prayer scarf from the Manang Valley. They are symbolic by coincidence only. I set the camera for a self portrait, and ten seconds later the wind pulls the knit cap from my head. I grab for it, and *click*, the camera catches me in action as I barely save my favorite hat, my *only* hat. To my back stands Tangi Ragi Tau, 2 miles away and 2,000 feet higher.

I should feel exaltation, but that's an emotion to share. My position, high and alone on a pinnacle of ice, is too exposed to feel anything but the need to go down.

I'm tired, but not devastated, certainly not so drained as at the end of a marathon. It's more like being halfway through a marathon. I stuff the bandanna back into the pack and I bury one end of the prayer scarf in the snow. Its free end flaps in the wind. The prayer scarf belongs here, but the bandanna does not. Nor do I. The time has already come to start down.

It's ironic to stay such a short time at a place that I've worked so hard to reach, but without pausing to consider this, I begin the descent. First I retrace my steps along the arête to the metal stake. I down-climb the spur with great care and only now do I realize that a fall would have sent me to the bottom of the crevasse. Once I'm across the snow bridge, I begin to relax. Strangely enough, from here on it's fairly easy—just keep going, mind my feet, and don't get lost.

The clouds move in and I must watch closely, following the track of ice-axe holes that I made coming up. It's not snowing, though the air is filled with blowing ice particles, resembling frozen fog. The spindrift begins filling the ice-axe holes and I increase my vigilance to stay on route. This is the stage where the Japanese faltered.

I come down with few rests, step after step, stopping only to scrutinize the route. Reaching the grooves that I dug in the snow, I turn around and back over the lip. It's steeper here, but the tracks are distinct—no chance of getting lost. Down and down, the descent is tedious and awkward: under the buttress, past the looming faces of ice, and down to my tracks of two days ago.

On the near-leveling of the pass, my legs swing freely, almost snagging on one another. Coming up to the camp, I hear a whistling sound, and I jump back as a barrage of ice drops from the overhang. The largest pieces all miss me.

Encased within the tent, I remove my crampons and boots. Night settles as I force myself to light the stove and set on a pan of snow. I notice that I'm talking to myself. "Yes, sure, it was a long climb and you're tired, but you have to get something to drink. You'll get dehydrated." It's good advice, but I fall asleep before the snow is melted.

I wake an hour later; I'm parched. The stove is still burning and the water is boiling. I drink and smile. "Thanks," I say.

"You're welcome," I answer.

"It was a good climb."

"Yes, you're right, " I reply. "It was a good climb." I smile again.

"Good night."

I see only the quiet darkness, and my eyes remain closed as I awake. When I turn, cold air assaults me through the top of the sleeping bag. The morning is not welcome; I don't wish to leave this place. Reluctantly, I open my eyes.

A rusted tin box sits on a straw mat, and the floor is remarkably uncluttered. My clothes and books are already packed. Sunlight peeks through the openings in the roof making a pattern of spots on the near wall. This is my last morning in Aiselukharka.

I rise with a shiver, and in a rush I pull on my clothes. Circling the room, I open the wooden shutters to admit the familiar sounds of the morning: the stone mill grinding daal, chickens fighting over breakfast, and a song on Radio Nepal being played too loud. The music comes from the main house. My seldom-used radio is Krishna Bhakta's payment for the last five months of food. The song is a story of spring—a time of planting and growing—so inappropriate.

In the center of the room sit the two bundles that I've packaged for the journey to Kathmandu. Two porters will have no trouble with the load. In my own pack I will carry the breakables and valuables. These include the gifts presented to me by the family: an army-issue *kukuri* knife and a shiny brass lamp. It's the mate to the tarnished lamp that I've been using these past two years. Chakra Lal and Ganga Ram of the ninth class arrive as I'm packing a few remaining items.

"*Sir, tapaai ahile jaanuhunchha?*—Sir, are you leaving immediately?"

"No. I must go to the school at ten, and after that I'll go."

"*Hunchha.*" Narayan nudges Ganga, prompting him to speak, "Sir? Please give us a remembrance."

"I have already—two years of classes. Isn't that so?"

"Yes, but some little thing, so that…"

"Narayan, didn't I once give you a photograph? And Ganga, didn't you receive a mathematics book from me?"

"Yes, it's true. *Hunchha.*" Narayan and Ganga look down at their feet and grin impishly. While I tie the loads, they take their leave. "*Namaste*, Sir. *Namaste.*"

Carrying my tin of water, I go out to the charpi in the back. The sky is like blue crystal and every leaf is coated with dew. I dawdle in the yard to contemplate the plum tree whose fruit I've never seen and to remember Aamaa's surprise over my harvest of multi-colored Indian corn.

I return to the house and find Krishna Bhakta talking with the two porters. They test the loads and we negotiate a price. They accept a fair wage though they remain disgruntled—it's a ritual. They will take the loads now and I will meet them on the way to Lamidada. As they leave, Krishna Bhakta admonishes them: "If you get there first, you are to wait until Philipsir arrives. Don't just leave the burdens at a shop. *Hunchha?*" They totter off in agreement.

Krishna Bhakta returns to the main house and I follow him up the narrow stairs to the top-floor kitchen. Aamaa is delighted to see me, for I rarely eat in the kitchen. She works at the smoky fireplace; the construction of a chimney-equipped cooking area is one of my many unstarted projects. She fries chickpeas in a round-bottomed skillet while the daal boils. The rice is already done and it sits covered on a stone slab. Aamaa perks up the fire by blowing on it through a bamboo tube: *whhoooo, whhoooo.* Nilam helps

293

by preparing the chutney. She grinds chillis and pepper on a board with a smooth stone. The morning is identical to any other.

Surendra comes up and Aamaa serves us while they chatter in Newari. Only Mahendra is missing. He has taken the water buffalo out to graze. Today's daal-bhaat is not the best. Perhaps Aamaa has rushed the meal for me. "*Mitho bhayo!* Delicious!" I say. When I've eaten two and a half servings, I'm full. After washing my hands at the stone sink, I return to my own room.

I have little to do. I brush my teeth and look around for anything that I might have forgotten. There's nothing, just the pans, wash basin, and sleeping pad that I'm leaving for Aamaa. At a sound on the stairs, I turn to see the entire family coming through the door. Aamaa carries the flat, sectioned plate used for tikaa ceremonies and pujaas, and from Surendra's fingers hang five flower garlands. Nilam unobtrusively slips a dozen mandarin oranges and a sack of pounded rice into my pack.

"Ah! I must get tikaa and flowers?" I grin.

"Yes. Yes," they say. "It's most essential."

I sit on the plank bench as they take turns. First a finger is dipped into red or yellow tikaa paint and applied to the center of my forehead, then a string of flowers is looped around my neck and the hands are pulled back in the sign of *Namaste*. We observe complete silence in a mood of disbelief. With each tikaa and garland, I return their *Namastes* and study their faces: Nilam, grimacing to make a perfect tikaa; Aamaa, first-time-ever frowning as she looks at me; Surendra, resembling his mother; Mahendra, resembling his father; and finally Krishna Bhakta, trying to smile, but with his lips turned down.

I stand and attempt to say "*Dhanyabaad,*" the ultimate expression of thanks, but the word sticks in my throat. We look at each other with our mouths closed, no one knowing what to do or say. At a death one mourns, when leaving on a trip one hopes for a safe return, but this is neither. We're stuck in a quandary of inaction. How do we face a "small death"?

294

"We have to go to the school, don't we?" says Surendra and his suggestion is accepted with relief.

"Mahendra, do you want to carry my pack?" I offer.

He smiles broadly; never before have I let anyone carry it for me. We troop down the stairs and four neighbor boys push me into the front on the trail leading to school. Up above, Aamaa hangs her head out of the window and watches us go.

As we walk, other students come down the hillside and form a long column behind us. Mahendra carries my pack with pride and the garlands around my neck swish from side to side with each step. I take a slight detour to get a final look at the slope above the dhaaraa. The crowd follows with comments about "Philipsir's trees." The trail winds along the edges of terraces, now dry and barren, and passes the cluster of houses where the Tailor lives. I'm disappointed that he's not home—perhaps he's out delivering a shirt or measuring a child for a new frock.

We move up between more fields and I look back at the growing line of people. They are deathly quiet. I shift the garlands slightly and I begin to understand that I'm leaving. Slowly, the tears well up in my eyes and flow down my cheeks, dripping down and watering the flowers about my neck. I don't sob or choke. I feel calm. The tears flow swifter, with ease, like a gentle rain.

A man stands by the side, waiting for the column to pass before joining in. He sees my face and the whispers circulate. "He has tears." "Philipsir has tears." I don't wipe them away. They run their course as they must.

The group scatters on the school ground, leaving me on my own. They busily arrange something, but I don't know what. We've already had two farewell feasts: one given by the school in my honor (even the Braahmans ate rice which was cooked by a man of the lowest caste) and another prepared by myself, an American lunch with foodstuffs imported from Kathmandu (peanut butter and jelly sandwiches, toasted cheese sandwiches, and tomato soup, all of which everyone ate, but few actually enjoyed).

Entering the school's ground floor, I look around the ninth grade's empty classroom. The too-few tables and benches are as wobbly as when I first came, the stone walls are still barren, and the blackboard has more pockmarks. Visible improvements are scarce. Have I actually done anything in the past two years? I completed various projects, helped to train new teachers, and taught over 1,500 hours of classes. The students definitely learned a lot and that can't be discredited. But have I changed anything? Was I supposed to? Would any change have been good? I think of the mountaineer who climbs clean, climbing *with* the mountains instead of *against* them, leaving no trace of his passage. When he's gone, the mountains are unharmed. The same principle applies to working in a strange land—the worker must be with the people and become one with them, but in so doing ceases to be an agent of change, and when departing, leaves the people unscarred. So I haven't changed the world, and that's no doubt the way it should be. As far as the Peace Corps is concerned, I've clearly done my assigned work and played my role as a goodwill ambassador, establishing international friendship. Though I doubt that Krishna Bhakta thought much about "international friendship" when he came to talk with me in the dark of so many nights.

I sit on one of the benches in the back of the room and remember all the lessons that the students had here, all the pieces of chalk that I used up on the board, and all the laughter that we enjoyed. It's easy to be nostalgic once all the problems are passed. I take a long look around the room, trying to indelibly record it all.

Outside again, I stroll around, making a final visit to some of my favorite places: my seat on the temple wall where I wrote letters to Kay, the dirt volleyball court where I broke my finger, the storage room where I graded exams and dreamed of climbing mountains, the stand of trees on the hilltop where I could sometimes be alone... The garlands make me self-conscious. I consider removing them as a sign of humility, but I decide not to. This is the village's day to treat me as though I'm someone special. Everyone's eyes are on me and I feel the tears returning.

The students and villagers begin assembling in front of the school, and when the teachers come parading out of the office, I know that it's time to join them. They take me to the front and place me by the statue of Sarasvati, the goddess of Wisdom and Learning. Everyone is here: the students and teachers, the Pradhaan Panch, other notables from Nawalpur, and onlookers from the village. Now, at last, with all of us packed together, the silence ends and the commotion begins.

The Headmaster starts a speech, "*Haamro pyaaro pis kor swayamsewakko dayaalo...* Our dear Peace Corps self-willing servant, whose merciful..." His words soon become too flowery and formal for me to understand, but few of us are really listening. He doesn't speak for long.

A black topi is produced, which the Headmaster places on my head. It's a few sizes too small and it sits atop my head like an overturned flowerpot. Next I'm decorated with more tikaas and garlands. The teachers, the Pradhaan Panch, Krishna Bhakta, Shyam Krishna the shopkeeper, and a representative student from each class all have a chance. Everyone else lightly applauds. The shorter students have difficulty adorning me with the strings of puffed corn and flowers. My topi is knocked off twice as they try to get the garlands over my head. And once it falls off when I stoop forward to help. The crowd enjoys the comedy, and I'm lucky enough to catch the topi each time.

The Headmaster presents me with a Letter of Gratitude, officially thanking me for my work, and then he hands me a framed model in relief of Pashupatinath, Nepal's holiest temple. Across the top of the glass is pasted the school's letterhead with its full title: *Aiselukharka Maadhyamik Bidyaalaya.* It's beautiful. I accept the gift with a *Namaste* of thanks.

The presentation is finished, but I need to say something, to publicly express how indebted I am to them all. "My friends," I begin as I look at the sea of faces, "these two years have felt like only two days..." Everyone is talking and moving around. "Aiselukharka has become like my true home…" I stop. The words sound empty and no one is listening to what I say. They are too busy calling to me: "*Namaste.*" "Please write us." "You must come back one time." It's like beginning a speech as the train is pulling out. It's time to go.

I put the model of Pushupatinath into the pack and lift it to my shoulders. Everyone has lined up into two long rows and I must walk down the center. All hands, including my own, are raised in a *Namaste*. I walk slowly down the aisle, turning from side to side, greeting everyone. *Namaste. Namaste. Namaste.* It seems unreal, as though this is all just a rehearsal.

Reaching the end of the two lines, I start off toward the trail that leads away from the school. I feel a sudden surge of emotion from the students. They refuse to let me leave so easily, but they won't stop me either. So everyone follows. Spontaneously, they step into line, forming a procession behind me. Like a long snake, we move across the athletic field and up the trail along the ridge. The school is left behind as we hike slowly up. We march higher and higher with no one willing to stop. Morosely the word is passed around that everyone will halt at the little pass where the trail begins the descent toward the river.

As we hike upward, the reality of it all becomes apparent, and when we reach the top, a lifeless silence prevails. This is truly the end—downhill one way to Kathmandu and downhill the other way to Aiselukharka. To stall for time, I take out my camera for a final picture. Not a single smile appears; every face is pained.

We have nothing more to do. We say "*Namaste,*" and "*Namaste,*" and "*Namaste,*" again. I turn my back and walk. Alone. Everyone stands frozen, watching me leave. Reaching the first bend, I turn around. No one has moved. I make a final gesture of *Namaste* and they all lift their hands to their foreheads in a silent benediction. I continue around the bend, and the hillside blocks them from view. They're gone. And I'm gone. I'm gone.

With each step, I feel that something is being wrenched out of me, the marrow sucked from my bones, leaving only an empty shell. The "small death" turns out to be my own. In a succession of steps, this person, Philipsir, has taken two years to develop from birth to maturity: arriving in Nepal, learning the language, adapting to the food and diseases, acquiring cultural sense, gaining acceptance in the village, becoming a productive teacher, and finally cutting the ties that bound him to another world. But speaking Nepali is irrelevant outside of Nepal and eating with the fingers would be considered crude in America. The role that I've assumed as Philipsir, the Nepali school teacher, has no existence outside of Aiselukharka. Leaving here means Philipsir's death. While my body goes on, the inner me ceases to exist.

I continue walking down from the pass. I'm aware only of the pack on my back and the rhythm of my steps: one, two, three, four... The slope beneath my feet is white and is unblemished by a trail. The whiteness stretches in all directions. The slopes of snow below the Tasi Lapcha are smooth and firm and my legs swing mindlessly, my body descending, a shell without a yolk.

Now I understand these past weeks of manic climbing, heedless to considerations of safety. I've been a zombie, an animated body with a mind long dead, recklessly climbing, trying to complete the small death that the departure from Aiselukharka left only half done. For six weeks I have climbed in a manner leading toward destruction, while at the same time I've reflected on the past two years in a process of reconstruction. I continue to descend.

My feet are encased in overboots and crampons, and the strap around my wrist holds the ice axe. The consumption of six days' worth of food and fuel has left my pack feeling relatively light. This combined with the downhill grade makes progress easy. The Tasi Lapcha is behind me and I work my way down to the northwest, steering clear of the difficult sections in the center of the slope. I must occasionally backtrack in search of a better route. This is the problem with descending—you can't see the troubles until you're on top of them.

As I down-climb a gully of snow, the surface abruptly gives way, opening a hole beneath me. As I fall through, my arms shoot out instinctively. My pack and elbows stop the fall, leaving me dangling chest deep. My legs kick desperately in the air, trying to catch a toehold on the side of the hidden crevasse. I hunch forward and dig in with the axe, pulling myself up and rolling sideways out of the hole. My heart beats wildly as I distribute my weight by crawling. The danger is passed before I have fully realized what happened.

The near catastrophe interrupts my thoughts and I concentrate more on climbing. In three hours I reach the relative leveling of the Drolum Bau Glacier. Here, at around 18,000 feet, the glacier is calm, but a mile south it turns at a right angle and plunges down a 1,000-foot cliff. This will be the crux of the descent from the Tasi Lapcha. Already it's midday.

Initially I follow the east edge of the ice where telltale scraps of trash point the way. Then I cross the half-mile-wide glacier, as I've been advised, and turn south again to reach the beginning of the rock. Below this point the glacier is a broken chaos of ice. It drops over the cliff like a frozen waterfall flowing at a pace measured in centuries.

I remove my crampons and my pack to make a downward reconnaissance. Only one route is possible. To the left is the tangled icefall and to the right is a rock wall. I follow the narrow line between the two. The way gives me an impression of previous use, but I find no definitive signs. Scrambling further down, I am convinced that this is the way. A voice appeals to me to save an hour: *Aw come on, go fetch the pack. This is only wasting time.* I persist further down to make certain that it's the right route.

Below me is a cliff—vertical and obscene. I look around, left and right. A dead end. I recall two bits of information that I've heard about this side of the pass: "An earthquake has altered the way" and "Take the right side of the glacier." But was that the right side going up or coming down? I climb back to my pack. The clouds of late afternoon fill the sky.

After fastening my crampons, I re-ascend the glacier and cross back to the left side. Moving down once again, I find more scraps of trash confirming the route. An hour later I come to the edge of the icefall, but here too are cliffs.

I can't believe it. There must be a way. I search. At one point the lower escarpment of rock reaches up to just 50 feet from the ice. Only 50 feet—the height of a five-storey building. A piece of broken basket shows this to be the right way. With proper ropes and equipment it would be possible, but I have almost nothing. My two pieces of webbing when tied together will reach 20 feet or so. I look down. A boulder protrudes from the ice, forming a ledge at about halfway. *OK, Phil. Do it!* Darkness begins to settle and the first tiny flakes of snow swirl in the air. I'm scared.

I put down the pack, remove one of the sleeping-bag straps, and cinch it tight around my waist. It's made of nylon, 1,000-pound-test. Leaving the pack, I clip my single carabiner and prusik sling onto the waist strap. I take the ice piton scavenged from Pharchamo and the webbing, and I begin down-climbing. I cut a few steps to get me lower, but soon it's too steep and I pound in the ice piton with the side of the axe. Now I tie the webbing to the piton ring and fasten the prusik to the webbing. I can slide this down as a self-belay, a type of protection, as I climb. The prusik knot should hold me if I slip. With more confidence, I'm able to climb down to where the webbing ends just above the ledge. Excellent. I enlarge the steps as I climb back to fetch the pack. The ungainly weight forces me to rely on the webbing as I bring the pack down. Leaving the pack on the ledge, I re-climb the pitch and remove the ice piton. Carefully now, I descend without a belay. This is my fifth time over these steps and I breathe deeply when I reach the boulder.

From the lowest part of the ledge, the ice overhangs slightly. With one end of the webbing still fastened to the dangling ice piton, I bring the free end around an ice-encrusted boulder and thread it back through the piton ring. This forms a noose that will pull the webbing increasingly tightly around the boulder. The lower end of the webbing swings 2 feet above the rock escarpment. Next I take a length of thin cord from my pack and tie one end to the piton ring. Once I'm down, I'll be able to pull on this cord, opening the noose and thus retrieving the whole thing. The far end of the cord reaches the bottom, or at least it seems to; it's too dark and snowy to see clearly.

I put my pack on and arrange the prusik. It worries me. I've never used a prusik knot on webbing before and I wonder if it can truly hold a fall. The strap around my waist worries me too. The material is strong enough, but what about the buckle? I tie a security knot into the strap's free end.

After a last check of the equipment, I step backwards over the edge and begin climbing. I look down with each step and I slide the prusik knot as I go. It soon becomes hopeless. I reach a stance on a verglas-covered boulder, but I am forced to lean backwards, away from the overhang. I must move to the right, but the holds are too far away. Chopping steps is impossible since I need both hands just to hold myself in place. I cautiously stretch out my right leg and get two crampon points lodged into the wall. I try vainly to jam my right hand behind a rounded knob of ice. I'm off balance and over-extended. Steel grates against rock and my left foot begins to slip. With a sudden sick feeling in my stomach, I realize that I'm about to fall. My left hand tries desperately to catch a hold, but it's too late. In an instant, the world rotates completely around and I smash into the cliff. *OhGodOhGod...* Then I'm in the air again and the ice rushes sideways.

I hang from the webbing, swinging side to side, with the ice axe dangling from my wrist and the heavy backpack pulling me backwards. My shoulder throbs. Just above me is the verglas-covered boulder. The strap around my waist pulls up against my diaphragm so that I struggle to breathe. Just ten minutes like this will cause me to pass out, though the added weight of the pack cuts the time even shorter. I must get down. I try to slide the prusik knot—it's jammed tight. I pull up on the webbing to get some slack, but the prusik still won't budge. Now I grab hold of the webbing and attempt to climb back onto the boulder. My hands are too weak and I make no progress.

I slump back with my breath coming in thin gasps. Self-defeat speaks to me: *You wanted to court extinction, so this is it. Just relax. You'll soon pass out, and the struggle will be over...*

"No!" I shout at the falling snow, rejecting destruction. Using my teeth, I pull my gloves off and let them drop. Next I release the ice axe, which clatters to the rocks below. It will be there if I get down. I should drop the pack too, but I'm afraid that it'll bounce over the edge and be lost. Clenching my bare hands around the webbing, I pull up with what little power I have left. The effort gains me an inch of slack—I can breathe again! As I gulp at the air, a portion of my strength returns. I begin to climb slowly. First I get my knees onto the boulder, and then, with my feet in place, I can stand.

My fingers have stiffened from the cold, so I untie the prusik with my teeth. I clip the webbing into the carabiner and pull it back against itself to form a loop. This I grip with both hands, hoping that they can hold the tension of this crude rappel as I descend.

As I lean back, the webbing slides around the carabiner and through my hands. The dark wall moves up. My hands hold, but the friction is incredible. The skin across my right hand is stripped away and the webbing becomes coated with blood. I don't feel it at all. The pack hits first. I'm at the bottom, looking up at the night. My hands are sticky with blood and the snow has stopped falling.

When I'm rested, I hunt for the ice axe and pull my gloves back on. To undo the waist strap is a job. The knot is wedged into the buckle—that last-minute decision to tie a safety knot has saved my life. After retrieving the webbing and the ice piton, I'm ready to go. I peer into the darkness. A sheer rock cliff drops out of sight, and I have no idea of how I'll get down. I step forward, putting my faith in instinct.

I can see only general forms. I climb one way and then the other. The crampons screech over the rock, and I doubt that I'll get down in one piece. I'm trying to descend 1,000 feet of vertical ice-covered rock, in the dark, carrying a full pack, at high altitude. *What are the chances are of surviving this?* I have no options. I climb as much by feel as by sight. I zigzag back and forth, making small delicate moves, step after step—for hours. Strangely, it's not cold. I can hear melted snow trickling over the rocks. My hands become drenched with ice water. Twice I stop to wring out my gloves. Then with astonishment, I look down and vaguely see the bottom—a ways to the left, back across there, and down.

My legs feel like rubber as I stand on the glacier. How long have I been climbing? I walk until I can feel a spot flat enough for the tent. I drop the pack and sit in the snow.

My fingers flex. I stare at my gloved hands, I look out at the night, and I stare at my hands again. I grin. I'm alive! My mouth opens and I laugh. I put back my head and the guffaws come louder. *Ha Ha Ha Ha...* I have to put up the tent. *Haw Haw Haw...*

This is all so silly. Who cares about mountains and Nepali or American roles? I'm alive! The person I was yesterday is dead, the person I will be tomorrow is yet to be born. Every moment of life—not just every two years of life—I must create myself for the next moment. Construction and destruction are inseparable. If poor Nepali Philipsir no longer exists, then neither does old American Phil. There's just me, Phil and Philipsir, born this instant. I'm alive!

I unpack the tent, but I only toy with the poles. I'm unable to fit them together. *Ha Ha Ha Ho Ho...* Oh, I can't stop laughing. *Haw Haw.* My stomach hurts. *Ho Ho Ha Ha.* I feel like Scrooge when he wakes up in the morning and learns that he hasn't missed Christmas. *Haw Haw.* I haven't missed my life! I would like to play with my toes! *Ha Ha Ha Ho Ho Ho.* I roll from side to side, doubled up with mirth. It's all so funny!

I laugh for a long time and in the midst of it I realize what day it is, and what day tomorrow is—the last day of April, my birthday! Tomorrow is my birthday, like today and every day. And I have an eight-day walk to Kathmandu in store for me. *Ha Ha Ha.* So put up the tent. *Haw Haw Haw Haw Haw...*

Epilogue 1985

Klaus continued to be alternately sick and healthy. At the end of his stay in Nepal he participated in the search for the body of Phil Cyr, a Peace Corps Volunteer who was bludgeoned to death and robbed by his four porters in western Nepal. Klaus flew home soon after. He now lives in Chicago, where he studies international education and the development of morality.

The rabbits grew to be fat and spirited. After a couple of months it was discovered that all three were males. One was eventually killed by a village dog and the other two were taken to Lamidada where they are hopefully fathering large families.

Kay lived with Kevin for just one year. She graduated with a degree in Environmental Planning and Management. After fighting forest fires for several seasons, she now works in a prescribed fire program with the National Park Service.

Pesout stayed in Nepal for a third year of teaching. He suffered severe injury to his right arm when he was stabbed by thieves in New Delhi. He now lives in Oregon and is married to Ann, another volunteer from Nepal.

Thomas continued his journey around the world. He attempted a two-man ascent of New Zealand's Mount Cook, but his partner had to be evacuated by helicopter after being hit by a falling rock. Thomas is now an electrician, installing the power system in a new building in Geneva, Switzerland.

Aiselukharka still boasts of having the best high school in the district. Each year, an ever-increasing number of students pass the SLC exam. Most recently Surendra passed the test, but Mahendra unfortunately did not. Many of Philipsir's students are now married and have children.

Krishna Bhakta grows gradually older. He is busy with village politics and local development projects. Aamaa is very proud of her sons, and Nilam is said to have grown into a beauty. They all wish that Philipsir would return.

The hostel is still without a roof. Work has been done to repair the walls that were damaged in recent monsoons, and the government has given funds to begin the roofing. The money isn't sufficient, but the Headmaster is confident that the building will be finished fairly soon. *Bholi-parsi.*

The trees were greatly damaged by onslaughts of goats and bad weather. Only one quarter of the original trees still stand. The village, however, has built its own nursery to grow trees for reforestation. So while the trees have died, the idea has lived.

Phil left Nepal in June 1980, and took two years to arrive in America. Along the way he lived on a kibbutz in Israel, canoed down the Congo River, hitchhiked across the Sahara, and helped to occupy a vacant house in the Netherlands. *The Two-Year Mountain* was written during a year's stay in Denmark. After completing his teaching credential in California, he has returned to Denmark where he works in an after-school program for both normal and handicapped children.

Autumn 1985

Homecoming, 2011

Salinas, California, March

All that was thirty-four years ago. Thirty-four years ago, when I first arrived in Nepal, fresh from university, determined to make a difference in the world, having no idea of what I was about to put myself through—being sick for weeks at a time, feeling desperately alone and isolated, struggling to teach in a foreign language, slowly adapting to Nepali culture, and ultimately leaving my village in tears. Three decades ago, when I threw myself into those near-death adventures: being rammed by a rhinoceros and solo mountaineering in the high Himalaya. On two of those climbs, I really should have died. That narrow escape from the Tasi Lapcha—tearing off a patch of skin—left me with a jagged scar between thumb and forefinger of my right hand. Sometimes I rub the scar, reminding myself that life is both precious and fragile.

Since then, I worked—for years at a time—in Israel, Denmark, Botswana, the Navajo Nation, Bolivia, and only recently back in California. Those three decades included teaching in four different languages, travels through fifty countries, and myriad adventures—abducted by pirates in the Congo, cycling the Kalahari and Namib Deserts, ice climbing in the Andes, and best of all, becoming a father. Being a full-time single dad means that my daughter has survived travels with me on four continents, including hiking the Inca Trail when she was seven and singing with the Bolivian National Opera, in French, when she was twelve. A more complete description of those decades can be found online at www.FarJourney.com

And what about Kay? We stayed in contact, and we've seen one another a few times, though we've never rekindled any romance. Besides never both being single at the same time, we've known that the type of relationship we had in college wasn't what we wanted as adults. She's been married and widowed, and has long worked as a ranger with the National Park Service.

During my first years away from Nepal, I occasionally reunited with my fellow Peace Corps volunteers, and I received a scattering of letters from Krishna Bhakta and from my former students. They told me about the trees, and developments at the school, and, most importantly, who had passed the SLC exam. Ram Prasaad sent me an exact accounting of his and Megha Nath's scores, demonstrating that he was still top boy by a margin of 687.2 points to 666.2. Their letters were hard to decipher. The Nepali letter-writing style is very formal and flowery. Even with dictionaries, I couldn't understand half of what they wrote. My Nepali language competence was degrading rapidly, and I worked for hours to reply to each letter. Meanwhile, the Nepali-U.S. schism of time, distance, and culture became increasing difficult to bridge. Eventually, shamefully, I didn't write any letters at all.

Now I teach high-school physics and astronomy in central California. It's all good. Most people don't know about my international background. They don't even know that my daughter was born in Botswana, the granddaughter of a famous witch-doctor.

My life in Nepal doesn't occupy much of my waking thoughts, but I have followed the news. In the past few decades, three stories from Nepal—all involving deaths—have generated the biggest headlines: the 1986 mountaineering disaster that left eight climbers dead high on Everest; the 2001 slaughter of the Royal Family by the Crown Prince; and the devastatingly bloody, decade-long Maoist insurrection that ended in 2006.

For the people of Nepal, news of the Royal Family massacre must have been unfathomable. I remembered how students in the village could hardly believe that *Newsweek* story about a brother and sister who had killed their

308

own father. The Nepali news media stated that after being ejected from a family party, emotionally unstable Crown Prince Dipendra, semi-crazed with alcohol and supposedly angered by parental rejection of his intended wife, had returned with automatic weapons and haphazardly gunned down his family. He murdered his father, King Birendra, and his mother, Queen Aiswarya, as well as his brother, sister, and five other relatives. He then shot himself. In a bizarre twist, while surviving in a coma for three days, he was pronounced King of Nepal. When he died, King Birendra's brother, Gyanendra—who was away in Pokhara during the massacre—was crowned King.

Just a year earlier, King Birendra had instituted a system of multiparty democracy, reducing his own power to the level of a constitutional monarch. This new system did not, however, solve problems of political corruption and developmental stagnation. In 1996, the Maoist-Communist Party of Nepal had declared a "People's War" with the goal of overthrowing the monarchy and establishing a People's Republic of Nepal. Urban bombings initiated the violence, with the rebels drawing support from widespread dissatisfaction with Nepal's slow economic growth. The government responded with a crackdown on political dissent. Hostilities grew. In 2005, King Gyanendra dissolved the government, declared a state of emergency, and shut down communications. This led to heightened violence. In 2006, during a ceasefire, parliamentary democracy was restored, and the government quickly voted to abolish the monarchy, ending two centuries of rule by the Shah family. The insurgency had lasted a decade, resulting in some 13,000 deaths. Former rebel fighters are now being absorbed back into society, while the government struggles to write a new constitution.

For me, these news stories didn't re-establish any real personal connection with Nepal. It all seemed far away. My Nepali life and experiences had become integrated into who I am, helping to shape my life attitudes and world view. I've never owned a car or a cell phone, preferring to live as low tech as possible. Looking around my house, Nepali prayer mats hang on the wall. The kukuri knife and brass oil lamp given to me by Krishna Bhakta sit on a shelf next to a Bushman bow-and-arrow set given to me by a !Kung hunter in the Kalahari. In the attic are two dusty boxes stuffed with old Nepali textbooks and papers.

I felt reasonably content with my internalized connection with Nepal until an email arrived from my British publisher, Hilary Bradt. She wanted to re-issue *The Two-Year Mountain*, which over the decades had achieved a historical aspect—a view of Nepal as it once was. I was hesitant about the idea. I knew that for me it would be emotionally difficult—dredging up memories of Philipsir, who died that small death when he left Aiselukharka; struggling once again with that internal divide between Nepali and American cultures; and facing the guilt I felt for writing so intimately about Krishna Bhakta and Aiselukharka without their permission or acquiescence.

Worst of all, I immediately understood that to do a re-issue right, I would need to go to Nepal and to Aiselukharka. I would have to find out what had become of the school, and the trees, and Krishna Bhakta, and Nilam, and Ram Prasaad Nepal, and… For decades I had lived an enjoyable fantasy of ignorance. I had imagined the trees growing, the school functioning, and my family prospering. This sugar-coated dream was preferable to facing the likely reality of deforestation, political destruction, and death. Krishna Bhakta had been in his late forties when I lived with him. If he was still alive, he'd be near eighty—in a country with a life expectancy of just sixty.

I ignored the email, but five months later, Hilary tried again. And I reluctantly replied. I suggested a journey to Nepal to report on the current state of the village. This idea was immediately seized upon, since it "would give the book an important extra dimension."

I was committed. I would go in the summer, during the monsoon, when I had time off from school. I began searching for information. I quickly learned that the Peace Corps no longer operated in Nepal. In 2004, they had pulled out following a Maoist bombing at the Kathmandu office of the

United States Information Service. All non-essential U.S. Embassy staff had been evacuated. I searched the internet for anything about the school and community. I found lists of schools on Nepal's Department of Education website, but Aiselukharka Secondary School wasn't mentioned anywhere.

Then I discovered that satellite images on Google Maps provided enough detail to see individual houses in the Nepali hills. But I couldn't find Aiselukharka. Over the next few months, I spent hours and hours scanning ridge lines, searching in vain for the school compound. *Was it completely gone?* Next, I climbed into the attic and dug through my dusty boxes of Nepali stuff, pulling out my old maps. I figured that I could do some simple triangulation to find the village, but it wasn't there. I continued the search, and finally, one night at 2 a.m., I found it. It was miles and miles from the map location, but the square-cornered *C*-shape of the school building was unmistakable. I zoomed in. I could see light shining through the upstairs windows onto the floor. *Huh? How could that be?* The roof was gone. The building looked abandoned, derelict. I was shocked. What had happened to the school? I could see the houses of the village, but the school building looked half-demolished. I was in a daze.

I continued to search for information, and a few weeks later I found a possible explanation for the derelict school. I discovered an on-line report from the *Watchlist on Children and Armed Conflict*. This was my first direct information about Aiselukharka. In 2004, Maoist rebels abducted two hundred students from the school. Soldiers held the students captive and forced them to chant slogans and listen to Maoist speeches for days on end. Students and teachers were threatened with "consequences" if they didn't join the movement. That was the standard Maoist strategy for recruiting child-soldiers.

The report said nothing more about the Aiselukharka school, so I was left to speculate if this Maoist abduction had somehow resulted in the destruction of the school building. The region had always been politically active. Krishna Bhakta and the school committee could easily have found themselves on the wrong side of the conflict. I woke repeatedly in the middle of the night worrying about this.

While browsing on-line, I was drawn toward descriptions of Himalayan peaks. Lobuche East, it turns out, was first climbed four years after I made that solo reconnaissance to the summit ridge. Kangchung West, now called Cholo, is currently deemed the highest of the Kangchung pair and has had very few documented ascents—it's just too nasty. Four years ago it was featured on a five-rupee stamp, under the name Mount Abi, with an elevation of 20,003 feet.

The most useful thing that I could do to prepare myself for the trip to Nepal was to re-learn the language. I pulled out my old Nepali language materials, including my sacred, military-green *Basic Gurkhali Dictionary*, published in 1960, and I began studying an hour or two a day. I created flash cards of a thousand vital vocabulary words, and I drilled myself as I walked to and from school. Each new word triggered a web of memories from Nepal.

Re-learning a language that I hadn't used for thirty years was a bizarre experience. Some words, like *mech* (chair), sounded totally foreign, as though I had never heard them before in my life. Other words, like *maachhaa* (fish), just came to me. I wasn't *remembering* them; they were just there, in my mind, locked in a separate compartment from memory. Like the way you know the word *water* in English, it's something that you just *know*, without remembering. During the process of studying Nepali, my body would occasionally give an involuntary shudder, as my mind took a small step inward toward *thinking* in Nepali.

I decided to write directly to my family in Aiselukharka. Emotionally, this was very hard. I guessed that there was less than a fifty-fifty chance that Krishna Bhakta was still alive. How can you write a letter to your father, who might be dead? The mere thought of it tore me up inside. Nor was it easy to write a complete letter in Nepali, using Devanagri script. In three days of linguistic and emotional struggle, this is what I composed (translated into English):

Shree Dearest Friend Krishna Bhakta,

Namaskar. I am wishing you deepest happiness. How much time has passed? Thirty years. I feel great anguish. How are you? How is all your family? Nilam's Mother and Mahendra and Surendra and Nilam? Day by day, I have continued to remember you.

What is all the news? Does the Aiselukharka Secondary School exist, or not? Does the school building have a roof, or not?

I am living in America, in California. I have one daughter. I teach science in a secondary school. I am coming to Nepal. I expect to arrive in Aashaad (mid-June). I will come to your house, but I will only be able to stay five days.

Your Dear Friend,

Philip

I made two copies of the letter, and addressed them to the *Family of Krishna Bhakta Himalaya*. I sent one by regular post and the other by certified mail, doubling the chances that one would arrive. As the weeks passed, I checked the mail each day with mounting expectation, but by the time that I left for Nepal, no letter had arrived from the village.

June 2011

Tribhuvan International Airport

W hen I landed here thirty-four years ago, with a group of young Peace
Corps Volunteers, we broke into spontaneous applause. Now, I arrive
with tears in my eyes. I never imagined that I would be back here. Memories
of my village and Kathmandu and high mountains all flood my mind, and I feel
overwhelmed. I close my eyes, taking deep breaths, and I try to control myself.

Changes are evident right from the start. The international arrival
hall has luggage carousels—two of them. And there is no haggling with
taxi drivers. Instead, two men stand behind a counter selling fixed-price
500-rupee taxi vouchers to town. Another man escorts me outside to the
first taxi in line, and off we go. I've been to large Asian cities before—Hong
Kong, Bangkok, Calcutta—but I'm not prepared for that kind of swarming
congestion in Kathmandu. On the way to the center of town, we are stopped
repeatedly by traffic jams. New garish buildings are going up on all sides,
surrounded by bamboo scaffolding ten storeys high. I have to crane my neck
to look up at them. Motorbikes race everywhere, ceaselessly honking. Years
ago, motorcycles were rare; now they're ubiquitous. Even young women are
driving them—wearing jeans. Women's attire has shifted. Traditional saris
have been replaced by the two-piece north-Indian *salwar kameez*, consisting
of baggy pants tight at the ankle, topped with a very long matching shirt,
and typically accented with a scarf. Many women are wearing Western-
style clothes, while the men are dressed in everything from the quasi-
governmental *daura-suruwal* (tight pants, shirt, vest, and *topi* hat) to T-shirt
and jeans. I don't see any suits and ties, but someone must be wearing them,

according to the American-style billboards advertising everything from computers to toothpaste.

Arriving downtown, I got a room overlooking Basantapur Square, just around the corner from Freak Street, which used to be Kathmandu's bargain hotel Mecca. I planned to stay four nights in Kathmandu before heading up to Aiselukharka—I would need that long to acclimatize emotionally. The days merged into a jumble of wandering the streets half lost, feeling like a tourist in a place that used to be home. Nothing looked the same, and I had to carry a guidebook to find my way around.

During my first full day, I headed out to see the old Peace Corps Office. I hoped that this would be one place that would at least *look* familiar—if I could find it. Getting there was a challenge. Even crossing a busy street was life-threatening. Standing at the curb, if I waited for a hole in the traffic, a mob of motorcycles would race into the gap at the last moment, and I would have to jump back. The safest method was to find a group of Nepalis who were also trying to cross, and to embed myself into the middle of the pack. When they moved, I moved, one lane at a time, forcing traffic to swerve around us in a terrifying game of chicken.

The Peace Corps office had been on a laconic country lane called Kamaladi (meaning lotus-*something*), but the dirt byway had been replaced by a paved runway for non-stop traffic. The office was gone. It had either been torn down or it was hidden behind high concrete walls.

I remembered one of the last times that I had been there. I had gotten into a conversation with a former Peace Corps Volunteer who after five years had come back on vacation. He acted unsettled about something. I asked him, "How is your village?"

"I don't know," he replied, looking away from me.

"You don't know?" I asked. "You haven't been back yet? When are you going?"

"I don't know," he said. "I'm not sure if I will go back." He folded and unfolded his hands.

I was dumbfounded. How could he come all this way, and not go home to his village? It didn't make any sense.

But now, thirty years later, it made perfect sense. I felt the same apprehension about going to Aiselukharka. Was it still home, at all? I've changed. They've changed. Will anyone even remember me? What was I going to say? *"Hey, remember me? I used to live with you all thirty years ago. Now, I'm here to look around, and see what's up."* I had ignored my family for three decades. What kind of reception did I expect? I wasn't the Prodigal Son; I was just a visitor.

I remembered an English professor at university who had told us a dream he had. He was returning home, but outside his town was a gate—a miniature gate—which was way too small for him to pass through. This was his subconscious mind expressing the time-worn theme: *You can never go home again.*

Part of my own anxiety was related to the poor state of my Nepali language. What if I arrived in the village, and all I could say was, *"Namaste. How are you?"* I was trying to use as much language as possible: in the hotel, in restaurants, asking directions, and listening intently to everyone around me. But I decided to give myself a boost by taking a language class. I hired Parbati Shrestha of the Intercultural Training and Research Center for a private two-hour Nepali lesson.

Parbati was a middle-aged Nepali woman with shoulder-length hair, wearing cream-colored pants and a matching paisley-print tunic. Her smile was constant and infectious. Not only did she enjoy her work, she was especially pleased to work with a student who was so highly motivated. Acquaintances have often remarked that I must be *naturally* good at languages. But that's not it at all. Any proficiency that I've ever had with a language has been due to working so damn hard: memorizing vocabulary lists, studying grammar,

316

listening constantly, and practicing, practicing, practicing. It's not easy or natural—it's *work*.

Still, Parbati and I had fun. Attempting to use Nepali only, I stumbled though an explanation of why I was there (a pilgrimage of sorts to my village), how my life had been in Aiselukharka (both wonderful and extremely difficult), what I had been doing since then (living and teaching all over the world), and where I was living now (in central California, as a full-time single dad). She stopped occasionally to write key vocabulary on a small dry-erase board: *te baayera* (because-of-that), *dungaa* (canoe), *ropnu* (to plant), *banaunchha* (build), and so on. Two hours passed quickly. I felt a definite jump in my fluency, but I was still worried—*Did I speak well enough to get by in the village?*

Parbati's classroom was in northern Thamel, in the prime tourist district, so to get back to the town center, I had to run the gauntlet of trinket hawkers and travel businesses. Walking down Narsing Gate, I was bombarded with a continuous pleading: *"T-shirt? You like? Come inside." "Where are you from, Sir?" "Singing bowl—I give you good price." "Rickshaw, Sir? City tour, two hours, very cheap. How much you pay?" "Come see. Yes, you like?" "Yes, OK, good, you buy." "Where are you going?" "OK, special for you, one hundred rupees." "Very nice, hand-made pashmina, very nice."* Because it was the monsoon season, tourists were at a premium, and the pleadings carried a tone of desperation.

I would eventually buy some embroidered T-shirts and brass ornaments for family, but I hated the system of haggling for a price. I always felt that I was being cheated. I preferred to be told a fixed price, take it or leave it. Still, the system of back-and-forth negotiation had a certain logic. No one *had* to buy any of these things, so no one was ever truly cheated. If you weren't willing to pay a certain price, you didn't have to. It resulted in the thicker-heeled tourists paying more than a poorer traveler. This made sense. Those who could afford it paid more. But where did I fit in? I walked around with the cash-poor attitude of a Peace Corps Volunteer, but I carried a supply of hundred-dollar bills stashed in my money belt.

Further down, out of Thamel, in Asan Tole, the crush of people intensified: men pushing bicycle carts piled high with aluminum cooking pots; uniformed students wearing tiny backpacks, strutting home, arm-in-arm, four-abreast; women in bright saris toting bags of vegetables bought at the market; porters carrying enormous wooden crates on their backs using the traditional *naamlo* headstrap; workers lugging lengths of pipe; and literally thousands of people walking up and down for no apparent reason. Through this mass of humanity came sporadic clusters of motorcycles. They honked their horns just in time for everyone to jump out of the way. Maneuvering through the crowds was exhausting. People bumped into me constantly, and the motorcycles were both annoying and frightening.

Interestingly, the only one who seemed unhappy with the crowds was me. All the Nepalis were having a good time. The press of people wasn't a hardship; it was a choice. Traditionally, the Newars—who built Kathmandu—constructed their houses very close together. Having a lot of people squeezed into a small space was a statement of social harmony. No one had to live or walk this close together. They could always take another route. Everyone seemed content with the crowding. Even the sound of motorcycle horns wasn't aggressive. Instead of an irritated *get-out-of-my-way* honking, it was more of a friendly *hello-here-I-come* tooting. I was the one who was out of step with the flow and mood of the traffic.

Each day I bought copies of the local newspapers. Many stories dealt with the recently arrived monsoon rains. In Mugling, roads were washed out. In one day, twelve people were killed and three went missing in landslides and flooding. Another five were drowned in Trishuli when a cable bridge broke. Meanwhile, rice planting was underway. *The Kathmandu Post* carried pictures from Pokhara of women running a race in the mud as part of a local celebration.

The Nepali-language papers were filled with advertisements for private secondary schools. The competition for students was fierce, with rival schools printing photographs and test scores of the top-quality candidates who had chosen their programs.

Politically, article after article bemoaned the government's inability to get things done. Roads were unmaintained. Insufficient power lines resulted in wasted hydro-electric power. Public school results on the School Leaving Certificate examinations were poor (compared to private schools). But the biggest gripe about the government was the deadlock in writing a new constitution. The three major political parties (UCPN-Maoists, Nepali Congress, and CPN-Marxist-Leninist), comprising 80 percent of the constituent assembly, besides disagreeing between themselves, also had infighting within their own parties. A major issue was the Special Committee for Supervision, Integration and Rehabilitation of Maoist Combatants. Some 7000 former combatants needed re-integration, but no one knew how this could best be done.

I found a particularly interesting headline: *Maoist Minister's Aide in Jail for Fraud.* The Maoists were suffering from the same problems of political corruption and governmental stagnation as the political parties that they had fought to eliminate. Governance was not an easy thing.

The topic that drew the fewest attacks from the press was health care. The improvements have been incredible. In the past decade, maternal deaths have been cut by half, and nearly half of Nepali married women use modern birth control. In 2002, abortion was legalized, allowing the safe termination of problem pregnancies. A third of Nepalis now use "adequate sanitation facilities" (toilets)—up from almost none when I lived here. The majority of Nepalis have access to a health post of some kind. HIV/AIDS is almost non-existent, at just half a percent infection rate. A third of the funding for health care comes from non-government sources, with $30 million a year coming from USAID. Still, 40 percent of Nepali children are malnourished, and Nepal ranks 140 out of 177 counties on the Human Development Index, which is a composite standard-of-living measurement.

An inescapable health issue plaguing Kathmandu is air quality. Kathmandu's explosive population growth (doubling every ten years) coupled with a disproportionate increase in motor vehicles (doubling every five years) has turned the air into a nasty soup of pollution. The amount of airborne particulate matter is twelve times the WHO's standard of safety. Many Nepalis wear face masks to filter the air, and young women don stylish masks that are color-coordinated with their outfits.

The population explosion was on full display the morning that I went out to the traffic circle next to the New Road Gate. I carried a photograph that I had taken from this exact spot thirty years before. The entire scene of the old photo contained just three vehicles: a bicycle, a bicycle-rickshaw, and a horse cart. That's all. Now, in the same field of view, I counted a total of thirty-five cars, four full-sized buses, five three-wheeled *tuk-tuk* microbuses, forty-two motorbikes, three courageous bicyclists, two trucks, and a guy in a wheelchair. No horse carts at all.

One afternoon I hike out of town up to the Swayambhunath temple that overlooks the valley. The city, though dirty, is commercially vibrant, with activity everywhere: men mixing cement with shovels to build a new wall onto a crumbling house, shopkeepers in tiny open-front stalls selling snacks and stationery supplies, a man cranking a bicycle-wheel grinding stone sharpening knives on the side of the road. Political slogans have been painted on random brick walls, and little shrines are scattered about. Even a non-descript rock poking out of the ground is religiously beautified with a splash of red powder and a *pujaa* offering of yellow flowers. There's also the ugly side: trucks spewing black smoke, hairless dogs eating roadside trash, and scab-covered children playing half-heartedly in a pile of dirt.

One unsettling surprise is a billboard for skin-lightening cream. It displays an attractive man's face, with right side lighter than the left, showing how *Fair and Handsome* bleaching cream for men can make your ugly dark skin light-colored and attractive—in just three weeks. I've seen skin lighteners advertised in Africa and in the U.S., but this is the first time I've seen this kind of product in Asia. Later, I read about a television ad campaign in India that "depicted depressed, dark-complexioned women, who had been snubbed by employers and men, suddenly finding new boyfriends and glamorous careers after the cream had lightened their skin."* It's troubling to see such blatant racism gaining a foothold in Nepal.

Swayambhunath is much as I remember it. Stupendous and exotic. A huge white *stupa* dominates the hilltop. At the base of the 365 steps that lead to the shrine is a group of blind musicians performing for donations. Rhesus monkeys prowl the hillsides, ready to snatch away food left unguarded by picnickers. Buddhist relics dot the path upward, and at the top a ring of brass prayer wheels encircles the stupa. A line of Buddhist pilgrims and Nepali tourists keep the wheels in constant motion, sending the prayer, *Om mani padme hum,* skyward. I take my turn walking clockwise around the stupa, spinning wheels as I go. In the past, I've often come to Swayambhunath for a respite from the city. It still holds that serenity. I just have to share the peace with a lot more people than ever before.

The iconic all-seeing Buddha eyes, representing Wisdom and Compassion, painted on the four sides of the stupa, are almost hypnotic. Those eyes have been reproduced on sculptures, in artwork, and on T-shirts. Interestingly, the squiggle on the face that looks like a stylized nose is actually the Nepali number *ek* (one), representing unity.

My last day in Kathmandu, before heading toward Aiselukharka, I have two important tasks. First, I have to check if I need a trekking permit, a so-called TIMS (Trekking Information Management System) card, to hike through Sindhupalchowk District. A hot, sweaty walk brings me to the Tourist Service Centre. A lady clerk listens to a general description of my route and determines that I don't need a TIMS card. That's because I won't

---

* www.telegraph.co.uk/news/worldnews/1556188/Indias-hue-and-cry-over-paler-skin.html

be entering any of the National Park or Conservation zones. Still, the notion that I might need an official stamped permit to travel home is disturbing—a symbolic declaration that my home is perhaps unreachable. Next, I have to buy a map. *Yes*, I need a map to find my way home. Double disturbing. I walk up to Thamel in a downpour. That's the nature of the early monsoon—roasting one hour and pouring rain the next.

While looking for a map, I'm surprised to stumble upon a bookstore that has three copies of *The Two-Year Mountain* for sale. I wonder if these dusty, plastic-wrapped books have been sitting on a shelf for twenty-five years, waiting for a buyer. The best map that I can find shows only half the route. According to it, a dirt road extends from Lamidada up past Melemchi along the Indrawati River, but I still plan to walk the whole way. It seems important to retrace the hiking route that I used in the old days.

I also go to the bus-park to ask about departure times for Lamidada. I expect to hear that there's a bus departing every few hours, but the agent says that buses leave every twenty minutes, all day long, until 4.20 in the afternoon. And I don't have to get a ticket in advance. I can just show up and go.

My last night in Kathmandu, I go out to have a big meal—vegetable chow mein and Tibetan *momos*, finishing with a chocolate crêpe. The food is great—Kathmandu has long been a culinary paradise—but the restaurant is contaminated with cigarette smoke. Nepali men are smoking more than ever before. It's a statement of status. Smoking a cigarette demonstrates wealth and sophistication. Fortunately, few Nepali women are following this fashion trend, but to enjoy the meal I have to sit with my head halfway out the window.

Kathmandu, to Lamidada, to Sipa Ghat, to Aiselukharka: Sindhupalchowk District

The bus churned and coughed its way out of Kathmandu and through Bhaktapur, passing continuous road and building construction. I couldn't tell where Kathmandu ended and Bhaktapur began. The individual towns of the valley have merged into one large metropolis. The bus had left the bus-park half empty, but we picked up more people at every opportunity. The aisle filled with goods. The most mysterious load was a 10-foot-long bundle of plastic sheets—bags or tarps or wrapping? The owner disappeared into the back of the bus, so I had no one to ask. My backpack ended up squeezed next to the driver atop a huge sack of rice. I shared my seat with a sweaty teenager wearing an incongruous *Hello Kitty* T-shirt. I tried to engage him in conversation, but he refused to speak.

Past Banepa, the highway climbed up to the edge of the valley. Out of the city, the hillsides shifted hue with the changing light—leaf green, jade green, and emerald green. Terraced fields covered the slopes in long, curved steps. Lines of women in brightly colored saris stood bent over at the waist, planting shoots of rice in ankle-deep water. At the top, the bus reached Dhulikhel, the small town where I had my first two weeks of language training all those years ago. Descending into the valley of the Indrawati River, the clouds parted, granting tantalizing glimpses of snow-covered peaks to the north. The broad sweep of the valley as we switchbacked downwards felt vaguely familiar.

The bus dropped me at Lamidada (not the same Lamidada where I flew in on my way to Everest). This was the trailhead—the grimy road-town filled with stray dogs that I had always passed through as quickly as possible. But this time, arriving in late afternoon, I needed a place to stay. I would be taking a leisurely pace—today the bus to Lamidada, tomorrow a hike to Sipa Ghat where the suspension bridge crosses the Indrawati River, and then a day-long climb up to Aiselukharka. I expected to find a sleeping place in the back room of a tea stall, but I was directed to a hotel 2 kilometers down the road. *"A hotel?"* I thought. *"In Lamidada?"*

After a short stroll, here it is—Hotel Zero Kilo and Restaurant—a three-storey brick building painted yellow and pink. One whole side is covered by a painted advertisement for *ASAAN Life Insurance Company,* and on the front are multiple artwork ads for *Reliance Paints.* I eat an unremarkable meal of *daal-bhaat,* and get a room with a simple bed, an electric light, and a ceiling fan. This *is* remarkable. I can't get over it—Lamidada has a hotel.

In the morning, I begin the walk toward Sipa Ghat. The former trail is now a dirt and gravel road, hot and dusty. I'm surprised by the amount of traffic—a parade of dump trucks, an occasional motorcycle, a bus each hour, and a few private cars. The day is debilitatingly hot, and the continual noise and dust of the trucks makes the walk miserable.

After a few hours, I stop to cool off at a village water tap. I intend to soak my shirt, but the water is being monopolized by a grizzled old man with a pair of large traditionally shaped aluminum water jugs. He keeps one jug filling while he carries the other away, back and forth, again and again. A plump woman in a simple village-style sari is also waiting for water.

Finally, on one of his trips, I ask him, *"Paani linu sakhchhu?*—I can take water?"

"Chha—OK," he says simply with a sideways nod of his head, and pulls one of his jugs out from under the flow of water.

I step forward and splash water on my head. Then I pull off my shirt. The old guy stares at my pale belly—my sweaty, slimy, sickly-white stomach—and he comments ironically, "*Kasto kaalo maanche*—Such a black man."

The three of us freeze in stunned silence. *Has he truly said what I think he said?* A moment passes. Then, in unison, we burst into laughter. He probably didn't expect that I would understand, but I did, and that makes it all the funnier. I nearly choke as I drench my shirt. The man and woman keep laughing and looking around for someone else to share the joke with. It's two minutes of pure hysterics.

I put my dripping shirt on, and remark how cool it is. I continue up the dusty road, feeling buoyed by a good laugh.

Two more hours of hiking bring me to the ridge-top, where the view opens up over the wide expanse of the Indrawati River valley. Down below I can see what the trucks are doing. Bucket loaders are digging gravel out of the river bed and filling the dump trucks. The riverbank is being used as a gravel quarry. The trucks, once full, drive off to wherever road construction is underway. I wonder who owns the mineral rights to the gravel, and if anyone local is profiting.

From this vantage point, I can see a cluster of buildings around the suspension bridge at Sipa Ghat. To the right rise the three ridges that lead toward Aiselukharka. Further up the river valley is the confluence of the Indrawati and Melemchi rivers. That's where the trail begins to Helambu— the place where that ugly stray dog, Sherman, adopted me, following me all the way home.

I descend toward the river.

Sipa Ghat is a mess of a place. When I was first here, Sipa Ghat consisted of the footbridge—just the bridge—no houses, no shops, nothing at all, not even a tea stall. Now, on each side of the road is a jumble of stores, homes, and businesses, placed so close to the rocky track that there is no space between the vehicles and the buildings. Merchants are selling food stuffs, kitchen utensils, cloth and clothes, medicine, and building materials. I peek inside a couple of roadside businesses. Inside one is a gas engine milling rice.

Another contains a pair of enormous closed-top stainless-steel vats used for pasteurizing milk. Sipa Ghat is thriving.

The side road down toward the footbridge is the opposite. The lower track is also lined with two rows of buildings, but the shop shelves are half-empty, houses are in disrepair, and businesses are boarded up or abandoned. The story tells itself. When the road first reached Sipa Ghat, the track to the bridge was the main thoroughfare, and it became a boom town. That was years ago. Later, when the road extended up the valley, this side track lost its importance. Businesses moved to the main road, and the area by the bridge deteriorated. It looks depressing.

Back on the motor-road, I ask about a place to stay, and a shopkeeper offers me a room attached to the main restaurant. The room is mostly underground, recessed into the hillside—dark and damp, with metal bars in the doorway—more of a dungeon than lodging. Fortunately, I meet a young man, Raju Rai, who is home on holiday from his college studies in Lucknow, India. He helps me find another place—an upstairs room with windows overlooking the road. Raju is an engineering student. His goal after graduation is to help fix the road system in Nepal. He's heard of Aiselukharka, but he knows nothing about Krishna Bhakta nor the school there. I am just a day's walk away, but I still have no idea who will be there or what the conditions will be. I keep wondering, "Is there a school there at all?"

In the morning, after a meal of Nepali milk tea, chick peas, and rings of dough fried in grease, I cross the suspension bridge over the Indrawati River, and begin the climb toward Aiselukharka. Right from the start, I am confused about the way to go, but plenty of people are around to point the way: men carrying 10-gallon cans of milk to be pasteurized in Sipa Ghat, a flock of boys in white Tae Kwon Do uniforms, women lugging enormous baskets of corn leaves for their animals. Despite all that, I get some bad directions. I had wanted to hike along the river a ways and then take the third ridge direct to the village, but I end up following a road under construction. A bulldozer has carved a scar through the landscape, turning a smooth path into miles of broken rock and uneven dirt. It is a wretched upward slog.

But then, in the mid-afternoon, a miraculous transformation slowly occurs—as I climb higher and higher, the ridges assume recognizable shapes, and the landscape begins to look familiar. With each step higher, the hillsides feel more and more like home. The track curves around to the left, toward the correct ridge—the ridge topped by Aiselukharka—and I pass through a stand of trees that I clearly remember. Now, I am excited—*really* excited. I am almost there.

Aiselukharka

Unexpectedly, the path curves *in front* of the ridge top, instead of around the back, and I become disoriented. I see some houses in the fields, but I don't recognize them. I'm coming in from the far end of the village, and the corn grows so tall around the track that I can't see much ahead. I come to a two-storey stone house with window-trim painted orange. I call to a woman sitting in an upstairs balcony, "*Krishna Bhaktako ghar yahaa chha?*—Krishna Bhakta's home is this way?"

"*Hajur?*—Pardon?" she questions.

"*Krishna Bhaktako ghar yahaa chha?*—Krishna Bhakta's home is *this* way?" I gesture up the muddy path.

"Yes, that way," she calls back. "Go that way, there, and you'll arrive. *That* way."

I pass a house that has glass in the front windows, and I laugh aloud. For years, I've had a recurring nightmare that Aiselukharka had become a stopover on a tourist trekking route, and that Krishna Bhakta's house had become a traveler's resthouse *with glass in the windows*. In my mind, glass windows had been the ultimate symbol of touristic degradation, but now the glass seems just a benign indication of development.

The path curves around the other way, past a garden of fruit trees, and down on the left is a small white-washed shop, with the front woodwork painted deep green. A sign hanging from the upstairs railing boasts a Red Cross emblem.

I repeat my call, "*Namaste.* Krishna Bhakta's house is…" But I'm interrupted by a voice coming from within the darkness of the shop, "That's me. I'm Krishna Bhakta." And he emerges into the light. It's him. He's here, he's here, he's here!!! I can't believe it. My mind does three complete summersaults. Krishna Bhakta sees me, and exclaims, "*Aoo, ooo!*"

I somehow take my pack off, and step forward. I put my hands together in a *Namaste*, but now my legs stop working. I drop to my knees, and Krishna Bhakta places his hands on top of my head, saying, "Thank you, thank you." I manage to stand, and I hold Krishna Bhakta's wrists in my hands. We hug. All apprehensions about how I'll be received vanish. I'm home.

He looks at my shirt, drenched in sweat, and he asks if I've come walking. But I can't answer. I'm crying and trembling and hyperventilating—all at the same time. I can hardly believe that it's really him, standing here in front of me. He doesn't look that much different—mostly bald now, with glasses, and a bit plump—but somehow he's still the same. He's wearing a dark blue, button-front, short-sleeved shirt, and a pair of below-the-knee cargo shorts. *Krishna Bhakta in shorts!* That's wild. I wipe the tears from my eyes. I manage to compose myself, but all I can say is, "Krishna Bhakta…"

He asks again, "*Hidera aaunubhaaeko?*—You came *walking?*"

I regain my voice. "*Hidera aaeko*—Yeah, I came walking."

"Why? A bus goes to Nawalpur."

"OK, but I *like* walking. You know that."

"*Malaai taahaa chha*—Yes, I know that." Krishna Bhakta suggests that we go to his house, but he's cut short by a middle-aged man who suddenly appears. He has a graying mustache and is wearing a white shirt and black *topi*. He asks expectantly, "*Ani, malaai chinnuhuncha, ta?*—So, do you know me, then?"

He looks somewhat familiar, but I don't know who he is. I say, "*Hmm.* Yes, I know you. But your name? I… can't remember your name…" (This will become a mantra in the coming days, as I embarrassingly can't recognize anyone.) Krishna Bhakta points over his shoulder, and coming to my rescue, he says, "Mahendra."

"Mahendra!" I shout. *How can I not know him?* Well, except that now he's around fifty years old. He's Krishna Bhakta's second oldest son. We shake hands, and I realize that I'm still hyperventilating. Mahendra remarks how strange it is that I've come walking the whole way from Lamidada. Krishna Bhakta mentions that Mahendra's daughter has also just arrived, coming from Kathmandu, where she goes to school.

That takes a moment to digest. Mahendra's *daughter?*

Mahendra remarks, "Yes, my daughter. And I'm a history teacher now. *Budho bhayo*—I've gotten old. Right, Sir?"

"Yes," I say, "we've all gotten old."

But Krishna Bhakta corrects me, "No, you and I, we haven't gotten old. Just him, Mahendra, he's gotten old."

I can't stop smiling. "And Surendra?" I ask.

"He's in Kathmandu." Later I learn that he has graduated *college*, and currently works as a drinking-water engineer in the city.

"What about Nilam?" I ask.

"She's in Kathmandu too," says Krishna Bhakta. "This is her daughter here." A very pretty girl with dimples wearing a cream-colored dress and black sweater moves closer, saying, "*Namaste*." Mahendra's daughter is right next to her. They are about the same age that Mahendra and Surendra were when I lived here. More than anything else, meeting Nilam's daughter brings home how much time has passed. A full generation has gone by.

I rub my head. This is a lot to handle. "*Mero maan bigrieko*," I say. "My mind is broken." I mention how both Krishna Bhakta and Mahendra have become a bit fat. This is a compliment. "And Aiselukharka has developed. There's electricity." I can see the wires between the houses. "That's your work, isn't it?" I say to Krishna Bhakta. "Bringing electricity." I remember that it was long his dream to bring electricity from Chautara to the village. Somehow, he has done it.

Krishna Bhakta tips his head in acknowledgement. "And we have water too."

"There's water?" I say.

"Yes, and a road is being built."

I kept smiling, like I was deranged. Finally, Krishna Bhakta said again that we should head home, and I shouldered my backpack. The shop—which I learned later was Krishna Bhakta's—was at the back end of his garden, so it was only a 40-yard walk to the house. I looked up, and there was my old room, with the same wooden shutters in the windows. The house had an additional covered storage area in front of my room area, but otherwise it looked the same.

Here was Mohan Devi, *Aamaa*, whom Krishna Bhakta always called "Nilam's Mother". She too was older, heavier, and wrinkled, but recognizable. She walked with a stifled gait. They ushered me inside the main house to a large upstairs room where I would sleep. There was a light bulb hanging by wires from the ceiling, and glass in the front windows overlooking the courtyard between the neighboring houses. Nilam's daughter, Nira, and Mahendra's daughter, Jesika, popped in and out, bringing tea and water, continually checking if I needed anything, and just sitting around, hanging out. For them, this was their summer vacation at grandpa's farm.

Krishna Bhakta and I sat cross-legged on the floor, and we talked about development in the village. Water had always been a big problem—that was the whole point of the trees that we had planted—but now the village had a system of water taps. Just outside, down in the courtyard, was a rectangular concrete pillar with a metal pipe sticking out, supplying water almost to the door. "*Kati wotaa dhaaraa chhan?*" I asked, "How many water taps are there?"

"Nine," replied Krishna Bhakta. He explained that the pipe brought water from the mountains high above Nawalpur. Water from that far up must have been at least reasonably clean. It was certainly a lot healthier than what we used to drink. The previous water supply was just the run-off from that little hillside where goats and cows were allowed to graze and defecate.

The new problem was that the pipeline came through a half-dozen other communities on its way to Aiselukharka. Anyone who wanted water between the source and Aiselukharka had automatic priority. Over the coming days, I learned that the taps were most often dry, with water flowing primarily between three and four in the morning.

All this was overwhelming—being in Nepal, in Aiselukharka, speaking Nepali, sitting with Krishna Bhakta, drinking a glass of sweet milky Himalayan tea, breathing in the distinct odor of the house's stone walls, hearing the snorting sounds of a nearby water buffalo. I felt like I was in a dream, and I just kept smiling. "*Katiko khushi laagyo*—How happy I feel!" I said. I was managing with my Nepali, and Krishna Bhakta was talking to me as though I had been gone only a week. My head was spinning.

Krishna Bhakta smiled broadly when he talked about electricity coming to the village. He was very proud of this achievement. The road, however, was a transient thing—it had already been washed out by this year's monsoon rains. No one knew when it might be fixed.

Next, I asked about the thing that was troubling me. "What about the school? It has a roof, or not? What has happened?"

Krishna Bhakta was uncharacteristically evasive, saying only, "We can go see the school tomorrow."

I wondered what he was hiding. It had to be something bad.

At the sound of voices, he went out, and returned in a few minutes, asking, "*Bhaat kaane?*—You'll eat rice?" He brought his fingers to his lips in the global gesture for eating. He led me through the door, and around the stairwell. Then he climbed out the window to a tiny balcony. From there, he stepped through a very low door that connected to my old room. My room was now the kitchen. The beams and roofing stones were coated with a thick black layer of cooking-fire soot, but Aamaa wasn't cooking on a fire. She was cooking with electricity. This was a revelation. I hadn't imagined that the electric power would be sufficient for cooking. The cooker was a simple red clay cylinder with a glowing electric coil inside. There was no smoke in the room. None! No coughing from smoke. No running eyes. The health benefits were staggering, but equally important was the freedom from firewood. No lugging of wood—and no cutting of trees!

The smell of *daal-bhaat* was intoxicating. I explained to Aamaa that I had been missing the taste of her *daal-bhaat* for thirty years. I took a seat on the floor, in the corner where I had previously had my sleeping mat.

She was surprised. *"Aamerikamaa daal bhaat chhaaina?*—In America there's no daal-bhaat?" she asked.

"You can cook rice and you can cook lentils in America," I explained, "but the taste isn't the same. The oil is different, and the spices are different. Even the rice is different. Yours is the most delicious, and I've been missing that."

Aamaa grinned happily. She filled my steel plate with a heap of rice, and added a scoop of *tarkari*. Tonight's vegetable dish was a blend of potatoes, beans, onions, and some other ingredients that I couldn't identify. She placed a metal bowl of daal next to my plate. Sitting on the floor and eating with my fingers seemed as natural as it had years ago. The taste and smells transported me to another time. This tasted so good. I looked around the room as I ate. A larger sink had been built into the wall, and a fireplace. They had installed some cabinets and shelves for cooking utensils. A towel hung from a nail protruding from the vertical roof support in the middle of the room. It looked like the same nail where I had hung my towel years before. It was somehow too familiar. I felt my body give a shake of confusion about the world I was in. I had the impression that I should be preparing lessons to teach at school tomorrow. I was losing track of reality.

I kept eating, gulping down a second helping of bhaat and tarkari. It was really, *really* good.

I slept well that night, but I woke early in the morning with a pounding headache. Random, unintelligible Nepali phrases were running around and around in my mind—all the words that I had been hearing without understanding. Even though I'd been doing surprisingly well speaking Nepali, a lot of language still eluded me. Those random unintelligible words had lodged in my brain, and were blasting my mind like a cacophony of chaotic noises. My mind was desperately trying to make sense of it all, which was both confusing and exhausting.

I felt better by the time we had eaten morning daal-bhaat. Krishna Bhakta and I walked to school together, taking a newly built upper trail. Mahendra came with us, along with a few others. We passed a small trail-side temple that had large mirrors attached to the front eaves of the roof. I knew that mirrors had religious significance, but I had never understood the meaning. I asked, "*Ainaa ke ko laagi chha?*—What are the mirrors for?"

Mahendra had a quick reply. "It's so that students can have a look at themselves on their way to school," he joked. We all laughed. It was funny, but I couldn't hold the humor for more than a moment. I was preoccupied with worries about what I would find at the school. Why had Krishna Bhakta been so evasive about the school roof?

We skirted the edge of a field of corn and approached the school compound. I looked up, and magically, there it was. I could see the upper wall of the school, but it wasn't the old school. It had been completely rebuilt, bigger—much bigger—and better, but in the same basic design. "*This is amazing,*" I thought, and I started laughing. The walls, of grey and white bricks, looked impossibly high, and the large glass windows were mounted in steel frames painted deep red. The ground floor looked complete, but the upstairs floor lacked windows. And the structure was intended to be three storeys tall. It was easily twice as big as the old school, in each dimension, but still shaped like a square-cornered *C*. Now I understood why the school looked derelict in satellite photos.

We enter a smaller building next to the new school, which serves as the office and storeroom. Krishna Bhakta introduces me to the Headmaster—a short man with a big smile, wearing a gray shirt and imitation leather sandals—and he introduces me to all the teachers. We exchange *Namastes*, and my story is passed around to everyone. I'm surprisingly greeted by two former colleagues, Gobindra and Rajendra, who were young teachers when I taught here. Now they are grey-haired. I have copies of old pictures, and we pass these around, telling stories and laughing. We laugh twice as loud when we discover that Gobindra and Rajendra can't recognize themselves in the photos. The current Headmaster was a third-grade student when I taught here. He had been too young to be in any of my classes, but he knew exactly who I was. He would have been one of the little kids that I had chased away from the windows when I was trying to teach.

We talk about the development of the school. Back when I had taught here, only six girls were enrolled in the entire secondary school. Now the ratio of boys to girls is fifty-fifty. *Double amazing.* Thirty years ago, we were ecstatic to have *anyone* pass the SLC Exam. Now the pass rate is 87 percent. Many of the students are able to pursue college-level studies in Kathmandu or elsewhere. Teacher wages have improved too, and retired teachers receive a fifty-percent government pension after twenty years of service.

I ask about Guru, the man who was once the school assistant. He's the one who brought me his dying nine-year-old son. Sadly, Guru passed away just three months previously. By sheer coincidence, I meet the son himself a few days later. He's married, and has kids. He has no recollection of long ago having been so sick.

The teachers are very interested in knowing exactly what year I taught at the school, but with Nepali calendar years not matching Gregorian calendar years I can't tell them. Then I remember that three lady NDS (National Development Service) teachers were here when I first arrived. "Yes, that's right," agrees Gobindra. They search through a stack of books and papers, and pull out a large ledger with a faded green cover. Rajendra flips through the pages, and finds what they have been looking for. He shows me two pages written in longhand in blue ink, and I recognize—shockingly—my own handwriting. They have unearthed my official completion-of-service letter.

Rajendra hands me the ledger, and I begin reading aloud. I manage only two lines before I choke up. I force myself to keep reading. I lose my voice to emotion again and again. Tears run down my face, as I relive the words that I wrote, as a twenty-something-year-old, three decades ago:

I'll write this in English because even after 2½ years in Nepal it's still quicker and easier for me to write in English than in Nepali. Also by writing in English not so many people will understand this and I won't be embarrassed by what I say. For two years Aiselukharka High School has been my home, my work, and my life. The good times have been much greater than the bad, and I've been extremely happy to be here. This school like others in Nepal has great problems facing it. Such things as students who don't study, teachers who don't teach, lack of materials, cheating on exams, and poor textbooks were sometimes upsetting to me. But I've had the chance to travel widely in Nepal and I can say that even with its problems Aiselukharka High School is doing better than most of the schools in rural Nepal. During the time that I've been here I've seen a lot of improvements in the quality of both teachers and students and I'm sure that this will continue. I believe that there is nothing more important to the development of a country than providing a good education for everyone. I wish the school the greatest success in continuing to provide the education that Nepal so desperately needs.

The one thing that I most want to say in these few words is to try to express my appreciation to all of you for the enormous amount of help that you've given me while I've been here. Arriving alone in a new and different place can be hard, but I was quickly made to feel at home, and you soon became both my friends and my family. There is absolutely no way that I can thank you all

enough for the love and the caring that you've given to me.
The good memories that I take from here I'll carry for the rest
of my life. I'm sure that I've not given even a small fraction of
what I've received. For the things of offense that I may have
done I'm sorry. Also I'm sorry that I was unable to offer more to
the school, still I tried my best. I wish that I had more to give
than just my thanks.

Philip Earl Deutschle
U.S. Peace Corps

After I had composed myself, we toured the new school building. The bottom floor was mostly complete. On the left side was a carpeted computer room, and on the opposite side was a large meeting room with large, polished-wood chairs. They had plans to put in more classrooms, indoor toilets, a kitchen, and hostel rooms. In the unfinished upstairs rooms were unplastered walls, stacks of window frames, piles of sand, and dismantled bamboo scaffolding. But even these half-done rooms had already been used for teaching. Algebra problems had been written on a ragged dry-erase board. Additional classrooms were needed because two years previously the school had added two grade levels, eleventh and twelfth, becoming an *upper* senior secondary school. The plan was to keep growing, adding two more grades, eventually becoming a *college*.

It was an ambitious goal, and typically audacious that they had begun a project before all the funding was in place. I remembered the school hostel that was never completed due to the lack of a roof. Krishna Bhakta, as President of the School Managing Committee, was a prime motivator behind these future developments, imparting his unflappable optimism to everything he touched. What they needed now was money—a lot of money—and somehow they would get it.

We went outside and walked through the other classrooms. Most of them needed a good cleaning and some minor repairs. I asked to speak with the tenth class, hoping to get a comparison to my students from years ago.

The students all stood at attention when Krishna Bhakta and I walked it. I gestured for them to sit. Their classroom was in reasonably good condition, with a white board mounted on the front wall. The students' long bench-table combinations were metal-framed with wooden plank seating. The boys' uniforms consisted of powder-blue button-front shirts and dark blue pants. The girls wore the same shirts, but with knee-length dark blue skirts. None of the girls had bare legs; they all wore long pants of various colors beneath their skirts. The girls sat on the left and the boys to the right, except for two boys sitting on the girls' side. Almost on cue, the students from the lower classes came running up and crowded around the windows to watch.

I tried to get the tenth class to practice their English with me, but they were very shy. I asked them what subjects they liked best (history and math), if they played sports (soccer), and what type of music they enjoyed (Nepali). They were very formal, standing at attention whenever they spoke. They asked me about my family, where I was teaching now, and how I learned Nepali. It was all very nice, but the one thing that I most wanted to ask them about was the Maoist takeover of the school. I wanted to know if they had been there, how scared they had been, and what had happened to them. But these were sensitive issues, and I didn't ask.

Later I did speak with a young man who had been a student at the school during the Maoist abduction. With some prompting, he recounted his story:

"*Hunchha*—Yeah, I was there. I was a ninth-class student. We were having history lessons. We didn't know anything was going to happen. We heard shouts outside, and other sounds. Soldiers came to the doors and windows. They had guns, rifles. That was my first time seeing a rifle, ever. We didn't know what was happening to us. Yes, I was *very* terrified. How many? One hundred and fifty soldiers, I think. The Maoist soldiers were all around the school, everywhere. Two of my friends got away running. The small children they sent home, but they kept the rest of us, the teachers too. I think so, yes, the soldiers they knew what to do. They were trained. They kept us for one week, like a prison. The soldier leaders taught us, lecturing to us about politics. They told us the Maoist way. They made us recite the Maoist way, many times. The teachers kept saying that they wanted everyone safe, no one hurt. Our parents in Aiselukharka and Nawalpur brought us rice and vegetables and water, and wood to cook. Our parents did anything the soldiers said to do. Yeah, we slept on the floor with blankets. The floor was hard! The soldiers watched us all the time, with guns. Everyone was frightened, but when they fed us we felt better. After some days, my friends were saying that the soldiers were right. The King was bad, and we should fight. The Commander said that bad things would happen to us if we didn't join the soldiers. After one week, they let us go. I think twenty students joined the Maoist army."

The Maoist recruitment had been ten percent successful. The young man who told me about this didn't originally join the Maoists, but later he went to Kathmandu and enlisted with the rebels. I didn't ask him about any of the things that he might have done as a Maoist soldier.

That afternoon, I stole some time for myself. At first, I went looking for a view of the village from a distance to take a picture. But I couldn't find a clear vantage point; there were too many trees. Next, I walked up the trail halfway to Nawalpur. I found the site of the old student hostel, but nothing remained—not even the foundation. The stones had been removed for construction of the new school building.

I returned to the village along the lower trail that passed by the *dhaaraa*. This was the hillside where we had planted all those trees. I had an old picture that I used to try to identify individual trees, but it was impossible. It was too overgrown. In fact, all of Aiselukharka was overgrown with trees. I smiled to myself. This was tremendous. The idea of planting trees had taken hold. Back by the site of the old hostel I'd passed a stand of trees that was clearly being managed. I'd seen full-size trees, along with smaller trees, and stumps. The trees were being used as a renewable resource. This was more than I could have hoped for. The preservation of the forest had been given an added boost in the past three years with the arrival of electricity. Now, instead of cutting trees for cooking fuel, everyone could just flip a switch. If years ago someone had suggested that the solution to deforestation was to use electricity for cooking, I would have said they were crazy. Now, it's a reality.

That evening, I opened my money belt, and counted my stash of hundred-dollar bills. I had decided to contribute some cash to aid construction of the school. I figured I could spare $1200 and still have enough to get back to the States. I told Krishna Bhakta that I wanted to make a donation, and I asked, "*Kaslaai dinchhu?*—Who do I give it to? To you or to the Headmaster?"

He thought about this for a minute. "First you'll give it to me, and then I'll give it to the Headmaster." From the way he said it, I knew that this was going to be a formal presentation. Krishna Bhakta explained that since the Headmaster was going away, we would need to wait two days to do the presentation.

I spent the following morning sitting in front of the shop with Mahendra, looking through old pictures that I had of the family and my students. As we talked, a tall middle-aged man arrived by motorbike. He greeted me, "*Namaste, Philipsir!*" He was one of my old students, but I didn't recognize him. He had to introduce himself—Mohan Bahadur. The name was familiar. We dug through the photos and found two of him—one a class photo and the other a shot taken during a volleyball tournament. As we talked and looked at the photos, I noticed how Mohan continually tipped his long head this way and that, as though the top of his head was too heavy to hold up straight. I remembered how he used to do that same thing in class, and I was suddenly able to bridge the gap in time. I could see the young boy's features in the old man's face—*Mohan!* I knew him. I knew his voice, his smile, his laugh, his gentleness. I knew *him*.

Mohan explained why he was there: "I heard down in my village that you were up in Aiselukharka. So, I had to come see you! And here you are!" He had *searched* for me.

I hadn't expected anything like this. Over the next few days, I met more and more of my old students, some by pure chance and others who intentionally sought me out. I got all kinds of news about everyone. An unexpectedly large number of my former students had become teachers, including Ram Prasaad Nepal—he was now Headmaster of his home-village school. Surendra Laal, who had been in my sixth-grade science class, came walking from a half-day away when he heard that I had copies of old class photos. Then there was balding Jagat Man, who owned a big market in Nawalpur. I had a picture of him—with an enormous head of hair—washing test tubes in a bucket. I began asking what they remembered about my time at the school, and they had some surprising things to say:

"We did that experiment with different kinds of rocks."

"And we made bubbles from those chemicals."

"I remember that you made us give long answers to questions, not just short answers like the other teachers."

"But you caught Narayan Prasaad cheating on a test!"

"Two students passed the SLC that year! That was a good year."

"You taught us very well. We learned so much. A lot of mathematics."

"Do you remember when Philipsir brought that snake to class? I was afraid to touch it."

"I touched it, but only its back. I wouldn't hold it. No, no, no!"

"Did you go with us when we went down to the river, swimming? That was really fun."

"No, but I went with Philipsir out at night to look at the stars."

"And we planted all those trees."

"We planted other things too."

They remembered things that I had completely forgotten about, like the time that I caught a bee and let it crawl around on my bare hand. It was an absolute celebration. I hadn't imagined that I would get a reception like this.

Each day that I was in the village, I felt more comfortable with my proficiency in Nepali. I understood more and more of what everyone was saying, and words that I hadn't used in decades suddenly popped into my mind when I needed them. I was truly *thinking* in Nepali again. Increasingly often, I had that bizarre feeling that I had slipped in time—that I was actually back in the 1970s, when I was living and working here. When this happened, I could feel my body physically trembling, and my head would shake as though I'd gotten a whiff of smelling salts. I wasn't just *thinking* in Nepali again; I was *becoming* Nepali again. I couldn't control it. This was often triggered by a distinctive smell, taste, or sound. Once it happened when Aamaa served me some sweet crackers that tasted identical to those original packaged Nebiko biscuits that were so popular in the past. I jumped back in time. The feeling was uncanny.

Aamaa pulled out the stops to feed me well. In the mornings, she had Jesika bring me tea, sometimes with biscuits or fried chick peas or an egg. Mid-morning daal-bhaat was always a tremendous meal. Then there was an afternoon snack, followed by evening daal-bhaat, and ending with a nightly offering of tea and biscuits. This was better than I had eaten when I had lived here, and I wondered if they ate this well all the time.

Each evening Krishna Bhakta sat with me, and we chatted about happenings in the village. We looked at old pictures, and I told him about what I had been doing for the past thirty years.

One of the local developments that I didn't ask Krishna Bhakta about was his new *charpi*. The family had built a permanent cement squat toilet in a small enclosure just outside the back door. It was flushed out with a pitcher of water, and everything emptied into a sewage lagoon on the other side of the garden wall. It was quite a development in sanitation. On my arrival in Aiselukharka, I had automatically reverted to the *water-and-left-hand* method of toilet use. It seemed totally natural. Other Nepali habits seemed equally natural to slip into, such as sitting on the floor, walking everywhere

342

in rubber sandals, and eating with my fingers. The one thing that I didn't get used to—that I had *never* gotten used to—was hitting my head on low ceilings and chest-high doorways. Seemingly unable to learn from physical pain, I managed to smack my head two or three times a day.

For my presentation of funds to the school I tried to dress up. I wore my long-sleeved shirt, and Krishna Bhakta donned his vest and *topi* hat. We did it in the large meeting hall inside the new school building. To start, the Headmaster rubbed red *tikaa* powder on my cheeks and forehead, and Krishna Bhakta placed a peach-colored ceremonial scarf around my neck. I gave a short awkward speech in halting Nepali, saying that I hoped this "small money" would be of assistance. I had wrapped the bills in a band of white paper. I placed the cash in Krishna Bhakta's two hands, and he then presented the money to the Headmaster.

The Headmaster handed me a framed "Praise Letter" handwritten in English on school letterhead:

Dear Philip Earl Deutschle
America

Sir

You are kindly thanked for your help in this school for two years working as Peace Corps Volunteer from America. After thirty years, you have again come to meet us in this school. You have assisted 1200 U.S. dollar as donation. We again hope in the future from you and your country. Shree Aiselukharka H.S.S. family heartily thank for it.

Krishna Bhakta Himalaya
President of School Managing Committee

Kunjar Mani Bhattarai
Principal / Head Teacher

Then we lined up and took rounds of pictures. They all knew that I had just one day left before I needed to depart, and now everyone was asking when

I would return. Without thought, I blurted out, "*Paanch barsa*—Five years. I will come back in five years." This was more than just the right thing to say; I truly meant it. I couldn't imagine staying away for another thirty years.

My answer made everyone smile. "And you must bring your daughter," they said.

"*Thik chha*—OK," I said, and I gave my head a sideways shake of agreement.

In the afternoon, I return to the school. I have heard that teachers in the region are meeting there for training, and that several of my old students are in the group. Actually, six of the twenty teachers in attendance are my former students. This is surprising. I only taught at the school for two years. How can so many have become teachers out of that small group? I can't help wondering if I had any influence on their career path.

We are all so pleased to see one another. We exchange news, and repeat much of the same conversations that I've had the previous days. After twenty minutes, we fall uncomfortably silent. There really isn't that much to say. What we need is something to *do*. Suddenly, I have an idea. "Let's play soccer."

"What? Huh?" is the stunned response, "Soccer?"

"Yes," I say. "Let's play soccer. *Right now*. Someone get a ball. Call those boys over there."

Mahendra gets a soccer ball from the school office, and we divide into teams. My team has the goal at the south end of the field—the side toward the new school building. We are a mix of schoolboys and old guys—Netra Ram, Gopal, Krishna Bahadur, Sita Ram, and some others. There is no referee. A couple of posts and two rocks serve as the goals. Gopal places the ball in the middle of the field, and we have at it. One of the schoolboys from my team runs up and gives the ball a tremendous wallop with his bare foot. The ball sails high through the air, nearly to the goal, hits a rock on the ground, and bounces back almost to where it started. Everyone on that side of the field rushes toward the ball, while I fall back in defense.

My old students play with as much ferocity as the young boys, only with less stamina. Several times the ball bounces too far west, dropping down into the temple courtyard, and play ceases while someone climbs down to fetch it. But if the ball goes too far east, that's the hillside covered with rocks and trees, so play just continues with those bare feet swinging madly at the ball amongst the boulders. No one complains.

Suddenly there's a shout, "Goal!" They've scored against us. I look across to determine the hole in our defense. It's Gopal. He's standing with his back to the ball, talking on his cell phone. *Cell phone?* Yes, there's cell phone coverage here in the middle of Aiselukharka—*if* you have the right service provider.

I manage to intercept the ball a few times, and with my long legs, I'm able to give it a respectable *thwack*. The best moments are when the ball hits a protruding rock or a hole in the field, and bounces in a totally unexpected direction or suddenly stops dead. This just adds to the absurd chaos of the game. And then they score on us again! Gopal isn't even on his phone this time.

We run up and down the field, kicking and hollering, and panting. One by one, out-of-breath players take seats on the temple wall as they grow too tired to continue. The game slowly fizzles out. Krishna Bhakta and Aamaa are well entertained.

When we got home, we had a photo session. Mahendra's wife, Sharda, plus Aamaa, and Jesika and two of her friends all played dress-up in different outfits. Along with Krishna Bhakta, Mahendra, and I, we took pictures in all the different combinations of people and clothes. Krishna Bhakta and I even tried to reproduce a thirty-year-old picture of the two of us kneeling in the garden. With a digital camera it was easy to take scores of pictures, and I promised to mail them prints when I got back to America.

The following day was my last full day in Aiselukharka. Krishna Bhakta and I walked to Nawalpur. From the day I arrived, he had been asking me when we would go to Nawalpur. I didn't know why the trip was so important to him, but it clearly was. It was a pleasant stroll. One of the young village boys, Imesh, tagged along with us. Along the way, Krishna Bhakta pointed out his various lands and places where the trail had been changed and improved.

In Nawalpur, we were treated to tea, snacks, and sodas in three different small cafés. I was introduced to some government officials, and everyone acted like we were visiting dignitaries. More of my old students appeared, and I told them all about what I had been doing.

Nawalpur had definitely grown, with twice as many shops and businesses as before. Most interesting, I met a young entrepreneur, Umesh Adhikari, who was establishing a wireless connection down to Melemchi so that he could provide internet service to Nawalpur. The World Wide Web was coming to the Himalayas, for an hourly fee.

The walk back to Aiselukharka was somber. I think that we were both anticipating the coming sadness of my departure. That evening's daal-bhaat seemed especially savory, with the portions of tarkari even bigger than normal. Afterwards, Krishna Bhakta and I talked about the route that I intended to take back to Kathmandu. I was thinking of hiking down to Melemchi, instead of to Sipa Ghat. From Melemchi, I could hopefully get a seat on a bus. It would be easier to get a seat where the bus originated, instead of in Sipa Ghat where it would most likely already be full. Krishna Bhakta agreed with that. We all went to bed early that night.

I wake to the clicking of goat hooves on the flagstones outside. I get up at sunrise and take a walk by myself—past the school, by the temple, down around the dhaaraa, and up through the fields. My rubber sandals make that distinctive *flip-flap* sound between my heels and the dried mud of the trail. I look at the shape of the distant hills, the pattern of stones on the houses, and the colors of the tiny flowers at my feet. I'm trying to ingrain every detail of the place in my memory. I can't fathom that I'm about to leave my Nepali home—again. How am I going to deal with this?

I return to the house for morning tea, followed almost immediately by an early meal of daal-bhaat. I carry my backpack down to the front porch, and lean it against a wooden support beam. I take off my rubber sandals, and slowly lace on my walking shoes. Changing my shoes marks a metaphoric transition from Nepali Philipsir back to American Phil. I try to push this thought from my mind. I'm barely able to keep it together.

I have a gift for Krishna Bhakta and the family. From California I've carried a copy of *The Two-Year Mountain*. Years ago I sent them a letter saying that I was writing a book about my life in Aiselukharka, but I never knew if that letter had arrived. Now I feel guilty about the book. Have I breached a trust of privacy by writing about them? Or by writing have I honored them?

I call to Krishna Bhakta, "*Baasnus, ta. Ma sanga euta upahaar tapaaiko laagi chha*—Please have a seat. I have a present for you." We sit together on a *gundri* mat out on the front stoop. Aamaa, Sharda, Jesika, and a few others from the village stand around us. I take the book out of the pink plastic bag that I've carried it in, and I hand it to Krishna Bhakta.

He carefully unwraps the red paper, and he turns the book over in his hands. At first, he seems confused about what it is.

I explain, "*Tis barsa agaagi maaile euta kitaab leke*—Thirty years ago, I wrote this book, about Aiselukharka, about my family."

"*Ah ha*," says Krishna Bhakta.

I begin flipping through the book, looking for pictures. I find a sketch of Shyam Krishna's wife at the little village store.

"*Ah*, it's the old store," says Aamaa.

And here's a sketch of Krishna Bhakta standing outside his house. "That's *this* house?" asks Krishna Bhakta.

"Yes, and that's *you*," I say. "This is where we are sitting right now."

"Yes, yes," says Aamaa, "This book is about *us*."

Krishna Bhakta begins to smile. "That's the dhaaraa. The old dhaaraa," he says.

"And here's the school, like it used to be." I want to show him the picture of the two of us in the garden, but I'm having trouble finding it. Here's a picture of me bathing, and students cooking. A shot of me climbing. Now I find it—the two of us.

"*Ah ha,*" says Krishna Bhakta, and smiles even broader. He discovers the page that has a sample of Nepali writing. We read it together, and laugh. Finally, he closes the book with a contented grin.

I look around at Aamaa and the others. In Nepali, I say, "You're not *just like* my family. You're my *actual* family."

Everyone smiles and nods. "Yes, that's right," they all agree.

"*Laa,*" I say. "It's time to go."

"And...when are you coming back?" asks Aamaa.

"The plan is to return in five years. But who knows?"

"OK, in five years," she states emphatically. "Yes, do please come. And you'll bring your daughter?"

"Yes. I will." I stand up, and shoulder my pack. There isn't much more to say.

We walk around the outer edge of the walled-in garden, toward the small shop. Here's where I say my farewells to Mahendra. Aamaa has stayed at the main house.

Krishna Bhakta and I, along with Jesika and a few people from the village, walk in silence up the trail headed north. Krishna Bhakta opens his black umbrella and carries it over his head, blocking the sun. I know that the path to Melemchi branches off at around the halfway point to Nawalpur, and I expect that he'll accompany me that far.

I feel emotionally lost, stretched between two worlds. My mind can't form coherent thoughts, as if I have a high fever. I feel a deep, deep sense of

348

Krishna Bhakta and his house

loss. It's not quite as bad as the small death that I endured when I walked away from Aiselukharka thirty-two years ago, but it's something like that. The difference is the pledge that I've made to return within five years. In addition, I'll be striving to raise funds to complete the school construction.

We all stop when we reach the fork to Melemchi. Krishna Bhakta says, "*Ma yahaa saama matra*—This is as far as I'm going."

Jesika gives me a *Namaste*, saying, "Travel well."

"Yes, I will, and I will be back. But also, you should come to America."

Jesika nods politely, but she knows it's unlikely.

I turn to Krishna Bhakta, and I say to him, "*Ke bhanna sakinchha?*— What can I say? There's nothing that can be said. Nothing."

I make the *ke garne* gesture by rotating my wrist with my fingers pointed upward—meaning that there's nothing that can be said nor done. *Ke garne?*

Krishna Bhakta repeats the gesture in agreement. He puts down his umbrella to give me a *Namaste*. He takes my hands in his. Then he reaches forward to give me an embrace.

Now the tears come to my eyes.

Krishna Bhakta holds up his right palm as though to say, *"Stop. It's OK. There is nothing more to be said nor done. It's OK."* But he still says nothing. He picks up his umbrella.

And I start to walk away, slowly down the trail. I feel empty inside, almost dead. But Krishna Bhakta is right. Everything will be OK. Right now, life is horrible—I feel sick inside. But, in time, in time, it will be OK.

Glossary

Aamaa Mother.

Acclimatization The process of adaption to life at high altitude, including changes in heart and lung performance, increased number of red blood cells, and chemical changes in body tissues. Acclimatization is about 80% complete after ten days at high altitude and 95% complete after six weeks. Upon descending, acclimatization is lost about as fast as it was gained.

Aiselukharka A Newari village of about 500 persons at 6,200 feet in the Sindhupalchowk District of north-central Nepal. *Aiselu-Kharka* literally means "Raspberry-Wasteland." The tasty orange *aiselus* grow on land that is not useful for agriculture. At least three villages in Nepal are named Aiselukharka.

arête A very sharp ridge of rock or ice.

bahini Younger sister.

bajaar Bazaar or market.

basnus "Please sit" (honorific).

belay Method of using a rope to secure a climber to a fixed anchor for protection against a fall.

bholi-parsi "Tomorrow, day after tomorrow." A catch-all phrase meaning that something will happen in a couple of days, in a few weeks, or perhaps not at all.

bidaa A departure or holiday.

Braahman A Brahmin, a member of the priestly class in the traditional Hindu caste system.

carabiner An oval ring of metal which can be opened or closed to join various pieces of climbing equipment, such as to connect the rope to an anchor or to connect the climber to the rope. Spelled *karabiner* outside the U.S.

caste The castes of Nepal should more rightly be called ethnic groups or tribes. To speak of the "Nepali people" or "Nepali culture" is to make a gross simplification. Dozens of languages are spoken in Nepal, representing extremely diverse lifestyles, religions, and cultures (e.g. Tamang, Rai, Newar, Sherpa, etc.) These groups are not arranged in a hierarchy; they are equal, but separate. They may intermarry, but they generally do not, just as an Italian will seldom marry a German. Traditional Hindus, however, who have no other ethnic affiliation (about 50% of the population) rank themselves according to religious purity. The Braahman is the highest, followed by the Kshetry, and lastly come the occupational castes: Damaai (Tailors), Sarki (Cobblers), Kami (Blacksmiths), etc. The mother tongue of the traditional Hindus is Nepali, which is now the national language.

CDO Central District Officer.

chang A Sherpa or Tibetan drink akin to beer, usually brewed from rice and served hot.

chapati An unleavened flat bread, like a tortilla.

charpi A latrine. Might be a Western flush toilet, an Eastern squat toilet, an outhouse, or just a hole in the ground.

Chautara A resting place for travelers, usually consisting of a stone platform and a shade tree. Also, the administrative center of Sindhupalchowk District.

chillum A vertical, hand-held pipe for smoking tobacco or hashish.

chiuraa Pounded rice, which looks like a crunchy cereal. The whole-grain rice is first slow boiled, then roasted, next pounded with a wooden pestle, and finally winnowed. Chiuraa is a Newari specialty.

chutney A relish made from spices, herbs, or fruits.

col A high pass between two peaks, not necessarily crossable.

cornice On a ridge, a wave-shaped curl of snow formed by prevailing winds. Cornices can be seen from one side only and a climber on a ridge-top risks falling through. Unstable cornices are also a major cause of avalanches.

crampons Sets of metal spikes that are strapped onto boots for climbing steep snow or ice.

daal-bhaat The twice-daily Nepali meal, consisting of boiled rice (*bhaat*), lentil soup (*daal*), vegetables (*tarkaari*), and sometimes meat, fish, eggs, milk, or yogurt. The rice and lentils complement one another to form a complete protein.

Dasai The greatest Hindu festival, the "ten-day" festival, that celebrates the victory of Durga, the Mother Goddess, over Mahisusur, the evil water-buffalo demon. Dasai is held during the two weeks before the full moon in the month of Asoj (mid-September to mid-October). The celebration includes the decoration of homes, family visits, feasting, and animal sacrifices.

DEO District Education Officer.

dhaaraa Flow or current. A water spigot or water supply.

didi Older sister. A friendly term referring to women working in shops or restaurants.

Durga The fierce manifestation of Shakti, the Mother Goddess. The wife of Shiva.

fisheries volunteers In the Terai, workers who taught methods of digging fish ponds and stocking them with carp for use as a protein source.

gamma globulin A protein extract of blood serum that is rich in antibodies and which is injected as a prophylactic against hepatitis. In Nepal, volunteers received gamma globulin injections every four months. Injections were usually given in the buttocks and volunteers could best relieve the swelling through vigorous dancing.

gaida Rhinoceros.

ghat Steps leading down to a river, used as a platform for cremations.

giardia (giardiasis) A type of dysentery caused by a flagellated bacterial infection in the intestines, characterized by chronic diarrhea, stomach gas, and frequent flatus.

Gurkha A term used for the Nepalis who serve in the British Army. The Nepali agreement to provide mercenary soldiers to the British Army allowed Nepal to remain independent even while all of India was under British domination.

guru Teacher. A religious advisor.

guthi Among Newars, a social body that oversees a piece of religious land and uses the proceeds to form a common trust fund to finance events or projects for the group's benefit. A *guthi* is usually organized along kinship lines.

Hajur Sir, Lord (honorific). Also used as an acknowledgement, or as a way to say "Yes," or as a question, "Pardon?"

half-letter The Devanagri script uses a syllabic alphabet; all consonants have a vowel sound attached (*sa*, *ta*, etc.) So to make a blend (*sta*), one must remove the vowel component of the first letter, forming a half-letter.

hawai jahaaj "Air ship," an airplane.

Himalayas The world's highest mountain range, lying along the southern border of Tibetan China, stretching through Bhutan, India, and Nepal. The highest point is Mount Everest, or Chomolongma (meaning "Mother of the World" in Tibetan), or Sagarmatha (meaning "Sky Head" in Nepali), 29,028 feet. A *himaal* is any snow peak.

hookah A tall traditional-style waterpipe, with a long tube for drawing the smoke.

howdah The seat or platform on an elephant's back.

hunchha Strong form of "to be." Can be used as "OK," "Yes," or "Yes?"

ice axe A mountaineering staff. At the lower end is a steel point. At the top is both a spike for climbing steep ice and a horizontal blade for cutting steps and handholds.

icefall A broken and crevassed section of a glacier where the ice descends a steep slope or makes a sharp turn. Icefalls are characterized by ice towers, called séracs, and vast crevasses.

ice piton A metal spike or screw which is driven into the ice for use as an anchor point.

ji Honorific suffix attached to names as a sign of affection and respect.

jutho Leavings of food. Ritual defilement, caused by touching the lips. Unclean. Mourning.

Kaancho A family's youngest son. Nepali language has words to designate sons and daughters ranging from the oldest to the fifth-oldest. Children are often called by their birth-order titles rather than by their given names.

karaayo Rabbit.

Kathmandu The capital and largest city of Nepal, population was 250,000 (1970s), currently 1.5 million in Kathmandu Valley (2010), elevation 4,500 feet. Kathmandu was founded in 723 AD by Newars. The name is derived from the famous wooden pagoda-temple, Kastha Mandap.

Ke garne? Literally, "What to do?" An expression of resignation.

khola Stream or minor river.

kosi Large river.

Kshetry The second-highest Hindu caste, traditionally the warrior caste. Kshetries adhere strictly to Hindu customs and caste rules. Their military leaders ruled Nepal for five centuries.

kukuri A large curved knife, used as an all-purpose cutting tool, but also made famous as a weapon of Gurkha soldiers.

la In Tibetan and Sherpa languages, a mountain pass.

Laa A Nepali expression that can mean, "Thank you," "Yes," or "Ah!"

lingu A large Maypole erected by Newars to celebrate New Year's Day. "Lingu" comes from the word *lingam,* a wooden or stone phallic symbol representing the god Shiva.

maanaa A unit of measure equaling about two cups.

machaan A raised platform for storing hay. The lookout towers of Chitwan National Park.

mani wall A Buddhist prayer wall, containing slabs of stone carved with religious text. Mani walls are common in the northern mountains. One must always pass with the mani wall on the right. *Mani* means "prayer" in Tibetan.

MIF kit Merthiolate Iodine Formalin, a chemical solution for preserving stool samples for later analysis. Pronounced *miff kit.*

mitho Tasty, sweet.

monsoon Around the Indian Ocean, a seasonal shift of the wind, characterized by heavy rains. Three-quarters of Nepal's rain falls during the monsoon period, from mid-June to the end of September. The heavy rains combined with the overcutting of the forests have caused severe erosion problems.

moraine A mass of boulders or gravel carried or deposited by a glacier. Lateral moraines are the long ridges of rock debris that accumulate on the sides of a glacier.

move In mountaineering, a shift of position. A set of movements in which both hands and both feet are shifted to new holds.

naamlo A tumpline. A headstrap that passes over the forehead for carrying loads.

Namaste An all-purpose salutation, both hello and goodbye, usually initiated by the person of lower position. Derived from the Sanskrit, *namas*, a bow. Pronounced *naama-stay*.

NDS National Development Service. A program which required Nepali university students to do a year of rural development work before they could complete their degrees.

névé Permanent snow that is in the process of turning to crystalline ice.

Newar An ethnic group in Nepal comprising about 4 per cent of the total population. Newars are divided into many sub-groups and castes, and are of both the Hindu and Buddhist religions. Newars are renowned in matters of trade and art.

paisaa The Nepali penny, with one hundred *paisaa* equalling one rupee. Money.

Panchaayat The village council, which elected representatives to the District Panchaayat. The National Panchaayat was essentially the parliament, but could only send recommendations to the King. The old Panchaayat System had no political parties.

pasal A shop.

Peace Corps Created in 1961, the Peace Corps provides skilled workers for Third World development. Volunteers are sent only to countries and to programs for which the host country has submitted a specific request. The three goals of the Peace Corps are to furnish needed manpower to developing countries, to give these countries an opportunity to know and understand Americans, and to give Americans a chance to learn of life in less affluent societies and to share this knowledge with the rest of America. Volunteers must be U.S. citizens over 18 years of age and are usually, but not exclusively, college graduates. They are given transportation and living allowances during a two-year service commitment. At the end of service, volunteers received a readjustment allowance of $125 for every month of service in 1980; this is now (2010) $275 per month. In 1980, 90,000 volunteers had worked in some 70 countries worldwide. By 2010, this had increased to 200,000 volunteers having served in 139 countries. Volunteers in Nepal worked in the fields of math/science education, water systems, bridge building, fisheries, English education, health/nutrition, reforestation, and lab technology. In 2004, the Peace Corps suspended its mission in Nepal following a Maoist bombing of the office of the United States Information Service in Kathmandu.

pipal tree In India and Nepal, a sacred species of fig tree, often used to shade a *chautara*. Also called a "bo tree," the tree under which Buddha found enlightenment. Sometimes spelled *peepul*.

pitch A section of climbing between two belay points, or an interval of climbing from one secure stance to the next. A pitch can be 50 to 250 feet of climbing.

piton A metal spike to be hammered into a rock crack for use as an anchor point.

Pokhara A town, or large village, located in the middle hills 96 miles west of Kathmandu, elevation 2,500 feet. The name is derived from *pokhari*, meaning pond. The Pokhara Valley contains several beautiful lakes.

Pradhaan Panch The head of the Village Panchaayat (village council).

prusik knot A hitch that can be slid up or down the rope, but which holds tight under stress. Prusik knots are useful for ascending a rope or for rigging a self-belay on a fixed line.

pujaa Worship. Can be a religious festival, a sacred ritual, or an offering of flowers, rice, money, etc.

raamro Good.

Rai A Hindu-Buddhist ethnic group living predominantly in Nepal's eastern hills.

recorder A European wooden flute, having eight finger holes. Also called an English flute.

RNAC Royal Nepal Airlines Corporation.

rupee Actually *rupiyaa,* the money of Nepal. Derived from the Sanskrit *rupya*, meaning silver. One rupee was about eight American cents in 1977-79. A rupee is currently (2011) about 1.4 U.S. cents.

sari A dress worn by Hindu women, consisting of a long cloth wrapped around the waist and draped over the shoulder. In Nepali, spelled *saadi.*

scree A region of boulders or smaller stones accumulated on a slope below a cliff. Loose scree can be laborious to climb and dangerous to descend.

seto mulaa White radish, shaped like monstrous carrots. *Mulaa* grows well above 6,000 feet.

Sherpa A Tibetan-like ethnic group living primarily in the high mountains, well-known as high-altitude climbers and porters. Sherpa men and women could have multiple spouses, though this was not common.

shraaddha A funeral offering to a god.

-sir An honorific suffix attached to the names of school teachers.

SLC School Leaving Certificate. Students must pass a standardized, national test (School Leaving Certificate exam) at the end of high school (tenth grade) to qualify for this diploma.

spindrift Powdered snow blown by the wind.

talus Same as *scree*.

Tamang A Buddhist ethnic group similar to Sherpas.

tapaai The honorific form of the pronoun "you."

tarkaari Vegetables.

Terai In Nepal, the low-altitude strip of land bordering with India to the south. The Terai contains dense jungle and is extremely fertile. It produces a food surplus that is exported to the food-deficient hills and to India. Other than Kathmandu, Nepal's largest towns and the majority of the nation's factories are in the Terai. Also *Taraai*.

Thoripaani "scarce water." Klaus's village in Khotang District was not actually Thoripaani, but Aiselukharka. The name in the narrative has been changed to avoid confusion with the Aiselukharka of Sindhupalchowk District.

thulo maanchhe Literally, "big man." A man of importance, such as a district official or a Pradhaan Panch.

Tihaar A five-day festival, occurring about three weeks after Dasai. Each day has a separate celebration. Sisters bless their brothers and gambling is permitted. The "Festival of Lights" represents the aspiration for enlightenment over darkness, and is celebrated with butter lamps or candles lining the windows.

tikaa A mark. A colored spot placed on the middle of the forehead to denote a religious blessing. Also worn by women as a cosmetic beauty mark.

timi The familiar form of the pronoun "you." Used for close friends, children, or subordinates. Can be used derogatorily.

topi The brimless cloth cap of Nepal, worn only by males. The color or style of a *topi* can identify a man's home region.

Tribhuvan The King of Nepal from 1911 (at age five years) to 1954, who guided the emergence of modern Nepal. Kathmandu's international airport is named after him.

tsho Lake, in Tibetan.

tupi The sacred Hindu top-knot, a tuft of hair at the back of the head. Hindu men often shave their heads, but the tupi must never be cut.

UNICEF United Nations International Children's Emergency Fund.

verglas A layer of ice on rocks, caused by the freezing of running water or by the condensation of mist. Verglas can create hazardous climbing conditions.

wallah In Hindi, a person associated with a particular type of work. A taxi driver might be a taxi-wallah, and a tea seller a tea-wallah.

webbing A woven nylon material used for harnesses, slings, straps, etc. Can be extremely strong, up to 4,000-pound test.

Yeti The "Abominable Snowman," the primitive man-monkey said to live in the high Himalayas. Some believe the yeti is Vishnu, who rises from a mountain lake; others believe it is a type of large snow ape. To see a yeti means death to the observer.

The Two-Year Mountain: Back to Nepal DVD

Filmed by Robyn Hutman and Matt Dickinson, this full-length, high definition film documentary vividly captures the author's emotional return to his village after a lapse of thirty-four years. In the wake of Nepal's bloody Maoist civil war, Deutschle discovers how the village has progressed in the three decades since his departure. Special features on the DVD include archival photos from both 1977 and 2011, and a video version of the narrated slide presentation from the author's original book promotion tour. Available through Bradt Travel Guides Ltd (www.bradtguides.com) or from www.FarJourney. com.